A to Z

26 Fun Steps to Sharpen your English

Abhijit Sengupta studied MA in English Literature at Delhi University and taught English in two Delhi University colleges before he joined the Indian Administrative Service (IAS) in 1972. He retired from the IAS in 2008 as Secretary, Ministry of Culture, Government of India. He was awarded the prestigious Pearson fellowship of the IDRC, Canada, in 1984–85 and received a Master's degree in Public Administration from Carleton University, Ottawa, Canada. He has served in many important positions in the Government of India and in the State Government of Karnataka. In 2014, Abhijit Sengupta was Chairman of the High Powered Committee of the Ministry of Culture to review the functioning of various cultural institutions. He has been a member of the Central Advisory Board on Culture and of the Governing Body of Kalakshetra Foundation, Chennai.

Sengupta retained a special interest in English literature over decades of government service. This book is the result of his love for what he feels is the most fascinating language in the world.

A to Z

26 Fun Steps to Sharpen your English

Abhijit Sengupta

hachette
INDIA

First published in 2017 by Hachette India
(Registered name: Hachette Book Publishing India Pvt. Ltd)
An Hachette UK company
www.hachetteindia.com

SRD

ISBN: 978-93-5195-190-2

Hachette Book Publishing India Pvt. Ltd
4th & 5th Floors, Corporate Centre
Plot No. 94, Sector 44, Gurgaon 122003, India

Typeset in Sabon Lt Std 10.5/14 by
Manmohan Kumar, New Delhi

Printed and bound in India
by Manipal Technologies Limited, Manipal

FSC
www.fsc.org
MIX
Paper from
responsible sources
FSC™ C104740

Contents

Preface

This book is a practitioner's view of English, not a dictionary or a textbook of grammar. A distillation of my experiences in teaching, reading, writing, communicating and working in English, it explores and clarifies the meanings of certain selected words as examples, and discusses broad aspects of grammar. But that is only a part of what this book intends to do. It is indeed to give you a peep into the nuances and the richness of a very complex, fascinating language and provide a brief glimpse into the beauty of its literature.

As I wrote this book, I kept in mind that some readers might want a book that did not take their English skills for granted. This book is for those who do have a reasonable knowledge of English, but may need to be a little more confident in its use. It is also for those who wish to revisit their skills and their understanding of the language, and to enjoy its subtleties. There are common words here, which we use frequently, but without appreciating their varied nuances. There are words we come across at work, in social conversation, or in the news, which we ought to know but may not be quite familiar with. There are of course some 'basic' terms used in standard English grammar, to remind us that the language does have a set of rules. And then there are fun words, to show a little bit of the quirky side of the language. There is, in addition, a sprinkling of literary terms and references, for what is a language without its literature? These references, except in a few places, are from English Literature, not American. Indeed the differences in the use of the same language, which this books touches upon, are significant – and as troublesome as left-hand and right-hand driving. George Bernard Shaw is believed to have once said, 'England and America are two countries separated by the same language.'

This book revolves around the fact that just 26 letters – five vowels and 21 consonants – have created today an enormous wealth of words, perhaps the largest lexicon in the world. English is the most widely used global language today, commonly used for interaction in global trade, international sports and world politics. The language seems to lend itself to communicating with others. How to do that, and do it well, is the starting point of our exploration. Have fun! Or, to use today's weird, incorrect but popular lingo, enjoy!

A

A short word, *a.* A vowel, the first letter of the alphabet. But it is a word in itself, one of the most important words in English. It symbolizes the beginning, the start of the most powerful, the most ubiquitous language in the world – the language of business, of academics, of international relations. In the beginning was the word. Today, it seems as if that word was in English.

The difference between *a* and *an* is in their use; the first is generally used before words starting with consonants and the second before words beginning with vowels, the letters *a, e, i, o* and *u*. *A doctor, a tractor, a sector; an orange, an Indian, an umbrella.* But there are exceptions, as you would notice with much of the English language. When the letter *u* at the start of a word is pronounced 'you', as with the letter itself, the preceding word is not *an* but *a*. *An usher* but *a user. An uncle* but *a uniform.* This rule applies even with words starting *eu*, with the 'you' sound. *An American tourist* but *a European traveller*. Another rare use of *a* before a vowel is with *o* when the word is 'one', because it sounds like *w* – *a one-way street* or *a one-word answer.*

The one exception in the use of *an* with consonants is when the letter *h* is pronounced softly. The difference is between, say, 'horse' and 'hour'. 'Hour' is said as if it was 'our', without the emphasis on the *h* – *If we ride a horse, we will reach the house in an hour.* It is the sound of the first letter of the noun that decides whether *a* or *an* is to be used before the word.

A and *an* are indefinite *articles* of speech, ('the' is the definite *article*). These two words are used when there is no emphasis to be placed – *a* book and not 'the' specific, particular book. *An apple a day keeps the doctor away.* In this common saying, *a* is used before 'day' because it could be any one of the seven days of the week; 'the' before 'doctor' is because, in a sense, you don't go to any doctor, you go to your chosen doctor. In a way, *a* is used the first time something is referred to; the next time the definite article 'the' may be used – *A boy was going to school; his friend called out to him and the boy stopped.* The definite *article* also gives an emphasis, or specificity, that the indefinite *articles* do not have – *a book of short stories* but *the best book of short stories*. There can be an explanatory adjective between the article and the noun – *a pretty picture*, *the tired footballer.*

There is no *article* before proper nouns, such as names of people – *Rama and Sujit went home*, not 'a Rama and a Sujit went home'; countries – *England is batting*, not 'an England is batting'; languages – *English is spoken in many countries*, not 'the English is spoken in many countries'; titles – *Mrs Bose might come*, not 'the Mrs Bose might come'; dates – *I was born in 1984*, not 'I was born in a 1984'. Proper nouns, such as names, do not use an article, except if a group or category is indicated. For example, we may introduce a person named

Mr Das by saying – *This is Mr Das*. But we might use an *article* if we create a specific category; if we are searching for someone, for example, we might say – *Is there a Mr Das here*? There are further distinctions. *He is a polite Englishman*, but *The English are a polite people*. Here, 'English' is not the language, but the people. When a noun is in the possessive form, the *article* vanishes – *a book* changes to *my book*.

A has another unusual use. There is a difference between 'few' and 'a few'; one is somewhat the opposite of the other. *A few persons know English grammar* means what it says, that some people know it. *Few persons know English grammar* means that not many know it. The first is countable – it could be a known number – while the second is not.

The use of *a* and *an* is significant in another way – in the indication of numbers. In Indian languages, there is no exact equivalent of *a* and *an*; in fact the definite and indefinite articles do not exist. In Hindi, for example, the explanatory word before a noun would be 'ek', or one. Like *ek kitab* – one book, not *a* book. In English, 'one' would denote an emphasis, specifically suggesting only one, and not any more than that. You would say – *Please give me a rupee*, not *please give me one rupee*, unless you wished to stress that you want only one rupee, and not two or more rupees. So, it is best not to translate literally from Hindi, or whatever be your mother tongue, into English as you speak.

The subject of mother tongues brings to mind the story of three young men at an English lesson. 'Tell us something in English about your mother tongue,' the teacher says. The first student replies, 'My mother tongue is Hindi.' The second says, 'My mother tongue is Tamil.' The third answers, 'My mother tongue is pink!'

And that brings us to the important matter of the *apostrophe*. If the third boy knew the difference between mother tongue and mother's tongue, his answer would have been different. The *apostrophe*, a comma dangling from above, indicates ownership – it tells us whether a shirt is *Arun's shirt* or *Aditya's shirt,* whether a ball is *Aruna's ball or Anita's*. After the noun, we have the *apostrophe* followed by an *s*. This denotes possession, in other words, a possessive noun. This is used for all living creatures. We can *pat the dog's ear* or *rub the cat's fur*. But generally, we do not use the apostrophe for inanimate objects. We do not keep a pen on 'the table's top', but on *the top of the table.* Or, the *apostrophe* is removed when we refer to *the table top*, or *the car door.*

A totally different use of the *apostrophe* is when it shortens a word. *It's* is the short form of *it is*. (Do not confuse the word *it's* with *its*. *Its* without the *apostrophe* indicates possession – *The dog could not find its bone.*). *Cannot* becomes *can't*, *will not* becomes *won't* and *did not* becomes *didn't*.

> Why is 'will not' shortened to 'won't' and not 'win't' or 'willn't'? The word 'won't' actually came from 'woll not', which is now not in use!

There are other examples, too. The word 'is' is often shortened as an *apostrophe s*. Be careful not to mistake 'who's', which is the short form for 'who is', with 'whose', which indicates whom something belongs to – *Who's the boy whose book is missing?* A common error occurs in the use of the word 'yours' – at the end of a letter one writes *yours faithfully* or *yours sincerely*, not 'your's faithfully'!

Pippa's Song, a beautiful short poem by Robert Browning (1812–1889), has an *apostrophe* in every line. Pippa, a poor little girl, sings –

The year's at the spring,
And day's at the morn;
Morning's at seven;
The hill-side's dew-pearled;
The lark's on the wing;
The snail's on the thorn;
God's in His Heaven –
All's right with the world.[1]

Have you heard of the Apostrophe Protection Society? It was started in 2001 and people from all over the world send photographs of examples of the wrong use of the *apostrophe*. You can check out *www.apostrophe.org.uk* for more.

The word *and* is one of the most important words in English. And so are *also* and *as*. The use of *and* is obvious – it joins two words, phrases and sentences. Sometimes, *and* opens a sentence or even a paragraph. Purists do not like this, but there is a continuity that is attached here, and an emphasis that is intended. Go back to the second sentence of this paragraph to *And so are...* to understand how *and* can be used to effect continuity.

[1] 'Pippa's Song', as it is popularly called, is from the play *Pippa Passes*, by Robert Browning; 1841. http://www.self.gutenberg.org/wplbn0002950688-pippa-passes-by-browning-robert.aspx?&words.

But if we give the word *and* an emphasis as we speak, it can give an additional, unintended meaning. Let's look at a famous nursery rhyme 'Jack and Jill':

Jack and Jill went up the hill
To fetch a pail of water.
Jack fell down and broke his crown,
And Jill came tumbling after.

If you stress the *and* in the first line, it might give the impression that Jill was not really supposed to go with Jack, or someone else was to go, but finally, Jill did. One should not invest any unintended significance to any idea by an unnecessary emphasis on *and*. Think of it this way. There are three *and*'s in the rhyme. How would it sound if you emphasized each one of them? By the way, why is there an *apostrophe* in 'three *and*'s'? This is because *and* does not have a natural plural form; the *apostrophe* has to take on a special use.

Also is similar to 'besides', but the usage is slightly different. Both mean 'additionally' but 'besides' hints of an element of separation, differentiation or comment. It has the same position as '*apart* from' which expresses that differentiation – *Apart from Raghu, who else was there?* is the same as *Besides Raghu, who was there?* On the other hand, *also* joins, it brings together – *He is a lawyer and also a novelist.*

As is a short word but with many uses. It stands for 'because' – *I did not go to work as I was ill.* It compares – *He is as tall as Ashok*. It suggests the frequency of an action, which is how often it should or could happen – *I go to the library as often as possible.* It indicates the way to do something – *Go as you like*. It means 'when' or 'at the very moment' – *As I entered the room I saw her.*

There are many other uses of the word, but two phrases are important – *as if* and *as is*. The first can be explained only by another phrase *as though*, which means giving an impression (and the impression given is generally not true) – *The ward boy behaved as if he was the doctor*. The other, *as is*, indicates a condition, usually a present state – *The car will be sold in an as-is-where-is condition.* This stops a buyer from later complaining of the condition of the car he or she has bought.

> *As if* is also a modern slang phrase, to mean 'not likely' or a simple 'no'. If a schoolboy is asked – 'Do you have many girlfriends?', the shy fellow might reply, 'As if.' Strange!

There are many words beginning with *a,* which are figures of speech or words of significance in English language usage. Let's look at some of them. An *abbreviation* is a short form of a word. *To abbreviate* is to shorten, as when we have 'ad' breaks for *advertisements,* which seem to go on forever. There should be full stops after *abbreviated* words, but this is given a go by nowadays. 'Re' for 'regarding' and 'ref' for 'reference' are common in today's business 'vocab'. Common and widely accepted are 'prof' for 'professor' and 'doc' for 'doctor'.

Acronyms are *abbreviations* of a specific kind. It is a combination of the first letters of the words. The Prime Minister's Office is called PMO for short; this is an *acronym*. There is a preference for *acronyms* that are words that can be pronounced easily. An example would be ISRO for the Indian Space Research Organisation, (pronounced 'iss–ro') which makes it brief, smart and easy on the tongue, and where we do not have to spell out each letter as in P, M, O. A word of caution here. There are some time-honoured ways of dealing with short forms – the CAG, short for Comptroller and Auditor General of India, is C, A, G, not, as some speakers on our news channels make it out, 'cag' rhyming with 'bag'! Those in the business of exports and imports would know that for *FOB*, 'free on board', each letter has to be stated; otherwise, the word 'fob' has other meanings.

Now for some basic grammar. What is an *adjective* and what is an *adverb*? An *adjective* describes, or qualifies, a noun – a person, place or thing – or a pronoun, which stands for a noun, or even another *adjective*. An *adverb* generally describes or explains a verb, or action – how, where, when, why and how much or to what extent. Be careful of the difference between an *adjective* and an *adverb*. *Dravid's exquisite batting* has an *adjective* to describe the quality of the batting, but *Dravid batted exquisitely* has an adverb to do just that. But just by adding '*ly*' at the end of a word, we may not get an *adverb*, and the same word can be either an *adjective* or an *adverb*, depending on its position in a sentence and what its use pertains to. In *Dravid's exquisitely timed drive*, the word 'exquisitely' is an *adjective* qualifying 'timed', which itself qualifies 'drive'. In English, the position of a word and its mix with other words, determines the nature of the word. Many words are both *adjectives* and *adverbs*, complicating the grammar all the more – *early, far, left, right, straight* and *well* are just a few simple examples.

An *adage* is a saying – words of wisdom as it were, which are generally derived from folk culture. A commonly known saying is *a stitch in time saves nine*, which means that if you spend a little time acting early you will save a lot of effort when things get worse.

An *aphorism*, on the other hand, is a witty way of saying something that is perhaps significant, perhaps sarcastic; it tells a truth very precisely. You would know of Murphy's Law – 'Anything that can go wrong will go wrong!' Then the Peter Principle – 'People tend to rise to their level of incompetence.' Oscar Wilde (1854-1900), the great British dramatist, said many pithy things; just one example here – 'I am not young enough to know everything!'

What about *alliteration*? Look at two very well-known ones – *Peter Piper picked a peck of pickled peppers* and *How high His Highness holds his haughty head*. A famous example comes from one of the greatest musicals of all times, *My Fair Lady*, that classic Audrey Hepburn–Rex Harrison film of 1964, which was adapted from George Bernard Shaw's (1856–1950) play *Pygmalion*. Professor Higgins, an expert in linguistics, takes up a challenge to turn a lowly flower girl, Eliza Doolittle, into a high-society lady. He teaches her the English language, with a proper accent, and one of the lessons in phonetics includes this line – *In Hertford, Hereford and Hampshire, hurricanes hardly ever happen*. Eliza, with her terrible accent, tries very hard; she says: 'In 'ertford, 'ereford and 'ampshire, 'urricanes 'ardly hever 'appen.'

An *anagram* is the clever rearrangement of the letters of a word or sentence to make another word or sentence, preferably with some connection – *butterfly* becomes *flutter by*. *A decimal point* is *I'm a dot in place*. Another one, truly inspired we should say, is *Chairman Mao – I am on a march*! Think of words where the same letters are rearranged; an example – *opts, post, pots, spot, stop* and *tops*!

And what are *antonyms*? The opposite of a word is the *antonym* for that word. A simple example would be *dry* as the opposite of *wet*. Sometimes, placing un- or in- creates the opposite meaning of a word, but these are not true antonyms. The opposite of *ease* is *unease*, of *definite* is *indefinite*. These are obvious. But a true set would be *ascent* and *descent* – climbing up and climbing down. Some words can have more than one *antonym*; for example, the *antonym* for *dark* is *light*, but it can also be *fair*. The *antonym* depends on the shade of meaning of the original word that you use. What is the *antonym* of *antonym*? It is 'synonym', a word with the same meaning!

A few tricky words? *Almost* looks like the combination of 'all' and 'most', but with only one *l*; it means 'nearly (all)'. You have to be careful about its place in a sentence as otherwise it can give a different meaning. It has to be placed just before the word it qualifies – *Almost all the candidates passed the test* is different from – 'All the candidates almost passed the test.' *Almost* should not be used as a replacement for 'most' – *most people* and not 'almost people', and if required then it should be *almost all the people*.

Although – note the single *l* again – means 'even though'. When using the word *although* in a sentence, the word 'but' must not be added – 'Although I was tired, but I studied for my exams' is wrong; the 'but' must go! *Altogether*, again with one *l*, means 'totally', 'entirely' or 'completely' – *It was altogether a new experience for him* – which is very different from *all together*, covering a whole group – *They were all together in the camp*.

One must be careful of some common errors, as with *access* and *excess*, *adapt* and *adopt*, and *affect* and *effect*. *Access* is 'a way in', 'an entry', while 'excess' is 'too much' or 'additional' – *Access to the website was blocked* but *He had excess baggage on his flight*. *Adapt* is to modify – *The writer adapted the old myths into modern stories*; *adopt* is to accept and make your own – *adopt a new style* or *adopt a baby*. In the third set, to *affect* is to impact – *My illness affected my studies* and *The effect* (or result) *of this was that I did badly in my exams*.

Another common error is the wrong use of *assume* and *presume*. To *assume* something is to believe that that something is true without ascertaining the facts; to presume is to take something for granted, beforehand, and therefore often self-importantly. *We assumed that the meeting would start at ten though it actually began at nine*, as against *The convenor presumed that everyone would know*.

A is an *article*, but there is more to that word. An *articled* clerk is a trainee, usually in an accountancy firm, who is attached to the firm (the origin of the word is the Latin *articulus*, or 'small joints'). An *article* is also a piece of analytical or descriptive writing in a newspaper, a magazine or a journal. And it can also be a piece or item – of furniture, or jewellery or clothing, and so on.

A is indeed a powerful letter. Add it to a word and it either gives a different form to the word or the word takes on a totally different meaning. 'Sleep', a noun, becomes *asleep* – *Your sleep is disturbed if someone shouts while you are asleep*. 'Part' becomes *apart* – *The technician took apart the whole machine just to replace one part*. You would notice that 'sleep' and *asleep*, 'part' and *apart* are related. But when 'foot' changes to *afoot*, or 'bet' to *abet*, the meaning changes. 'Foot' of course is a part of your body and is also a measure of length; but *something is afoot* means that something, usually nasty, is about to happen. A 'bet' is a wager, where one has a sure expectation of an outcome – *I bet we will win the match* – while to *abet* is to instigate – *He was charged with abetting the murder*. One who *abets* is an *abettor.*

At is an important word. It explains where you stand in a particular context or position. It expresses an association to a place – *I am at home* (which indicates my location), and also to an activity – *I am at work*, or to a condition – *I am at ease*. Therefore *I am at an interesting point in the book* is different from, say, *I am on the last page of the book*, which is very specific. *At* also refers to rate, indicating speed – *He was driving at a hundred miles an hour when the car overturned*, or value – *Onion prices are now at an all-time high*.

After all the analysis of *a*, we must remember the word *alphabet*. There is no plural – 'alphabets' is often used, but is entirely wrong; *letters of the alphabet* is correct. The *alphabet* is the totality of the letters which help create a language; in English, as we know, there are five vowels and 21 consonants. The word itself comes from a combination of 'alpha' and 'beta', the *a* and *b* of the Greek alphabet.

What is the *ampersand*? It is the character &, which stands for *and*. It was the last letter of the alphabet; while repeating the alphabet, a student would say, '*a,b,c …x,y,z* and per se (on its own or by itself) and'. That became *ampersand*. That letter was shifted out of the alphabet but is still used as a short form of *and*. It is also used as *&c* to form 'etc.' because & began as a combination of *e* and *t*; the Latin word *et* means 'and'!

A very common mistake occurs with @. This symbol technically stands for *at* and not 'at the rate of'. In commercial terminology, this is written as, say, 2 *apples @ Rs 10 each = Rs 20*. Here the price of one apple becomes the rate, and therefore we read the equation as 2 *apples at the rate of Rs 10 equals Rs 20*. But it is also correct to say 2 *apples at Rs 10 each*. (With the use of 'rate', the word 'each' is not necessary since 'rate' implies only one). The symbol @ has now become common in Internet usage as the expression of an address; it could be *ABC@xyz.com*. Here you would read it as *ABC at xyz dot com*, not 'at the rate of'. This is an address, a location, and not a price per unit.

B

To *be* is to exist, the most philosophical concept of humankind. The primary reality of the world is our *being*. (To emphasize the point, we call ourselves human *beings*!) There are various intricate concepts of grammar that the word *be* can take us to; we need not get into details, but remember that words and phrases such as *is*, *am*, *are*, *was*, *were*, *will be*, *can be*, *could be*, *could have been*, *might be* and a host of such terms are derived from *to be*.

The word *be* is sometimes added at the beginning of another word to denote a related word or activity. *Because* comes from 'cause'. 'Calm' becomes *becalm*, that is 'make calm'. But sometimes, the new word has nothing at all to do with the original word. Entirely opposite are 'stow' and *bestow*. The first is to put or stash away – *She stowed away the woollens carefully for the next winter*. The second is to give away, such as an award or title – *The King bestowed a knighthood on him for his achievements.*

Been with 'have'/'has' or 'had' is the past participle of *be* – *I have been to his house* or *He had been out jogging when the theft happened*. Note that *been* here did not need another verb with it. Otherwise one might say *I have been going to his house for many years*, but *been* has its own place and meaning. Remember the nursery rhyme:

Pussy cat, pussy cat, where have you been?
I've been to London to see the Queen....

A very difficult aspect of English is its tricky spelling and pronunciation. There are so many words in English that are spelt the same way or sound similar, but have very different meanings. Or sometimes, the same word has many uses. The letter *b* abounds in them. Let's look at a few everyday words to see how they are used in a fascinating variety of ways.

Back can have many uses. A *back* is the opposite of 'front' and used not only for humans and animals, but also for inanimate objects – the *back of a book* or *the back of a chair*. It is a rear area, as with the *back of a building* or the *back of beyond* – the latter an exaggerated way of referring to the location of a remote place. There are a number of meanings to the word. The simplest, of course, is of someone or something not moving forward but in the reverse direction – *Go back the way you came*. It shows support, as to *back a candidate*, and also expectation – *We backed our team to win*.

The addition of a word after *back* changes its use. To *back up* is to have in reserve or provide an alternative; from this we get a *backup battery*. *To back out* – to go back on a promise; *to back off* – to retreat from a stated position; *to back away* – to move back; *to back down* – to climb down from a stand taken earlier. To do something *behind one's back* is to do it without the knowledge of the other person. *Back to back* is a set of two, one after another – *India won back to back matches to reach the finals*. *Background* refers to the past history – *To explain the background to the whole problem will take very long. Background* also relates to *behind-the-scene* activity – *They worked quietly in the background for their candidate. Background* music is what you hear in a film. A *backgrounder* is a note that explains the basic issues leading up to the matter on hand; in business, it could explain the history of a product or the firm itself. *Backdrop* refers to the scene at the rear – *They posed with a tree as the backdrop*. The *backstage* crew in a play are those who are not the actors, but do the lights, sound, sets, costumes, makeup and so on.

Bad and **bade**? *Bad* is the opposite of good, and everyone knows the word. But *bade*, pronounced the same way as *bad*, is the past tense of *bid*. To *bid goodbye* is to say goodbye or take leave of someone; the past tense is – *I bade him goodbye for the last time*.

Bear rhymes with *bare*, and it is not pronounced like 'beer'. The word *bear* has so many meanings. It is, of course, a furry wild animal, generally brown, but black in some parts of Asia and America, and also white in the Polar regions. *Bear*, as a verb, is to admit, allow or take on – *to bear the cost of a project* – or undertake a responsibility. It also means 'to tolerate' – *I could not bear his taunts*. The past tense is *bore* – *He bore with all my complaints patiently.*

Bare is 'uncovered' or 'unclothed' – a *bare body*; or 'simple' or 'basic' – *the bare Act without explanations*; even 'only' or 'mere' or 'just about'– *He passed with bare minimum marks* or *He barely passed the exams*. The word can also be a verb – *He bared his soul to me*; the past tense of *bare* is *bared*. What about *bare necessities?* These, of course, are the minimum provisions, of food and clothing, which one needs to eat and live, to keep going. It is also the title of a very popular song from the animation film *The Jungle*

Book, made in 1967, one of the film versions of Rudyard Kipling's (1865–1936) collection of stories of that name, published in 1894. In this film, Baloo, the sloth bear, sings '*bare* necessities', the fun is in the pun on *bear* and *bare*:

Look for the bare necessities
The simple bare necessities
Forget about your worries and your strife,
I mean the bare necessities
Old Mother Nature's recipes
That bring the bare necessities of life.[1]

In modern financial management, *bears* and *bulls* have a special place. The stock market, through stock exchanges where a company's stocks or shares are purchased or sold, rises and falls, depending on various economic factors. When the market rises, and quickly, it is a *bull* run; when it falls, or is sluggish, it is *bearish*.

Bow and *bough*. *Bow* itself has many meanings and two ways of pronouncing the word. *Bow*, when it rhymes with 'no' and 'so', is the weapon that Rama used as a warrior prince, and so did Arjuna. *Bow* is also the word for a piece of ribbon tied in a particular shape and worn in the hair or as a necktie, in a way that two triangular pieces of cloth stick out on two sides of the knot. It is also the front of a boat or ship. The other *bow*, which rhymes with 'cow' and 'now', is the bending from the waist before a superior

[1] Written by Terry Gilkyson • Copyright © Walt Disney Music Company; from The Jungle Book, released 1967.

person to show him respect. (It is also the sound of a dog barking, *bow* or *bow-wow*.)

This *bow* also sounds the same as *bough*, the branch of a tree. We do not often use this word in normal speech nowadays, it is more a word used in poetry. There is a well-known English nursery rhyme, which is believed to be the earliest such written in America in the early sixteenth century. It goes like this:

Rock-a-bye baby, on the tree top;
When the wind blows, the cradle will rock;
When the bough breaks, the cradle will fall,
And down will come baby, cradle and all!

To **break** is to make a whole into smaller parts, pronounced the same as – but is very different from – **brake**, to stop suddenly or slow down. A *brake* is an instrument or a gadget that helps you to stop, and it is the action itself. But careful, for a car, the word is inevitably used in the plural, *the brakes*. Let's look at this example – *If you do not brake in time, or if the brakes fail, you will break down the front gate*. But *breakdown* as one word, a noun, indicates a collapse, usually the *breakdown of a car* or the *breakdown of law and order*. *Breakfast*, to break your night's fasting, has to be said fast, not slow; the 'fast' is not elongated; the 'a' almost does not exist! There is also *breakup* – a sad situation created, say, by *the breakup of a marriage*. As a noun, *break* can be used also as a time gap – a *coffee break* or *lunch break*, a *break* from the regular work. *Break*, the verb, becomes *broke* in the past tense –*The mug broke when he dropped it*. *Broken* is a qualifier, too – *He found the broken mug* or *He found the mug already broken*. But *broke* is also slang for 'being without money' – *He went broke after his business failed.*

Then, *book*. If you are reading this you are reading a *book*, a noun. But as a verb, you can reserve, or *book*, a table at a restaurant or *book* tickets in advance for a play or a film. A policeman can *book* a person for an offence, by recording the charge. A *bookie* is a person who accepts bets in gambling as in horse racing. But to *go by the book* is to strictly follow the rules.

A *board*, with a lowercase *b*, usually refers to a piece of cardboard or a thin piece of wood, on which are drawn various designs and systems for playing a game, such as chess or Monopoly or Chinese Chequers. It can also be just a flat piece of wood. Since wood is used for most stage flooring, a play that is being put up is said to be *on the boards*. Similarly, a *billboard* is a *board* where announcements or information is put up; it is also called a hoarding. *Board* is also the food provided, usually at a lodging house to a *boarder* – many small hotels have signs that announce *boarding and lodging*. One might also be a *boarder* at a *boarding school*, where students stay for their studies, unlike day scholars, who come from home to school daily for classes. To *board* a bus or a train is to get on to it. A *Board*, with a capital *B*, refers to a group of persons who formally run a business firm or some other institutions.

But is a powerful word, a joining word, a conjunction. *But* implies a comparison, or a balancing of different views or positions. *I have a big nose, but he has a bigger one* – a comparison. Or, *I like cricket, but she prefers football* – a presentation of two views. *But* has yet another role, *but for*. This phrase is the same as 'had it not been for' or even, in some cases, 'without'. *But for his goal, his team would have lost the match* means that without his goal, or had it not been for his goal, the result would have been different and his team would have lost. This is an example where two independent words join to create a totally different meaning. English abounds in such combinations. *Butt* sounds the same as *but*, *but* it has a very different meaning. A goat might *butt* you with its horns in you *buttocks*, also called *butt* for short. A *butt* in your *butt* might make you the *butt* – the target – of jokes among your friends.

By, bye and buy are three words that sound the same, but have different meanings. We need to be sure of when to use which word. The first of the three, *by*, usually denotes who or what has done something, and this act can be implied. *The poem written by Rabindranath Tagore* or *the poem by Rabindranath Tagore* – both are the same, Tagore being the author of the poem. In the second example, the word 'written' is implicit. There is an element of possession, or ownership, in this *by*. The word also means 'in the vicinity or direction of' – *He went to the house by the sea.* It can also indicate the way he went – *He went by the shortest route.* A *bypass* is a way around, usually, a hill or a town, and a *passerby* is one who is going along the way.

Then there is the use of *by the way*, and a less popular version *by the by* or *by the bye* – both meaning 'incidentally'. As you can see, the phrase is used to refer to something in passing. *By and by*, means 'sometime in the future' – *He will realize his mistakes by and by. By and large* means 'on the whole' or 'overall'. *By all means* stands for 'certainly' – *By all means do what you like.* To learn *by rote* is to learn by memorizing. A *bylaw* or *by-law*, however, has nothing to do with *by* in the usual sense. This *by* is derived from the

Old Norse word for town or settlement; England has many places whose names end with *by* – Rugby, Derby, Grimsby, Whitby and so on, and the practice went abroad. Willoughby is a city in Australia; it is one in the USA, too. What is the difference between a law and a *bylaw*? A law is enacted by a legislature; a *bylaw* is a rule by a subordinate body, such as a municipality; thus municipal *bylaws*.

Bye, of course is the word nowadays used casually to take leave. But it comes from 'goodbye', which in turn comes from the phrase 'God be with you'. In cricket, a *bye* is an extra run which is taken even when the ball has not been touched by the bat or the batsman's body.

To *buy* is to purchase something, to acquire after paying money or some other item of value for the object purchased. We have spoken of the *bough*, but *bought* is the past tense of *to buy*, and rhymes with 'cot'! *I buy lots of books, I bought ten yesterday.* Then again, *bought* is different from *brought*, which is the past tense of *bring*.

There is also *bi*- which is twice in a given period – for example, *bi-weekly* or *bi-monthly*. But is *bi-weekly* once in two weeks or twice in a week? Both the uses exist and to avoid any confusion, it is best to say 'twice a week' or 'once in two weeks', which then would be 'once a fortnight'. Generally, though, a *bi-weekly* train would be twice in a week; it would be unusual for it to be only twice a month (in which case someone might call it a *bi-monthly*). And for twice a month, it is safer to use 'fortnightly' as is done for magazines that come out twice a month (though there are 26 fortnights and not 24 in a year of 12 months!) This is an example of the limitations and the awkwardness of the English language.

This one is for computer geeks. You do know, don't you, that *blog* comes from 'weblog', an online journal or personal diary on the web? There are a few hundred million *blogs* on the Internet, and this form of self-expression has become a powerful tool for creating social opinion. Have you noticed the visual pun on the two sets of words – 'we blog' and 'web log'?

C

The letter *c* is a phonetic puzzle; it is a chameleon that can sound either like *k* or *s*. At times, words beginning with *c* use the *k* sound and at other times the *s* sound – the *k* sound as in *cat*, *cow* and *cup* but *s* as in *city*, *civet* and *place*. Indeed, *c* is more often used as a *k* sound, and when used as *s*, it is followed by *e*, *i* or *y*, as in *cellar*, *centre*, *circle*, *city* or *cyst*. C sounds like *k* if it is the end letter – as with *arc* or *attic* – and also if it comes before *a*, *o* or *u*. The word *cynic* starts with the *s* sound but ends with *k*, yet it is *s* at both places in *cynicism*, because the ending of the word has changed! When *ic* has *e* afterwards, then the sound is *s* not *k* – *ice, spice, rice* and *mice*. The same applies to *c* between *a* and *e,* as in *ace*, *lace* or *race*. There are always exceptions. *Celtic* is pronounced 'keltik', but the use of 'seltik' is equally accepted. Unlike in our Indian languages, where a single letter of the alphabet suffices, it takes a combination of *c* and *h* to make the sound *ch* for *chacha*, the Hindi word for 'uncle', and for *chap*, *chart* and *choice*. But *ch* can also work as *k*, as in *character*, *chaos*, *chorus*, *chameleon* or *chemistry*. And indeed, it can also be pronounced 'sh', as with *charade* or *chateau;* as you can guess, these are French words originally.

C has a number of uses as just a single letter. If, in history, you come across *c.* 1000 AD or *c.* 2000 BC, the *c* stands for *circa*, that is, approximately, about or around 1000 AD or 2000 BC. The letters AD refer to 'Anno Domini', 'in the year of Our Lord' in the Christian era, not 'after death' as some believe it to be, while BC refers to 'Before Christ'. (Nowadays it is common to use *CE* for '*common* era' and BCE for 'before *common* era').

As a capital C, it is the Roman numeral for 100; the Latin word is *centum.* On the other hand, the small *c* is the abbreviation for *cent*, usually today one hundredth of a dollar. C stands for *centigrade*, which is a measurement of temperature, as we all know. But only scientifically inclined persons would know that *c* is also the speed at which light travels through a vacuum, it is *constant* at 299,792,458 metres per second!

When you write a letter to someone, you often *cc* it to someone else. This comes from the phrase '*carbon copy*', where a copy is taken by putting a sheet of carbon paper between two sheets of writing paper. This gave rise to the '*cc*-ing' that one may do in sending e-mail to more than one person. But if you did not wish to reveal the names of the recipients to each other, you 'bcc' it, that is a blind carbon copy.

C is also a programming language. It was developed in 1972 at the Bell Labs for use with Unix and later expanded into C++. But why C? Because, it followed an earlier programme called B which had been created in 1969. C, used as programming system software and as an intermediate language between machine languages and higher languages, became very popular in the 1980s. Did you know that there is also a programme called D?

Call is a simple word with complex uses. When you *call* someone, you speak to that person – *The teacher called her to discuss her work*. You shout out if that person is a little far away – *I called out to Sheila in the park*. When you *call* someone by a name, you give that person an identity – *We call her Ayesha*. If you give your pet a name, you *call* her by that name – *Our pet cat is called Chubby*. But you also use a phone to *call* someone – *Please call me in the evening*, you might say. A *caller ID* system allows the phone number of the *caller* to be displayed on the receiver's phone system; modern technology reduces the chances of making anonymous phone *calls*. Again, with telephone technology, we have *call back* facilities, where, if the number you have *called* is engaged, the *called* person's phone *calls* you back automatically when free. And *caller tunes*? Mostly terrible stuff!

But such a direct use of *call* limits its use; there are other uses, too. *It's your call* means 'you have to decide' and to *take a call on* (different from *taking a phone call*) is to take a decision. When a person retires of his or her own volition, or stops the work he or she is doing as a matter of personal choice, he or she *calls it a day*. *Call for* could be to send for – *The Government called for a report*. It could be a public slogan or demand – *The people called for the resignation of the minister*. To *call upon* is to ask for and expect a positive response – *The Government called upon its citizens to contribute to the flood relief effort.* It need not be from a position of authority, but there is a hint that the *called* person(s) is/are expected to listen – *The protestors called upon the government to reduce corruption.*

When does a word begin with a *capital* letter, the larger version of a letter of the alphabet? A simple matter, but which needs a mention. In English, the first letter of a sentence invariably begins with a *capital* letter. Names of persons, places or things, too, begin with a *capital* letter – *Dhruv, India, Kolkata, my pet cat Chubby*. Some categories also begin with the *capital* letter because they pertain to religions – *Christian, Hindu, Muslim, Sikh, Jain* – or because the words have an origin in words that themselves begin with a *capital* letter; from *Bengal* we have *Bengali*, or *Assamese* from *Assam*, *Chinese* from *China*, or *American* from *America*. Strangely, our ego makes us speak of ourselves by using 'I' with a *capital*; recently a few writers have used the small 'i', but this is not the popular usage. The common pronoun 'he' is written as 'He' when we refer to God, irrespective of the religion we follow. The poet *e.e. cummings* (1894–1962) (his full name is little known – Edward Estlin Cummings) wrote poetry deliberately without *capital* letters; note how his name avoids the *capital* form.

The word *capital* has many meanings. A *capital* is the seat of government of a country, or a province – *Reykjavik is the capital of Iceland*. Money is *capital*, especially in its use in business. In the realm of classical economics, *capital*, in the form of money or goods, is one of three basic factors of production, the others being land and labour. *Capitalism* is a concept in economic theory, which is that the private ownership or control of the three factors of production leads to profit-making for the owner of *capital*. And finally, if you think your friend is a wonderful person, a jolly good chap, he is a *capital* fellow! Today you would probably say 'he's cool'.

A quick look at words which begin with both a *capital* letter and an ordinary letter, the first used as a proper noun – *august, eve, general, lent, major, march, may* and *sue* are examples of words that change meaning when used with the capital letter at the start; they may even be pronounced differently as with 'august'. 'August', the month, uses a capital 'A' with the stress on the first syllable 'aug'; when 'august' is used to mean 'eminent' or 'distinguished', the stress is on 'gust'. Such words are *capitonyms*!

Case is a multiple-use word. It is a holder – a suitcase holds suits (and others clothes), a bookcase holds books, a cigarette *case* hold cigarettes and a spectacle *case* holds a pair of spectacles. It is a particular incident or happening – *In this case, the advice was wrong*. It could be a matter for police investigation – *The police registered a case of murder against persons unknown*. It also stands for a matter in court, which is diarized with a *case* number – *The court case went on for ten years*. It could be a set of numbers, specifically or as a general overview, especially in health matters – *Three cases of meningitis were admitted today* or *The number of cases of diabetes is increasing every day*. In slang, we might criticize a person saying – *He's a sad case*.

English grammar, too, has the *case*, an important but not commonly used concept. A *case* is the grammatical function of a noun or a pronoun. There are three main *cases* – subjective, objective and possessive. In modern terminology, the words quite explain themselves; let us look at a few pronouns as examples. *I, he* and *she* are of the subjective *case*, the subject of what is being said or done; *me, him* and *her* are objective *case* as 'objects' of the action, and *mine, his* and *hers* are possessive *case*. *I told her of this new book of mine* has all three *cases* in the sentence. There is also a vocative *case*, where you 'invoke' someone – in *Son, I love you*, the first word is vocative.

All letters using the *capital* form are in the uppercase, while those using the smaller form are in the lowercase. *CASE* is uppercase, *case* is lowercase. Uppercase letters are all of the same size; in the lowercase, *b, d, f, h, k, l* and *t* spread up and are called 'ascenders' while *g, j, p, q* and *y* go down and are 'descenders'!

Let us look at other important grammatical terms beginning with *c*. What about a *clause*? In traditional grammar, a *clause* is a group of words that has a 'subject' and a 'predicate' (a verb or a group of words with a verb). A long sentence may have a number of clauses. A simple rule is that a *clause* should make sense by itself, though it may not be a full sentence. The more *clauses* there are in a sentence – which is then called a *compound sentence* – the more complex the sentence. A sentence can be expanded to provide 'add-ons':

I went home.
I went home as soon as I could.
I went home as soon as I could and watched the cricket match on television.

Each sentence increasingly explains a little more the circumstances surrounding my going home; there is an increasing number of *clauses*. There are various types of *clauses* – adverbial, adjectival or relative, infinite, participle, conditional; look up details if you like but that is not essential for you to understand the basic concept. You would have noticed, though, that there would be at least one independent *clause* which can stand on its own – *I went home* – and there could be one or more dependent or subordinate *clauses*, which do not have a complete meaning on their own.

A *comma* (,) is the symbol for a brief pause in a sentence – *He travelled to Delhi, Mumbai and Bengaluru.* A *comma* is often placed after an opening, introductory word, phrase or *clause*. *Yes, let us go*. A common error is the wrong positioning of the *comma*. *If we go, we should not be late* has the introductory *clause* 'if we go'; often a *comma* is wrongly placed after 'if'. Of course, *commas* separate a set of words which are together required to describe something or explain a situation. *It was a big, fat, black cat*. Or – *A cat saw a mouse, scrambled down the tree, rushed across the lawn and jumped on the mouse*. Note that 'and' is usually used before the last phrase or clause of a sentence. And, usually, there is no *comma* before the last 'and', but many experts find this incorrect.

The reason? Suppose you were to write – *Bharat took his parents, Govinda and Radha to the movies*. How many people went to the movies? If his parents' names were Govinda and Radha, then only three, including Bharat, had gone; a *comma* would be required after 'Radha' to clarify that they are his parents. But if Govinda and Radha were his brother and sister, that would make it five people who had gone to the movies. In which case, to show that Govinda and Radha were in addition to the parents, one might need a *comma* after Govinda. That is why some purists believe that it is the correct form. The *comma* before the 'and' is called the serial *comma* or the Oxford *comma*. Why Oxford? Because, traditionally, it was used by the Oxford University Press.

There are also the *colon* (:) and the *semicolon* (;), the latter being a stronger pause than the *comma*. A *colon* is usually placed before listings, or before a quotation, as at the end of this paragraph. A *semicolon* separates clauses which are quite independent of each other, but where the writer feels that a larger thought process can bind the *clauses* together. You will know the difference in the use of the *comma* and the *semicolon* if you look at Charles Dickens' (1812–70) magnificent description of the days of the French Revolution in *A Tale of Two Cities* (1859):

> *It was the best of times, it was the worst of times; it was the age of wisdom, it was the age of foolishness; it was the epoch of belief, it was the epoch of incredulity; it was the season of Light, it was the season of Darkness; it was the spring of hope, it was the winter of despair; we had everything before us, we had nothing before us; we were all going direct to heaven, we were all going direct the other way – in short, the period was so far like the present period, that some of its noisiest authorities insisted on its being received, for good or for evil, in the superlative degree of comparison only.*[1]

Then the powerful *conjunction*. Words like *and, but, for, yet, though, if, as, after, while, since* and *unless* are

[1] Charles Dickens, *A Tale of Two Cities*; originally published 1859. These are the opening lines of the novel.

conjunctions that join two or more words, phrases or clauses. *My friends went to see a film but I went home.* Because they coordinate between two words or matters, these are *coordinating conjunctions*. There are pairs of words, called *correlative conjunctions*, where two words are used together, *both...and*, *neither...nor*, *either...or* are examples – *Either you are wrong or I am.* Some are also called subordinating *conjunctions* as they join a dependent clause with the main one – *Though it was a holiday, I went to office for a meeting.* But such fine distinctions are not really necessary in our use of correct English.

Take a look at some words that begin with *co*. The two letters at the start of a word as a prefix, implies 'together', as in your *co-worker*, a person working with you, or a *co-passenger*, one travelling with you. *Did you study in a co-educational school?* Not in all words starting with *co*, however, would the letters form a prefix, certainly not in *cot, coat, cough, comb* or *cost*! But when it is a prefix, the *co* is pronounced separately to rhyme with 'so' before the rest of the word is pronounced. Sometimes there is a separation of the *co* from the rest of the word through a hyphen, at other times not; this is a matter of usage. But English is a tricky language; a *coop* is a tiny space as with a hen *coop* (to rhyme with 'stoop'), while a *co-op* is a *cooperative*, from which we also get *cooperation* ('co' being pronounced separately here)! Depending on the style being followed, such words may be spelled with a hyphen after *co* (*co-operative*) or without one (*cooperative*).

Co. in business is the short form of *company*. *Com* is the short form of *commercial* in its use as a top-level Internet domain, as for example ABC@yyy.com, which was introduced in 1985. We also have country-wise Internet domains such as, say, *co.in*, which indicates the country India, *co.ca* for Canada or *co.nz* for New Zealand and so on. A dotcom *company* is one which does its business almost entirely on the Internet.

Come is a simple word, but its uses are many, especially with other words. Repeated, as in *come, come,* it is a gentle rebuke. *Come* or *came* is added to 'about' – *The meeting came about* (happened); 'across' – *I came across a pup* (met or noticed or found by chance); 'after' – *The goonda came after me* (followed) or *Nine comes after eight* (follows in sequence); 'along' – *My studies are coming along well* (progressing); 'around' – *He came around* (recovered) or *He came around to my views* (changed his views); 'at' – *The dog came at me* (attacked); 'back' – *The team is on a comeback trail* (returning to a position); 'between' – *Do not come between us* (cause a break up); 'by' – *He came by to see me when I was ill* (dropped in) or *A good detective novel is difficult to come by* (obtain or locate); 'down' – *He came down in his car* (travelled) or *He has come down in the world* (lost his position).

Then we have *come* with 'in' – *The news is just coming in* (becoming available or arriving); 'into' – *She has come into money* (acquired wealth); 'off' – *The meeting did not come off* (happen); 'on' – *He comes on as a bit of a fool* (appears) or *The lights come on at six* (are put on or displayed); 'out' – *The true story came out* (was revealed); 'over' – *Do come over* (visit); 'through' – *His intentions came through clearly* (manifested); 'to' – *He came to after a few hours* (revived after losing consciousness) or *He came to the house* (arrived at); 'up' – *She came up with a wonderful idea* (proposed) or *He came up the ranks* (rose in level); 'upon' – *We came upon a beautiful garden* (discovered); 'with' – *He came with me to the party* (accompanied) or *He came with new ideas* (brought along).

There are a host of other meanings and those given are only a sampler. But we need to be careful in using the word. *Where do you come from?* is awkward and a sign of poor English; it is better, instead, to ask *Where are you from?* In reply, it would be poor English to say *I come from Kochi*, or even worse, *I am coming from Kochi*; it simply is *I am from Kochi*. (*Coming from* is fine if you are asking someone who has just arrived, probably unexpectedly, where he has *come* from.)

Come on, apart from the examples earlier, has three colloquial, or commonly spoken, meanings. One is to *call* for quick action – *Come on, let's go!* The second is a polite rebuke, a mild scolding – *Come on! You are capable of better work*. The third is slang for showing interest in someone – *He was coming on strongly*.

Commit, has two *m*'s and one *t*, but *committed* has two *m*'s and two *t*'s. To *commit* has several meanings. One may *commit a crime*, that is 'do it'; for that the judge may *commit that person to a jail term*. But a person may *commit* himself to doing something – *He committed himself to the cause of helping street children*. Or, more commonly, *He is committed to the cause of helping street children*. From this comes *commitment*, a vow or pledge, dedication, loyalty or devotion to a cause.

> Committee, the word for a group of people to study or examine something, has three letters repeated, two *m*'s, two *t*'s and two *e*'s in pairs, perhaps the only example of its kind in English.

There are *comparative* and 'superlative' forms of words. 'Fast', 'faster' and 'fastest' – the 'er' creates the *comparison*, and the 'est' the superlative of the adjective 'fast'. There are two ways to *compare* something with something, two ways of making *comparisons* – with 'as...as' or with 'than'. *I am as tall as he is* means that both are of the same height. The other form is with 'than' when the two are not of the same height – *I am taller than he is*. With 'as', the level or quality is the same, with 'than', it is not the same. There is a saying, '*comparisons* are odious'; why do you think that is so?

To *compute* is to *calculate*, to figure out. Arguably the oldest known mechanical *computing* device is the Antikythera mechanism, found in 1901 by a diver in the wreckage of a ship off a Greek island of Antikythera, near Crete? It is believed to be over 2,000 years old! When this device was found, our present day *computer* had not been invented and experts could understand its significance only decades later!

Con is the opposite of 'pro'; it means exactly that, 'opposite' or 'against', but in a plural form. Arguments for and against are the *pros and cons* of an issue – *The political party weighed the pros and cons of a mid-term election.* To *con* is to cheat or swindle – *The swindler conned the businessman of ten thousand rupees.* A less common and somewhat old meaning is 'to memorize' – *to con by rote* is to learn by heart. *Con* as a prefix is 'together' or 'with' – as with *conjoint* or *conjoined* twins. Think of *conduct* – 'behaviour' as a noun, or as a verb, to organize, guide or transmit; think of a duct or a conduit, which carries something, such as water or electricity.

What is a *contranym*? It is a word that has two *contradictory*, entirely opposite, meanings. To sanction is to permit, it is also to block or boycott. To refrain from doing something is to stop doing it; it is also a repetition, like the refrain of a song. To trip along is to go along happily, almost dancing; it is also to stumble! There are a few dozen such words.

A few common errors that we make must be mentioned here. *Cost* is a noun; as ordinarily understood, it is the price of something. *What is the cost of the book?* is considered to be the same same as *What is the price of the book?* But actually, the amount of money taken to produce one copy of the book is its *cost*, and a profit margin is added to fix the price. That is the difference between *cost* and price. Indeed, if a book is not selling well, it might be sold at the *cost price*! But *cost* can be what one might have to suffer or lose – *The accident cost him his life*, or *The delay in reaching the office for the interview cost him the job*. Here, *cost* is a verb but even in the past tense, it is not 'costed', it remains *cost*. There is no such word, except in one very limited way. The process of calculating the expenses in manufacturing a product is *costing*, and one could perhaps ask, in accounting jargon – *How was this costed?*

To *compliment* someone is to praise, to speak well about him or her – *I complimented him on his dress sense* or *The principal complimented her on coming first in class.* On the other hand *complement* is an addition or improvement – *After the recent recruitment, we have a full complement of staff* or *Good cheese complements good wine.*

Then we have the mix up between *counsel* and *council*. *Counsel*, as a verb, is to give advice – *the teacher tried to counsel the boy to behave better*; as a noun, a *counsel* is a lawyer – *My counsel argued the case very well in court. Council* is an assembly of legislators or elected representatives – *a council of ministers* or a *legislative council*. From these one gets *counsellor* and *councillor*. A *counsellor* is a professional who listens to the problems of others and advises them – *counsels* them – on how to handle those problems. A *councillor* is usually one of a few elected people who run a town or city *council*. There is a third word, *consul*, which is used for a certain category of diplomats, whose office is the *consulate*.

Court has many meanings. It is an area for playing certain games, like *a tennis court*. In the days of yore, kings had their *courts* where the ministers and *courtiers* gathered and public decisions were taken. It is, today, a place where legal cases are heard by a judge and decisions handed down. One might *court arrest*, that is, allow oneself to be arrested as a form of protest. You could also *court trouble* if you do or say something which could get you into trouble, encouraging that trouble to happen. And a young man may also *court* a young lady, a rather old-fashioned concept today, but to try and win a lady's affection is something men will do as long the world exists! *The ball is in your court* means that you have to take some steps about resolving a matter.

Cricket, anyone? We need not spend time on the insect *cricket* which makes a sound by rubbing its wings together. The passion of many million Indians is the game of *cricket*. In old French, *criquet* was a type of club, and perhaps the game of *croquet* has the same origin. In old English, *cricc* meant a *crutch*. Of course, a *century* in cricket is a hundred runs, but *c* is the scorer's short form for *caught*.

> What is *culture*? It's a very difficult question to answer. It is the way a people live and behave; it also expresses the maturity of a people in terms of the creative arts and aesthetic appreciation of the arts. Who is a *cultured* person? It may not be wrong to say that the more well behaved you are in society and in your personal world, the more *cultured* a person you are. To have good social manners, be concerned about others, to be helpful – these are perhaps a few basic signs of being *cultured*.

D

D-day is generally used in military terminology as the day for a pre-planned attack. The most well known D-Day is 6 June 1944, when the Battle of Normandy of the Second World War began, the start of the final effort of the Allied Expeditionary Force to free Europe from Nazi rule. The first day of examinations, of a new job, of any difficult effort, might be called *D-Day*. This is not quite *doomsday*, though it might appear to be that way to some people! *Doomsday* is the last day of the world, in traditional Christian belief – the day of reckoning which will bring *doom* or ruin to all mankind.

A *dash* has so many meanings. It is, for one, a punctuation mark of many uses. It separates two parts of a word or numbers. It is also used in place of brackets, or to separate two parts of a sentence. There are two types of dashes – the em dash and the en dash; the em dash is the same width as the capital M and the en dash that of N. What is the difference between the three forms – the em and en dashes and the hyphen? The M dash is used, generally, to express an aside, a brief shift in thought; *The boy – though he was born poor – rose to become the Mayor of London.* It separates a fresh matter in a sentence – as in brackets or parentheses. It also gives a pause – if there is only one em dash in two parts of a sentence. The en dash is used to separate numbers, say phone numbers; *my phone number is 011–23456789.* Or it can separate places, as in *the Delhi–Agra express train*, or people, as in *a mother–daughter relationship*, where the two words it joins are of equal importance. There is a slight difference between the en dash and the hyphen; the latter is slightly shorter, and is used when two different words have to be put together to make a new concept – *a well-known person.* But the difference between the dashes and the hyphen, in daily use, remains somewhat theoretical.In publishing, the en dash often replaces the em dash and when it does, it is used with a single space on either side unlike the dash, which has no space on either side.

The American poet Emily Dickinson (1830–86) was a very frequent user of the *dash* in her poetry. Look at these four lines:

'Heaven' – is what I cannot reach!
The Apple on the Tree –
Provided it do hopeless – hang –
That – 'Heaven' is – to Me![1]

A *dash* is also a run, a rush, to the school gate when you are late, or to shelter to escape from the rain. We have the hundred metres *dash* at an athletics meet, for example. It is quick action like *dashing off* a letter to the editor when you want to protest about something in the newspaper (provided

[1] https://allpoetry.com/Heavenis-what-I-cannot-reach.

you still read one)! It is also an act of violence – to *dash* something to the ground, or against a wall, is to throw it and smash it. Similarly, to *dash one's hopes* is to destroy one's hopes. A *dash* – a very small amount – of mustard in the salad may make it tangy. A *dash of colour* in an otherwise dull room? Again, a little bit. There is, of course, the *dashboard* of a car, where the instruments panel is placed. The term was earlier used for a board in front of the driver of a horse carriage, which prevented the mud or snow thrown up by the horses' hooves from reaching the driver.

Data is a word we use almost daily – in mathematics, economics and other social sciences, and in computer terminology; so much so that we do not stop to think about it. *Data* is a set of facts, generally formulated in numerical terms, which, when processed, gives us information about something. *Data* is a plural word; the singular is *datum*, but is rarely used because we rarely use one single piece of *datum*. But it is one of those words commonly treated nowadays as a 'mass' noun where one says *The data is wrong* for a set of *data*, and not 'The data are wrong'.

De, at the start of a word as a prefix, means the opposite of the word. On the other hand, *d* is even more important at the end of a word as a suffix; '-ed' puts action into the past, and changes the tense! *Detoxify, demystify, demilitarization,* these are words where the rest of the word, excluding *de*, has its own meaning. Indeed, in these cases, for all practical purposes, *de* and the rest of the word can be separated by a hyphen. But this rule has its obvious limitation; it cannot be that *defy* is the opposite of 'fy', *demand* the opposite of 'mand' or *demit* the opposite of 'mit'! (No hyphen is possible with these words, that is the test).

De jure and *de facto* are two terms that are used quite commonly in English, but are taken from the original Latin *de* meaning 'about' or 'from'; here it is not a prefix. The first relates to law and legal matters, the latter to a fact, but not necessarily legal. *When the King died, the prince was still young; the Queen was the* de facto *ruler and the prince was only the* de jure *Head.*

Dear is one of the most common words in English, because it is the word you use to call someone you love, and it is the word that starts most letters. You address a person you write to with the word *Dear*, even if you were to write something in anger. When do you use *my dear*? It is to express a closer friendship or relationship; at times it can be used by a superior in a condescending way to a junior. And *dearest* is obviously for the person who is *dearest* to you, the person you love. But *dearest* is a bit of an old-fashioned term in today's world. Perhaps *darling* is better? Be careful of the correct usage for formal writing.

Dear, dearer, dearest. Interestingly *dearer* is not a term for addressing anyone. One could perhaps say *She is dearer to me than anything else in the world.* It is generally a comparative form of *dear* as in 'expensive' – *Things are getting dearer every year.* It is in this context that we have *dearness allowance*, a special part of one's pay to compensate for an increasing cost of living.

Degree has so many uses that it is difficult to explain its nuances. We have already seen the use of the 'comparative' and the 'superlative', which is the use of *degree* in grammar. But in common usage as a measure of comparison, it is a differentiation – *a case of second-degree burns*, or indication of a level – *His encouraging words gave me a degree of comfort.* Temperature is based on *degrees*, water freezes at zero *degree* – 0° – Centigrade and boils at 100° Centigrade. In terms of physical space, any circle has 360 *degrees* – the earth, the moon, the sun, the planets. You get the sense of limitation – 360° being that limit. A college *degree*, a BA, or a University *degree*, an MA, shows the level up to which a person has studied.

Defer has two meanings. To *defer* is to postpone. It is also to bow down, but no one has to do that literally, physically – *I defer to your superior knowledge. Deference* is the showing of respect and regard – *In deference to the court's suggestion, the lawyer withdrew the appeal.* And *deferral*, from the other *defer*, is 'postponement' – *The deferral in the proceedings meant that the accused remained in jail a week longer.*

The *difference* between *defer* and *differ* can come into focus in, say, a court matter. The court may *defer*, that is postpone, the passing of a judgement and two learned judges may *differ*, or disagree, in their views. *Difference*, at the start of this paragraph, is the abstract noun; one may have a *difference* of opinion with a friend, when one disagrees with his views. *Different* means 'another' or not the same – *We have different views on the subject* or *This is a different story*; 'various' or 'many' – *There are different versions of this story.* We also have *differently* – *He is a strange fellow, he does everything differently.* A physically challenged person is a *differently abled* person.

An error we often make is in using 'demanding for'. It is only *demanding*; *demand for* is correct only when the word is used as a noun, not as a verb. *Our demand for justice* is correct, but 'we demand for justice' is wrong, it should be *we demand justice.*

A set of similar words is *desert* and *dessert*. The first has two meanings. A *desert* is a land with little or no vegetation, such as the Kalahari *Desert*. The second meaning is 'to abandon', or 'to leave without permission' – *The sailor deserted his ship*. The lack of people can make a place *deserted*, left to itself, also abandoned – *The beach wore a deserted look at night*. The other word, *dessert*, is the sweet or pudding you might have at the end of a meal. There is also *dissertation*, which is long essay on a subject, especially one written for a university degree or diploma.

Yet another set of similar words are *drought*, *draught* and *draft*. The first word, rhymes with 'out' and refers to agricultural conditions when insufficient rainfall leads to a shortfall in agricultural production and a shortage of water and foodgrains. The second has several meanings and is often misspelled nowadays as *draft*. A glass of beer from a tap is a *draught* of beer; an unwanted inflow of cold air into the room is a *draught* of air, a certain *dose* of liquid medicine is a *draught* of medicine; the *depth* of a ship in water is its *draught*; bullocks used to till the land are *draught* animals. A *draft* is a cheque issued by a bank which can be encashed at the receiver's bank immediately. It is also a first, rough, possibly incomplete version of a book or a document or a drawing – *This is a draft of his speech*; so, as a verb, it is to draw up an outline of a speech or some other document – *He drafted a speech*. *Draft* also refers to compulsory military enrolment – *During war a country's young men may be drafted for war service.*

Deter is to try and prevent someone from a certain action – *His threats did not deter me from carrying on with my work*. The past tense has two *r*'s – *deterred*; so does the noun *deterrent* – like *a nuclear deterrent*, a nuclear capacity that *deters* others from going to war against a country which has nuclear weapons. To *determine* is to decide, to fix – *The survey determined the city limits* – while being *determined* stands for being firm or resolute – *He was determined to come first in class. Determinate* means 'specifically defined' – *a determinate set of numbers*. A *determinant* is a factor in a decision-making process – *Interest rates are a key determinant in the demand for new housing*. It is also a mathematical term; a *determinant* is a value used in linear algebra or in calculus.

A ***determiner***, in grammar, is a word that *determines* the noun we are talking about and creates a noun phrase. They indicate what we are talking about – *this pen, my pen, your pen* and so on. They are either specific – for example, *his, its, my, our, the, their, this, that, those, which, your* – or general – *a, an, another, any, other, what* and so on. One rule is that we generally do not have two *determiners* together, it creates confusion; we cannot say – 'Your that pen was on the table'. To indicate which pen and also its ownership, we have to say – *That pen of yours was on the table*. As usual, there are exceptions, such as 'a few' or 'any other'.

We all know what a ***dictionary*** is – a list, in alphabetical chronology, of all the words in a language, with their meanings. The English word *dictionary* is believed to have been created by John of Garland, an academician; sometime in the 13th century, he wrote a book called the *Dictionarius* to study Latin *diction*, the correct way to speak.

A fairly frequent prefix is *dis*-. It implies the opposite of the original word. In the papers one reads about corrupt officials being caught by the authorities for assets *disproportionate* to (not in proportion to) their known income. *Disqualification* is the opposite of 'qualification', *disappearance* is the opposite of 'appearance', and *disprove* the opposite of 'prove'. Again, not all words beginning with *dis* have an opposite word. *Disturb* does not have an opposite word 'turb'. And, *distress* and 'stress' have a common, not opposite, meaning.

Do is just that, to *do*, work, exert, act upon, accomplish, complete some action. It needs mention though that *do* also has an element of emphasis, not just that one should *do* something, but that one should certainly *do* it, and well – *Do your homework*, but with emphasis, it becomes *Do do your homework*. The difference in emphasis is between *I study* and *I do study*.

In today's busy living, *to do* lists of things one intends to do are important, but in elegant Victorian English, *a to-do* referred to a confused, bothersome situation – *Oh, no! What a to-do!*

One has to get a sense of the difference between *do* and 'make'. Both are words indicating action, but 'make' is somewhat specific. *I do my work*, but *I make my own breakfast*. But be careful, in modern slang, you can ask – *Did you do lunch?* when enquiring if someone has eaten their lunch. There is also *make do*, which is to manage with what one has – *The poor boy has to make do with only one pair of trousers*. The opposite, or negative of *do*, of course, is *do not* or *don't*. This can lead to, say – *Do not do anything wrong*, or – *Don't do anything I wouldn't do!*

Do's and *don'ts* is a tricky use. The phrase together means 'a set of instructions' – what to do and what not to do. The difficulty is with the use of the apostrophe. A second apostrophe, when *don't* already has one, is awkward. Some try to remove the apostrophe from do's and don'ts, but that leads to 'disk operating systems'. Generally people write *do's and don'ts*, which reduces the awkwardness of two apostrophes in one word.

Dogma is a strong belief in something, a doctrine of faith, and generally in a religious context. Often these are basic principles or tenets of a religion, a set of core principles. But political ideologies can also be *dogma*, not to be questioned. When one believes blindly in a viewpoint to the exclusion of other views, he or she is *dogmatic*. If you read *dogma* backwards, it reads '(I) am god'!

A *dot* is a tiny circle, a round spot. But *dotty* means 'somewhat mad' or 'scatterbrained'. A *ditty* is a song, a tune. And *ditto* means 'the same' or 'repeat'; it is indicated sometimes in a column or list by two inverted commas below the original item being repeated.

Drama is a form of literature, which is enacted on stage, but it may also be read – as with any other form of writing. As a consequence, it also can refer to situations which are theatrical or emotionally charged, such as a *hijack drama* or a *political drama*. *Dramatic* pertains to exaggerated, theatrical behaviour or spectacular action in real life. A *dramatist* is a person who writes plays. A play is a specific countable piece of *drama*, one play or ten plays; *drama* is the genre, the type of writing. There is no plural created by adding *s* to *drama*. It would be incorrect to say 'She has written ten dramas'; the correct form is *She has written ten plays*. The term *dramatis personae* refers to the cast of characters of a play, and is, therefore, sometimes used to describe the persons involved in a *dramatic* situation.

> The greatest *dramatist* of all time has to be William Shakespeare (1564–1616). Four hundred years after he passed away, he still remains the world's most well known literary figure. He has written 38 plays, some of them the most incredible *dramatic* work, and as if that were not enough, he also wrote 154 sonnets, besides other poems. His plays have been translated into at least 80 languages.

E

E is the most common letter in the *English* language. It is used over 11 per cent of the times letters are used in *English*; in other words if there were a hundred letters used in common words picked at random, it is likely that *eleven* of those letters would be *e*. It is, in Internet times, especially relevant as the abbreviation for *electronic*, as in *email* or *e-commerce*. The letter *e* is also the abbreviation for a number of other words – such as for *error*, *east* and *English*. In bills given by many shops for purchases, one might notice a phrase at the bottom, *e and o e* – it stands for *errors and omissions excepted*, to 'cover' for any *errors* that the billing might have made. The letter *e* is a constant in mathematics; it is the base of natural logarithms, the number being 2.7182818284. . . .

In what is arguably the most famous *equation* in physics, the famous physicist Albert Einstein (1879–1955) calculated that $E=mc^2$. *E* stands for energy, *m* for mass and c^2 is the square of the speed of light; the *equation* expounds his special theory of relativity. In his own words, 'It followed from the special theory of relativity that mass and *energy* are both but different manifestations of the same thing.' There is a famous limerick:

There was a young lady named Bright,
Whose speed was faster than light;
She went out one day,
In a relative way,
And returned on the previous night.[1]

The letters e.g. stand for the phrase *for example*. It comes from the Latin phrase *exempli gratia*, which means 'for the sake of an *example*'. If this phrase is used, there is no need to add 'for' in front of *e.g.* as then we would have 'for, for example'. There is also no need to add an *etc.* after *e.g.*, as the *example(s)* does/do not in any case make a full list. And what is *etc.* or *et cetera*? It is Latin for 'and so forth' or 'and other things'. There must be a comma before the *etc.* and a full stop after. *At the stationers' we get envelopes, paper, pencils, pens, etc.* There must not be an 'and' before the *etc.* A similar phrase is et al., which means 'and others'. It is usually used for persons, and a short list of people followed by *et al.* would cover the whole group; in listing the many authors of a book, for example, one could find the first author's name, followed by *et al.*; note the full stop, since *al.* is the short form of *alia* ('among others' is 'inter alia').

E has a major role in the formation of prefixes, such as em-, en- and ex-. *Em-* and *en-* are added at the start of a word to make it function or to put it into effect. *Embalm* is to put a balm, a liquid coating, over a body; *empower* is to

[1] See http://quoteinvestigator.com/2013/12/19/lady-bright/for the story on sourcing.

give power, such as *to empower women's groups to speak up against gender discrimination*. *Ensure* is to make sure; *enjoy* is to get joy; *entrap* is to trap; *enliven* is to liven up; *ennoble* to make noble. But obviously, not all words beginning with *em* or *en* have that implication. *Ex-* implies 'former', such as an *ex-student* of a college.

There are words or phrases starting *en* which are pronounced in the French manner, as the words are originally from that language. The phrase *en* is then pronounced like 'on'. *En route* is like 'on route'; it means 'on the way'. *Ennui*, pronounced somewhat like 'on–we' is a feeling of boredom, of lethargy. *Entourage* – for example *the President's entourage* – is the group comprising the staff and companions who might travel with the VIP (here, as in some other similarly ended words, the 'age' is pronounced in the French way roughly as 'aazh'). An *encore* is the additional short performance of a performer when the audience asks for a repeat of an enjoyable performance; it is the call itself at the ovation given to a great performance, requesting some more.

There are two opinions about the way to pronounce *envelope*. The paper cover in which we put letters or other papers used to be frequently pronounced 'on–velope' though that French-influenced pronunciation is nowadays not often followed. There is actually a community Facebook page on this – It's Envelope, Not Onvelope! There is also the verb to *envelop*, and that is not pronounced 'on'; it means 'to cover' – *The clouds often envelop the mountains*. *To push the envelope* is to go beyond the normal boundaries of any thought or action or to do something that has never been done before. *Back-of-the-envelope* calculations are quick, rough calculations, especially to get a broad indication of results or trends – *My back-of-the envelope calculations show that we will finally make a profit this year.*

East is the direction 90 degrees from north and south and opposite west on a compass; it is the direction in which the sun rises as it is the direction of the earth's rotation on its axis. *The East* is also sometimes used for the culture, the ethos, the way of life, of the *East* as a whole. *Eastern* pertains to the *east*, and we have *Eastern* philosophy, *Eastern* attitudes and so on. The cultural divide between the East and the West was sharply distinguished by Rudyard Kipling (1865–1936), the India-born British writer, who wrote *The Ballad of East and West*, published in 1889:

Oh, East is East and West is West, and never the twain shall meet,
Till Earth and Sky stand presently at God's great Judgment Seat.[1]

Each and *every* are words that are sometimes used incorrectly. They are similar in meaning at times – *Each year the birds come here from Siberia* or – *Every year the birds come here from Siberia*. But *each* represents one, individual year, and is a singular noun, while *every* is collective and represents all the years together. *Each* is used when two are involved – *He held a stick in each hand* or *Each one helps the other*. If *each* is used in comparison, the pronoun 'of' is sometimes awkwardly added – *Each of the news channels is giving the same story*; in *Every news channel is giving the same story*, there is no 'of'. *Every* is often time related – *The clock strikes every hour* or *He goes to*

[1] http://www.bartleby.com/246/1129.html

school every day specifies periodicity, that is, how often something happens.

The *earth* is round, we know, and there are so many ways of proving it. And yet there still exists a Flat *Earth* Society, even in these modern times, whose mission is to promote the concept of a flat *earth*! A bestselling book by the economist columnist Thomas Friedman (1953–), *The World is Flat* (2005) argues that the world is now a 'level playing field' and provides equal opportunities for entrepreneurs anywhere on *earth*.

Earth is also the soil on the ground, which is cultivated for growing crops. If there is no rain we say that the *earth is parched*. A *scorched earth policy* is the way an army destroys everything around it as it retreats, so as to make things difficult for the enemy. This is a very unfortunate military strategy, as it ruins the lives of the civilian population of that area. *Earthing* is connecting an electrical device to the ground or earth. Perhaps because it is invaluable, we speak of something expensive as having cost the *earth*. *What on earth, why on earth, how on earth* – are all exclamations to stress a point, but with a sense of disagreement. *What on earth did you do? Why on earth did you go there? How on earth did you go?*

A quick word about *eight*. This number between seven and nine, is a Fibonacci number (check for that word in Chapter F). An *eight*-sided figure is an octagon, and an octopus has *eight* tentacles. There are *eight* corners of the earth, if you take into account north, south, east, west, north-east, north-west, south-east and south-west. In Hindu mythology, there are *eight* guardians of the directions – the *ashta dikpalas*. The number is important in many religions. In Christianity, the New Testament was written by *eight* men; the Dharmachakra in Buddhism has *eight* spokes and symbolizes the *Eight*-fold Path.

Either has two uses. As a sort of opposite of 'neither', it is used in a positive comparative context, while 'neither' is used in a negative way. *Either batsman should do well* means that any one of the two is expected do well, while *Neither batsman will do well* means that both will not do well. In another form, this would be *either of the batsmen* or *neither of the batsmen*, where *batsmen* is plural but *either* remains singular. The other use is in conjunction with 'or' – *Either you should go, or I* or *Either Rita will get the job, or Vinod will.*

The word *else* has many uses. It means, first or in addition to – *What else did you do?* Or – *Who else came to your place?* It can also mean 'in a different way' and can be in relation to a person, place or time – *I am meeting someone else*, or *You have to take a taxi, how else will you get to the meeting on time?* Or – *My home is far away, where else can we meet?* It is used with 'or' as an alternative – *Please study hard, or else you will regret your laziness when the results come out*. That does sound like a threat which is a fourth way of using the word – *Study hard, or else!* Nowadays there is a fifth use – *That was something else*, meaning 'very different' or 'special'!

To *elect* is to choose, in political systems, usually through a ballot, during the process of *elections*. The *electorate* covers those who are eligible to vote. What is the difference between an *election* and a referendum? The first is where individual candidates are chosen through a voting process; the second is a system in some countries where important policy issues are voted for or against, as it is referred to the people by the government to elicit or seek out formal public opinion for a decision.

The difference between *electric* and *electronic*? *Electronic* systems need *electricity* to start up! This is not a physics class, and so only a very simplistic definition can be attempted here. *Electric* pertains to – it is the adjective of – *electricity*. When *electricity* passes through 'passive' systems it remains *electricity*, but is then transformed into heat, light or motion for *electrical equipment* – an electric cooker, an electric bulb, a vacuum cleaner. When it passes through some 'active', complex component such as a transistor, it is an *electronic* system. *Electricity* is the flow of *electrons*, which can be started and stopped, but *electronics* is about systems for controlling that flow. The word *electric* is also used to describe a certain charged up atmosphere – *The air was electric at the concert, the audience was spellbound*. The *e* in *email*, *e-business*, *e-commerce* and other such terms, as we have seen earlier, stands for *electronic*.

English is the language most widely spoken and understood in the world. It has become the language of international commerce and diplomacy. But it is spoken in many different ways; even in England, modern slang and the Queen's English are very different from each other.

There are many fun poems and stories about the crazy language. Here are the first lines from one:

I take it you already know
Of tough and bough and cough and dough?

Others may stumble, but not you,
On hiccough, thorough, slough and through?
Well done! And now you wish, perhaps,
To learn of less familiar traps?
Beware of heard, a dreadful word
That looks like beard and sounds like bird,
And dead: it's said like bed, not bead –
For goodness sake, don't call it deed![1]

Look up a whole set of such poems at the website *www.spellingsociety.org*. But do not be embarrassed if your English is a little weak; after all, we have learnt it, and were not born into it. So we should be able to laugh a little at ourselves when we come across a gem like this one, a letter reportedly written by one Mr Okhil Ch Sen to the authorities at the Sahibganj Divisional Railway Office in 1909, which, one believes, led to the setting up of toilets in all railway coaches. This letter is well known, but as a classic example of wrong *English*, is worth recalling:

Dear Sir,

I am arrive by passenger train Ahmedpur station and my belly is too much swelling with jackfruit. I am therefor went to privy. Just I doing the nuisance the guard making whistle blow for train to go off and I am running with lotah in one hand and dhoti in the next when I am fall over and expose all shocking to man and female women on platform. I am got leaved at Ahmedpur station. This too much bad, if passenger go to make dung, the dam guard not wait train minutes for

[1] http://spellingsociety.org/uploaded_misc/poems-online-misc.pdf

him? I am therefor pray your honour to make big fine on that guard for public sake. Otherwise I am making big report to papers.

Your's faithfully servent
Okhil Ch Sen[1]

English is a 'mad' language. In what other language do people drive in a parkway and park in a driveway? Why is there is no egg in an eggplant, no ham in a hamburger, no butter in a butterfly; why neither apple nor pine in pineapple? Is there any other language where people play at a recital and recite in a play? Why should 'oversee' and 'overlook' or a 'wise man' and a 'wise guy' mean the opposite? If the plural of mouse is mice, why is the plural of house not 'hice'? We can go on and on. . . .

But, with all its strangeness, *English* is indeed a loveable language. It has produced some of the finest writing in the world – great classics in poetry, prose and drama – and we are the poorer if we are unable or do not find it worthwhile to at least dip into those works. Much of the technical and scientific literature of the world is in *English*. Because of the complexity of the language, and yet its worldwide use, it is all the more necessary for us to be correct in its use. Today, we have 'good' for 'well', 'cool' to mean 'great', 'hot' for 'wonderful' and 'like' for nothing at all at the start of a conversation – the language is going through an upheaval.

An *epic* is the term for a very long poem which relates the life of one or many mythical heroes, of kings and queens, of gods and goddesses. The two important Indian *epics*, written in Sanskrit, are the *Ramayana* and the *Mahabharata*.

[1] Displayed at the National Rail Museum, New Delhi

The *Mahabharata* is generally considered to have been written before the *Ramayana*, though it pertains to a later period. The *Ramayana*, believed to have been told by the sage Valmiki in approximately the 4th or 5th century BCE, has seven 'books' or *kandas*, narrating the events in Rama's life. The *Mahabharata*, written by Vyasa, possibly around the 8th or 9th century BCE, describes the devastating war between the Pandavas and the Kauravas at Kurukshetra. At the heart of this *epic* of 18 *parvas* or periods, is the counsel given by Lord Krishna when he advises Arjuna to do his duty at the field of battle. This is in the *Bhagavad Gita*, the fountainhead of much of Hindu philosophy.

There are two significant Greek *epics*, the *Iliad* and the *Odyssey*, both attributed to Homer, around the 8th or 9th century BCE and a Latin *epic* poem by Virgil, the *Aeneid*, written around 29 and 19 BCE. The *Iliad* describes the ten year Trojan War, when the Romans laid siege to the Greek city of Troy but does not describe the end of the war. What happens then is described in the *Aeneid*. The *Odyssey* tells of the travels of Odysseus, also known as Ulysses in Roman myths, who takes ten years to return home to Ithaca, and has many adventures during his journey, but is able to return to his wife Penelope who has waited steadfastly for him. An odyssey is today the word for an *epic* journey, actual or emotional.

An ***epigram*** is a short comment which generally causes amusement. English poets such as John Dryden (1631–1700) and Alexander Pope (1688–1744) were famous for their wit. Pope's famous line, 'Fools rush in where angels fear to tread', is a classic example.

Another great name is that of Oscar Wilde, who advised us – 'Always forgive your enemies – nothing annoys them so much.' Mark Twain said – 'Don't let schooling interfere with your education.' Epigrams use language cleverly to make a subtle point.

An *epigraph* is an inscription on a monument, or a short comment or quotation at the start of a book or the chapters of a book. An *epithet* is a word or short phrase that describes a person – for example Mahatma is an *epithet* used for Gandhiji. There is also a strange device, the *transferred epithet* – *I lay on my sleepless pillow.* Actually, it was I who was sleepless and not my pillow. What happens is that the modifier, the description, is shifted from the animate to the inanimate, giving it an unexpected turn of phrase. One of the best examples of this is the opening lines of a poem by W.H. Auden (1907–1973):

Lay your sleeping head, my love,
Human on my faithless arm.[1]

An *epitaph* is what is written on a tombstone of a person who has been buried. It can be serious or funny, as in an *epigram*. In Kohima in Nagaland, India, is an *epitaph* of the soldiers who gave their lives, in March 1944, during the Second World War, as they battled to repulse the Japanese army. It reads:

[1] Edward Leeson; ed., *The New Golden Treasury of English Verse*; Pan Books, 1980; p. 459.

When you go home, tell them of us and say,
For their tomorrow, we gave our today.[1]

An *essay* is a piece of non-fiction prose, explaining the thoughts of the *essayist* on any subject under the sun. In English, some of the early *essayists* were Sir Francis Bacon (1561–1626), Joseph Addison (1672–1719), Charles Lamb (1775–1834) and William Hazlitt (1778–1830). There is another, related, meaning of *essay*. It is an attempt or an effort. It is often used as in *to essay forth*, to go forward – *He essays forth every morning to the centre of town*. The writing of *essays* is indeed an attempt to go forth and express one's views. Today, some of the best blogs are *essays* on the Net.

Etiquette can be the subject of a whole book; here we must touch upon it very briefly. It is the way we behave with other people, the way we act in a social context or a code of conduct. *Etiquette* can be as direct as using the correct fork and spoon to eat with, but it is much more. It is the way we show good manners and polite behaviour. But good manners are not easy to come by – how many of us say 'please', 'sorry', 'thank you' and 'excuse me' as a matter of habit?

Ex followed by a hyphen, *ex-*, has a specific role. The use of *ex-* as 'former' is quite common; we say *ex-Prime Minister* or *ex-employee*. But if the person is dead, then *ex-* is normally not used. One does not, say, use ex-PM or former PM to refer to Jawaharlal Nehru; one would normally speak of Jawaharlal Nehru who was prime minister or the first prime minister. Actually, if a distinction has to be made, the

[1] http://www.ww1cemeteries.com/other_cemeteries_ext/kohima_war_cemetery.htm

immediate past person would be *ex* and those before him or her would be 'former'. If there is a doubt about which word to use, 'former' is safe! *Ex*, without the hyphen, means 'without' or 'outside' – like *ex gratia*, a payment outside the norms or rules, made as a special case. *Ex officio* is used for a position held because of another regular position – *The Vice President of India is,* ex officio, *the Chairman of the Rajya Sabha.* And one's *ex* in slang is one's former spouse or partner.

Extra is 'more' or 'additional'– *He gets an extra newspaper over the weekend* or *He puts his extra income into a separate bank deposit.* It comes originally from 'over and above' or 'beyond', and *extra* then is a prefix. *Extraordinary* is that which is beyond the ordinary. *Extracurricular* is outside or beyond the curriculum. In films, one may have *extras*, usually those who are in crowd scenes or similar shots with lots of people but no speaking roles. In cricket there are *extras*, too, runs not off the bat, and fielding positions such as *extra cover*. In games like hockey or football, if the scores remain the same at the end of the regular time, there is an *extra time* played. One sees *extra-terrestrials* (also spelled 'extraterrestrials') in films, characters from outside the earth. Stephen Speilberg's 1982 film *E.T.: The Extra-terrestial*, was a super-hit.

Though *e* is the most used letter in the English alphabet, there is a very unusual short novel of about 50,000 words without the use of the letter *e*! In 1939, Ernest Vincent Wright (1872–1939) – whose own name started with *E*! – wrote *Gadsby*, which was given the subtitle – *A Story of Over 50,000 Words Without Using the Letter 'E'*. This type of clever writing is called a lipogram.

f

F, the sixth letter of the English alphabet, has a range of meanings as an abbreviation. Perhaps of most common use is *F* for *Fahrenheit*, the measurement of temperature introduced by Daniel Gabriel Fahrenheit (1686–1736). Though the world has generally moved to Celsius, a few countries, notably the USA, continue to use the *Fahrenheit* scale. There is also *f* as a notation in mathematics that stands for *function*; *f(x)* reads *function of x* and expresses a relationship between an input value of x and its output. But in scriptwriting and screenplays, *fx*, without the brackets, stands for *effects*. *F1* is *Formula One* racing, based on *formula*, that is, the rules that govern the motor sport.

F has an important role in academic work. *F* as a reference or citation in a book stands for '...and *following* page (or paragraph or section)'. Therefore page 100 *f* would refer to pages 100-101, while pages 100 *ff* would be for a few undefined pages from page 100. *F* also stands for *folio*. In printing, *folio* is a folded sheet to make four printed pages. *Folio* is also a particular page size, about 15 inches in length. Some rare books were earlier printed in *folio*, including

Shakespeare's first *folio* of plays, published in 1623.

In modern times, *F* is a programming language, a subset of *FORTRAN*. The original version, which derives from Mathematical FORmula TRANslating System, used to be in all capital letters, though later versions do not use the capitals. *FORTRAN* was developed by IBM in the 1950s for engineering and scientific computation.

Three related words beginning with *f* and of much importance to human thinking are *fact*, *fiction* and *fantasy*. We use the word *fact* all the time, but what does it mean? The word *fact* is from the Latin *factum* which means 'something done'; it is a given actuality that can be proven, something true, and generally not disputed. There are different uses of the word. *In fact* begins a statement of something that is supposed to be true, though many people pass off their opinion by starting off with *in fact*! The same is the case with *as a matter of fact*. *A factual error* is one in which something stated or written is not true. Sometimes, *fact* can be used in an opinion that cannot be proved – *It is a fact of life that we all go through difficulties at times*. One cannot say 'true fact' as a *fact* is expected to be true in any case.

Fiction is the opposite of *fact*. It is something not true, and therefore is used for a written work of the imagination. It is the commonly used word covering all novels; short *fiction* is the term for the entire range of short stories – *His latest work of fiction is brilliant* or *This book of short fiction is very disappointing.* Nowadays there are various categories of *fiction – literary fiction, commercial fiction, young adult fiction* and so on. Very, very short *fiction* is *flash fiction*, usually considered to be shorter than three hundred words. Writing which does not tell a story and is not a work of *fiction*, is *non-fiction* – biographies, essays et al.

The difference between *fiction* and *fantasy* is interesting. *Fiction* deals with imagined characters and situations in the real world, those that can exist or be possible. *Fantasy* deals with imaginary characters, places or events that are outside the realm of possibility, such as the world of Harry Potter. (Wonder then, why *science fiction* is *fiction*, when it is largely based in outer space and the future, which is totally *fantastical*).

A related word is *fable*, generally used to describe a story of long ago, with strange creatures and talking animals, which has some moral advice for the reader. *Aesop's Fables* are the most well known of such stories – around 65 tales told by a seventh-century Greek slave (some say he was African). In India we have the even more ancient tales of *Panchatantra*, a set of 87 stories in five books, believed to have been told sometime in the third to fifth century. Each of the five parts has a larger story within which various tales are interwoven and one story leads to another. From the word *fable* comes *fabulous*, or wonderful, beautiful, terrific – *You are looking fabulous in your new dress* or *Thanks, that was a fabulous treat you gave us.*

As with other letters of the alphabet, *f*, too, has a number of commonly used words that have a wide, dispersed use. A simple word – *fair* – has multiple meanings. It generally implies 'unbiased' or 'just' – *it was a fair decision* or 'reasonable' – *a fair sum of money*; it stands for 'favourable' – *We had fair weather and there was no rain*; and 'moderate' – *He was in fair health* or *She did a fair amount of work*. In that sense, the phrase *fair to middlin'* denotes average – *The wheat was of fair to middlin' quality*. *Fair* can pertain to skin colour – as an English concept, a *fair maiden* is a pretty girl. *His handwriting is fair* is when it is clear and easily readable. To say that there is a *fair chance* of something happening means that there is good possibility of that happening. It also indicates some size – *A fair number of people had gathered*. There is a special use of the word in English, to substitute 'quite' or 'totally' – *It fair took me off guard*. In present-day international commerce, some importers seek a certification of *Fair Trade* for products to indicate that no illegal practices have been adopted; that, for example, there has been no exploitation of children in the production process.

The other totally different meaning of *fair* is the temporary market where stalls with entertainment such as games, and food, are available for those visiting the *fair*. In medieval times, these *fairs* were a popular way of selling goods. In India, *fairs* or *melas*, are held on the occasion of religious festivals – the Kumbh Mela is the largest congregation of humanity at one place. In Hindu mythology, gods and demons fought a 12-day war over a *kumbh* – a pitcher of divine nectar. A half or Ardh Kumbh festival is held annually and a full Kumbh Mela every 12 years.

And on to *fare*. It is the cost of a ticket, normally in transport, such as *the bus fare* or *the taxi fare*, but the driver could also say that he has a *fare* when speaking of the passenger. *Fare also* relates to food and the variety or quality of it; *What is the fare today*, one might ask about the menu as one sits down to a meal. And there might be *mouth-watering fare on the table*. *Fare* also relates to performance – *How did you fare in the examinations?* To *fare well* is to do well, that is the result of an effort. But to bid *farewell* as one word is to bid goodbye – it comes from the phrase *fare thee/you well* – wishing that the person you are bidding goodbye may do well in future.

The word *fall* has many meanings. *Fall* is the drop of an object from a height thanks to the pull of gravity. One may *fall to the ground* or *fall from a tree* or *fall sick*. There is *fall to* which is to begin forcefully, or 'attack' – *The children fall to the food every day at lunchtime as if they have not eaten for a month*. The past tense of the verb *fall* is *fell*. But *fell* has its own meanings, too. To *fell* is to cut down – *The woodcutter felled the tree*. In an old style, *fell* also suggests cruel or unfortunate; *in one fell swoop* denotes one savage act. *Fall out* is the result (of an action) – *The fallout of one boy bunking class was that we were all marked absent*. And to *fall short* of a certain level is just that – *In his parents' eyes, he fell short of the high standards they had set for him*.

Is there a difference between *fall* and *fall down*? Actually, there is, though it is not easy to explain. 'Down' is added when a person or an object *falls* when that was otherwise unexpected. *Fall down* generally implies a quick, hard action. *Fall*, by itself, without 'down', is generally used for something coming down from above, perhaps an expected or anticipated action. The difference is slight; it is between *The child fell down* and *The child might fall if you don't hold her*.

Fall stands for autumn in the USA and Canada, but usually with 'the' in front and with a capital F; it is the season starting around mid-September. In many temperate lands, the leaves on the trees take on colour as they dry and *fall*, like the autumn leaves in the poem – red and yellow and brown. It coincides with an academic term that begins in August-September; the *Fall term* comes before the Winter term and is generally the start of the academic year. *Landfall* is the touching of land by a cyclone from the sea. *Nightfall* happens when night *falls*; the day breaks, it never *falls*! *Downfall* has nothing to do with physical things; it is the loss of one's position, wealth and power.

Follow means 'to go after'; the dog *followed* his master; if that were a human obeying a spiritual master, he would be a *follower*. In today's world, it is the way you keep track on social media of what someone is saying. A group of people interested in a particular personage, activity or sport would be a *following* – *Motor sports is new to India but already has a large following*. Sports terminology uses the word *follow* in many ways. *Follow through* in cricket is the steps a bowler takes while bowling, after he has released the ball; in golf, it is the continued forward movement of the club after it has hit the ball. In both cases, it is the completion of a natural movement. These are only two examples; the word *follow* and its derivations obviously find many uses outside sports.

Fast is an interesting word. To *fast* is to avoid eating; this is a way of observing certain religious events in many communities, but politically, it is also a way of expressing protest. Mahatma Gandhi made it a very powerful tool in his non-violent movement against British rule in pre-independent India. A period of *fasting*, too, is called a *fast*. *Fast* also expresses speed, as an adverb in *He is going fast* or an adjective in *This is a fast car* – the opposite of 'slow'. This is used in a game like cricket – a *fast bowler* would be one who can bowl consistently at a high speed, generally at about 140 km per hour.

But *fast* also has the very opposite meaning. To *hold fast* is to hold on firmly, either something physical or in thought – *He held fast to the belief that the earth was flat* or *He held fast to the plank of wood in the midst of the flood waters;* note the use of the 'to'. To *fasten* is to tie up very firmly. *Fast* is also 'permanent', not liable to fade – *These clothes are made with fast colours*. And *He was fast asleep* means that he was in deep, undisturbed sleep. There is also an unexpected meaning, the origin of which is unclear – a person believed to be living a dissipated life, or is supposed to be of loose moral character, might be called a *fast* person; unfortunately, in a classic example of gender bias, it is more often than not used for women who lead *a fast life*. On the other hand, one sees in Indian usage – 'Ram and Hari are fast friends' if they are very close friends; this is not correct usage though.

> What is a *figure of speech*? It is a device in the use of the English language by which a word or a phrase goes beyond its literal or apparent meaning. The correct use of a *figure of speech* comes with practice in its use. There are well over a hundred of them, but only a few are commonly known. Some of these devices are referred to in the relevant chapters elsewhere; a few examples are *alliteration, euphemism, hyperbole, irony, metaphor, simile, onomatopoeia, oxymoron, pun* and *proverb*.

The word *fine* has many interpretations. The first is the usage of the word as something good. To the question 'How are you?', you might say '*I am fine*' if you are well. The weather is *fine* if the sky is clear and the temperature is neither too high nor too low. Related to this is the use of the word *fine* as 'accurate' or 'acute' or 'of good quality'. A knife may be *finely sharpened*, the student may give a *fine answer* and the cloth may be of *fine quality*. You may also *fine tune* your response or your speech to improve it. But the opposite is also true – an imposition of a penalty, usually of money; *The motorist had to pay a big fine for violating the traffic rules.* (Have you come across this joke – 'A *fine* is a tax when you have done wrong, a tax is a *fine* when you are doing well'?) The term *fine arts* covers the range of visual and performing arts. *Finery* is expensive clothes for a special occasion – *She was dressed in her finery for the feast.*

Final – the last. *This is the final episode of the serial.* Or, a little incorrect but a very common term – *the final exams begin tomorrow.* From that word we have *finale* – pronounced 'fin–al–ay' – *The fireworks were the grand finale of the entertainment programme.* Then *finality* – the definite ending to an act or discussion usually implying a decision or completion – *There was no finality to the argument. Finals*, in plural, is the *final* game of a tournament which decides the winner of the tournament – *Germany won the finals of the 2014 Football World Cup.*

To *fix* something is to set it right or repair it – *My watch is going slow, do you think you can fix it?* – and to set up or put up, perhaps on a wall – *Can you please fix this nail for me?* Strangely, it can be the problem itself – *You have put me in a fix*. It is also to settle or firm up – *I have fixed the meeting for tomorrow*. We may also say – *He is so fixed in his ideas that it is difficult to talk to him.* In slang, a *fix* is a dose of heroin or such narcotics. Also in slang, it is a solution to a problem

– *Is there a fix for this problem?* But a *fixer* is not one who *fixes* a painting on your wall, or repairs your watch; he is someone who can get things done through bribery or other underhand means. That is where the term *match fixing* also comes in. And *fixture* – it is a programme *fixed* generally for sporting events, such as Manchester United's 'home and away *fixtures*'; it could also be an attachment such as a light *fixture* or a plumbing *fixture*. One might use the word sarcastically for a regular at an activity – *He is a regular fixture at the races.*

There are certain offshoots to the word *fix* – *affix, pre-fix, and suffix*. (Note that with pre- there is no second *f* as in the case of the other two words.) To affix is to put or attach or add, such as to *affix a seal*, or *affix one's signature*. 'Pre-fix', is to place in front or ahead of, or to *fix* in advance – *The taxi rates are pre-fixed*. Here one uses the hyphen; it clarifies that it is not the grammatical term 'prefix', which is discussed more in Chapter P. 'Suffix' is to fix after, to add at the end. 'Suffix' is also a grammatical term – see Chapter S – but it is used as a word by itself – *The doctor suffixed his long list of degrees after his name on his name board.*

Here are some interesting sets of words – *flee* and *flea*, *'flu* and *flue* and *flew*. To *flee* is to run away, as from some danger – the past tense is *fled* – while a *flea* is a tiny bug, generally only a couple of millimetres in size, often found on a dog and other pets. A *flea market* is a place where cheap articles and second-hand goods might be sold. The origin is not clear, but in the USA, early markets of this kind had horses for sale; since horses are known to carry *fleas*, could that be the cause of this term? *'Flu* with an apostrophe is the short form of influenza, the word is correctly used with 'the' before it – *Do you have the 'flu*? A *flue* is a pipe or duct, usually in a heater of a furnace, while *flew* is the past tense of the verb *fly*, to move or travel by air. The *fly*, as a noun, is no doubt one of the most irritating household insects. A limerick from Ogden Nash (1902–1971) goes:

A flea and a fly in a flue
Were imprisoned, so what could they do?
Said the fly, "'let us flee!'
'Let us fly!' said the flea.
So they flew through a flaw in the flue.[1]

The word *for* is a multi-dimensional preposition. It can indicate intention, as in *He stood for elections*; in other words, he wished to be elected. But *He stood for probity in public life* means that he supported honesty in the public sphere. It can be a reservation – *This is a home for the elderly*; an indication – *This parcel is for Mr Kannan;* a geographical direction – *He left for home*; an attempt to obtain or seek – *The lazy fellow aimed only for pass marks in the exams*; a time period – *The boy had to wait for an hour before he could get a bus*. The use of *for* in the context of duration has an interesting twist – the phrase *for long* is always used in the negative; one says *I did not stay for long*, one cannot say 'I stayed for long'; for that one would say *I stayed for a long time*. In computer terminology, a *for* loop allows *for* the reiteration and repeated execution of a code. *For* also expresses a desire – *Oh, for a hot bath at the end of the game*!

There are many tricky words beginning with *f*. *Fore* and *four* are examples. *Fore* means '(in) front', 'ahead of', always

[1] https://www.poemhunter.com/poem/a-flea-and-a-fly-in-a-flue.

indicating something before something else – *Humayun's tomb was built before the Taj Mahal*. The word *forefathers* refers to one's ancestors, those before one's father. To *foretell* is to tell *beforehand*; to *forewarn*, to warn *beforehand* of something about to happen. The *front* legs of an animal are its *forelegs*. *Fore* is a matter of perspective, not only in time but also in space. *Foreground* is the *front* part of a painting or a photograph, the opposite of 'background'. To come *forward* is also to come to the *fore* – *The youth of the country must come to the fore to remove corruption from public life*. At the same time, to *forego* is to give up – *He decided to forego his lunch every day to save money for his poor mother.*

Four is a very important number. It is the smallest composite number, divisible by 1 and 2, and also equal to the sum of its prime factors, 2 and 2. There are metaphorically '*four corners*' of the earth, in the *four* directions – north, south, east and west; *four* mathematical rules – addition, subtraction, multiplication and division; *four* seasons – spring, summer, autumn, winter; the *four* elements in ancient Greek thought – air, water, fire, earth. In all religions, the number *four* has some significance. In Hindu philosophy, the *four* aspects of life are *dharma*, *artha*, *kama*, *moksha*; the *four Vedas*, the earliest and principal scriptures, are the *Rig Veda*, *Sama Veda*, *Yajur Veda* and *Atharva Veda*. The fundamental tenets of Buddhism are based on the *four* Noble Truths – Dukkha, Samudaya, Nirodha and Magga. There are *four* holy books in Islam – *Torah*, *Zaboor*, *Injeel* and *Quran*; and *four* sacred months – Muharram, Rajab, Dhu al-Qi'dah and Dhu al-Hijjah. In Christianity, there are *four* gospels – in the New Testament these are the gospels of Mathew, Mark, Luke and John – and the *four* Horsemen of the Apocalypse; the *four* Horsemen are beasts that come out of seals in God's hand, ride *four* horses, white, red, black and pale, and represent conquest, war, famine and death, *foretelling* the Last Judgment. Indeed the number *four* is very important in all faiths.

Five, which comes after *four* numerically, not alphabetically, is also significant in many ways. It is the third prime number, and a Fibonacci number (A Fibonacci sequence starts with 0 and 1, and is the sum of the previous two numbers – 0,1,1,2,3,5,8,13....) As with *four*, *five* is also significant in philosophical and religious terms. The *five* elements of both early Greek philosophy and Indian belief are earth, air, water, fire and ether. The *five* elements in Chinese belief, the Wu Xing, are water, wood, fire, earth and metal. From the *five* Pandava brothers of the Mahabharata to the *five* wounds of Jesus and the *five* pillars of Islam – *five* has much significance. Muslims pray *five* times a day. Sikhs have *five* sacred symbols – *kesh* (uncut hair), *kanga* (a comb), *kara* (a steel bracelet), *kachcha* (shorts), and *kirpan* (a sword); they also revere the *five* men, the '*panch pyare*', who, in 1699, first formed the Khalsa.

Form and *from* are similar words, with a wide range of meanings and a typing error can be very misleading. *Form* is the performance level of a sportsman – *The batsman was in great form and scored a double century* – or of certain performers, including animals such as racehorses – *The form of that racehorse has not been impressive*. It is also a document in which information has to be filled in, such as *an application form* for a job. *Form* also includes shape – *It was a hideous form that emerged from the shadows* – or manner – *an unusual form of protest*. There are a number of *forms* or systems in mathematical formulations. Indeed the word denotes structure, and brings us the words *format* and *formal*. *Former* means 'earlier' or 'previous' – *The former principal was invited to speak to the students.* The other word, *from* indicates the starting point. It can denote origin – *He is from Bengaluru*; be the starting point of a journey – *He travels from home to office every day by bus*; the start of an activity – *He joined duty from today*; the start of an interaction – *A warning from the referee to the player went unheeded.* It can be the beginning of a time period – *He is away from eight to eight every day.* Incidentally, we might have *form* and *from* side by side, and then it's even more important to not create a typo – *Dravid's form from the previous series had continued.*

Here are two fascinating words. One is *floccinaucinihilipilification*, one of the longest words in English. It means the consideration of something as useless. The other is *friggatriskaidekaphobia*, the fear of *Friday* the 13th.

G

G is a tricky letter in terms of its sound. Some words with *g* have the letter pronounced as *j*, the soft *g*, especially when *g* is followed by *e* or *i*, but not always (*get*, for instance, is the hard *g*). Within a word itself *g* may be pronounced as *g* or *j*. *Gentleman*, *genteel*, *genius*, *gypsy*, *age*, *cage*, *change*, *range*, *allege*, *college* are some words in which *g* sounds *j*. Words such as *engage*, *gauge*, *grange*, *gorge*, *gorgeous* have the strong *g* first and then the soft *g*. *Geography* has it the other way. *Ginger*, *George* and *georgette* have two j sounds. The complexity of pronunciation is even more with words like *analogue*, *analogous* and *analogy*, where only the last of the three words has the *j* sound for the *g*. So, are there any common rules? Well, *g* followed by *a*, *o* and *u* is the hard *g*; with *e* and *i* it could be either the hard *g* or the soft *g*, more often the latter. A rare exception is in the use of the old-fashioned *gaol* which is the same as 'jail'. If placed between *a* and *e*, *g* has a *j* sound – *age, adage, carnage, rage, verbiage* and so on. G between *d* and *e* is also *j* when *e* is the last letter – *badge, edge, hedge, ridge, nudge*.

Is there any unexpected attribute to *g*? Well, it seems to express something which is larger than the norm or the average, both in physical and non-physical, aesthetic terms. *Galaxy*, *galactic*, *gargantuan*, *giant*, *gigantic*, *grand*, *grandeur*, *grandiloquent*, *grandiose*, *great*, *greatness* – all imply larger, or *greater*, than the ordinary. Perhaps *gorgeous*, too. Tucked into words, *g* is found in *big*, *large, huge and humongous*. And of course, *God*, the omnipotent, omniscient, omnipresent Being who has no boundaries, who is limitless. We shall look at some of these words as we go along.

However, let us begin *g* with a set of seven short, three-letter words, most of them used somewhat colloquially, more in ordinary conversation than in formal writing – *gab*, *gad*, *gag*, *gal*, *gap*, *gas* and *gay*. The first is to talk a great deal, often incessantly – *For heaven's sake, stop gabbing*; it is also used in a specific phrase – *Raj has the gift of the gab*, meaning that Raj is fluent in conversation (and can talk you into agreeing with him). In theatre, the word *gabble* is used for a quick rehearsal only to recite the lines, so that the director can check if the cast have learnt their lines. The second word, *gad*, linked to 'about', is used in a negative way; to walk about or go around aimlessly – *She gads about town all the time*. A *gadfly* is an insect that hovers around horses and cows; in human terms it is a person who is always hanging around in an irritating way.

Gag has many meanings. A *gag* is something – such as a piece of cloth – stuffed into the mouth to stop someone from speaking and so an action preventing someone from expressing one's opinion – *The Government has issued a gag order*. To *gag* is also to choke and retch or throw up;

the past tense is *gagged*. A *gag* is a short, funny tale as well. Those who specialize in writing storylines with a pile of *gags* thrown in, are called, yes, *gag writers*.

Gal, we all know, is a short, slang form of *girl*. A *gap*, say in a wall, is a break between the two parts of the wall; *gap* is also a difference, such as in time – *Between him and his brother there is a gap of ten years*; or in income – *There is a big gap between his pay and mine*. *Gap analysis*, in corporate terms, is the study of the difference between the potential of an organization to perform and its actual performance. *Gas*, apart from the standard chemistry meaning – one of three common states of matter, the other two being 'solid' and 'liquid' – also is the short form of *gasoline*, the American term for petrol. As a colloquial word, *gas* signifies verbose, useless talk – *He gasses all the time about himself*. (Note the spelling with the additional *s*.) Till a few decades ago, the word *gay* meant 'carefree' or 'happy'; today, it is the term for a male homosexual person (the term for such a female is 'lesbian'). The correct use of the word is essential. And yet, the noun for *gay* is *gaiety*, which though not very common, continues to have its original meaning.

To *go gaga* over something is to behave in a rather silly, excited manner or to be infatuated – *He went gaga over meeting his favourite film star*. A *gaggle* is a group or a flock, usually *a gaggle of geese* – *geese* being the strange plural of *goose*, the bird – but is also used in some ways for an assortment of people – *A gaggle of schoolchildren was waiting for the bus*.

A few words about size show how difficult it is to explain why a word is used in a particular context. *Gargantuan* means 'huge' or 'massive', it is something *gigantic*. Is there a difference in the use of the two words? Not much.

Gargantuan generally is for something very large but without a physical shape and not measurable – *He had a gargantuan task before him. Gigantic,* from the Greek *gigas* meaning *giant*, is also not physically easy to measure, such as a *gigantic tsunami.* But it is more likely that *gigantic* would indicate shape and size, more than the abstract *gargantuan. Giants* themselves are mythical, huge creatures generally in human form; in literature they are sometimes good and gentle, but often not. *Giants* are plentiful in old Greek and Roman mythology, such as Cyclops and Titans; in Indian myths, characters like Kumbhakarna, who slept for six months at a time and ate enormous amounts when he awoke, are popular. In *Gulliver's Travels*, Jonathan Swift (1667–1745) created the Brobdingnagians, a giant race, and Lilliputians, the very opposite.

The word *get*, with its past tense of *got*, is simple, but when added to other words, has different meanings. The most common use is for possessing, obtaining or receiving something – *What did you get for your birthday?* Or *The old man finally got his pension.* You can *get over,* or overcome, the loss of a friend. To *get away from him* requires an effort at moving away from a person. To *get away with murder* is to manage not to get caught for that crime, but *he can get away with murder* can also be used to say that he can *get* away with anything! To *get away for a holiday* also requires a special effort at *getting* leave from work and planning the trip. To *get through the examinations* is a very happy thought, but one needs to *get down to one's studies* to do that, otherwise one may *get into a mess. Get him on the line*, the boss tells the secretary, to talk to someone on the phone. To look at all uses of the word could take a whole book, but two more uses can be mentioned here;

one is about moving from a certain state of being or living, and the other is about moving someone or something physically. Here are lines which include both, from a song in the musical *My Fair Lady*, where Eliza Doolittle's father, a tramp, is about to marry:

I'm getting married in the morning,
Ding dong, the bells are going to chime,
Girls, come and kiss me, say how you'll miss me,
But get me to the church on time.[1]

General with a capital G (another capitonym) is a rank, given at the highest level of the army; unless there is a rare Field Marshal above that. But with a small *g*, it indicates something all pervasive, common – *the general public* or *the general opinion.* With *generally*, one gets a synonym for 'usually', 'commonly', 'by and large' – *The meeting went generally along expected lines* or *It is generally cold in these parts.* To *generalize* is to make a statement that *generally* but perhaps not accurately covers all – *All politicians are corrupt.* That may not be true, but such a *generalization* is common. A *generalist* is one who is not a specialist in anything. Have you heard of *GATT* – the *General Agreement on Tariffs and Trade*, a multilateral trade agreement of 1948, which continues to be the basis of international trading norms?

God is the Supreme Being in all major religions, however different be that religion's understanding of *God. God* is of a single form, though many *gods* and *goddesses* may be

[1] https://www.britannica.com/topic/My-Fair-Lady-musical-by-Lerner-and-Loewe

venerated in certain faiths. Those who do not believe in the existence of *God* are called atheists; those who only doubt *God's* existence are agnostics. In today's scientific world, an international group of scientists have been working on locating a certain particle which they believe would be the source of all matter; this is called by some *the God particle.* There are a number of idiomatic uses of the word *God.* Some of them are *thank God – Thank God, he was not seriously injured in the accident*; *God forbid – If, God forbid, he needs any surgery, it will not be a major one*; *God willing – God willing, he will be well soon*; *God only knows – God only knows when the surgery will be over.*

Good refers to a moral concept; there is also a social concept of the *common good.* The abstract noun, *goodness*, refers to the virtue or the quality of a person or thing – *the goodness of milk*, for example, and drinking a glass a day of it might do someone *a world of good.* The word, in all its variety, would cover something favourable – *good news*; appropriate – *good behaviour*; with visual appeal – *good looks*; pleasant – *good times*; logical – *good reason*, and so on. There is also an interjection of surprise – *Goodness! How did he climb over that wall!* Then there is a less used old-fashioned phrase – *Goodness gracious!* Another slang interjection – *goody!* – is a juvenile, very British, manner of expressing delight while *goodies* is the word for sweets, or such sweet eatables. But the most common use today of *good* is to reply to 'How are you?' with 'I am good'. (This is also a common response when asked if one is comfortable, or if one would like to be served more food or drink.) Till a few years ago one would have said 'I am well', but modern ways of social interaction are fast changing.

> How did *good* not become 'gooder' or 'goodest' in comparison, but 'better' and 'best'? This is not clear, but as someone has said, 'Never let "good" come in the way of "best"'! A popular example of the comparative is in this rhyme:
>
> *Good, better, best, never let it rest,*
> *Till your good is better and your better best.*

Google is now a household name; the word was created by the misspelling of the mathematical number *googol*, which is 1 followed by a hundred zeros! *Google*, the Internet search engine that has revolutionized the process of seeking information using the Internet, was started by Larry Page (1973–) and Sergey Brin (1973–), in 1996. There is also *goggle*, which is to look wide-eyed at someone or something. *Goggles*, or sunglasses, are usually coloured glasses for the eyes to protect the eyes from the sun or wind.

A very common word in our daily use is *government*. Note the capital G if we use it for a specific *government*, such as the *Government of India*. The *government* is the totality of the ministers in the Cabinet, the administrators and the staff – all who combine to look after the common people. The *national government* is a commonly used term when the capital G may not be used. We also have the State or provincial *governments*; note that state, without the capital S has a different meaning. We will discuss that later in Chapter S. The *n* in *government* is not sounded, so the word sounds like 'guv–er–ment'. To *govern* is to rule, and here the *n* must be heard!

Great describes something or someone extraordinary. It could be a matter of size, as with *Great* Britain – the larger Britain comprising England, Scotland, Northern Ireland and Wales. There is the *Great* Barrier Reef off the coast of Australia and the *Great* Wall of China. *Great* could be the word for 'wonderful' – *He is a great chap* or *It was a great performance*. The abstract concept is *greatness*, or 'eminence'. As Shakespeare wrote in *Twelfth Night*, '*Some are born great, some achieve greatness, and some have greatness thrust upon them*'. In its common usage nowadays, *great* could be the response to a question like 'How are you feeling?' Or, for that matter, to 'Shall we go out for dinner?'

Grammar is one of those strange palindromes – send the *g* to the end of the word and you get *grammar* backwards! It has three letters, *r*, *a* and *m* twice each in forming the word. One must note, also, the spelling of the word; it is 'ar' at the end, and not 'er'! *Grammar* is the set of rules of a language that together gives logic to a language, and allows one person to understand the use of the language by another person. Many people communicate in a language without knowing the written rules of the language. *Grammar* consists of its syntax and its morphology. Syntax refers to the logic and principles by which sentences are structured, while morphology relates to the logic of words, parts of speech and so on. There is also semantics, the larger aspect of nuance, inference and subtlety in meaning, which, strictly, goes beyond standard *grammar*. A *grammarian* is an expert in *grammar*; *grammatical* pertains to *grammar*. It is believed that the first book on English *grammar* was a *Pamphlet for Grammar* written by a certain William Bullokar in 1586. Today, a search online for books on English *grammar* shows up about 2.67 million entries, and *www.amazon.com* has nearly 45,000 books on *grammar*!

G does not have many words that stand for *grammatical* terms. One of the few is the *gerund*. It is a noun formed out of a verb – *Running is a good way to exercise.* It is useful to know the difference between a *gerund* and a present participle, which also ends in 'ing'. A *gerund* acts as a noun. A present participle has other roles; it can be an adjective – *a pair of running shoes*, or a part of a verb – *He goes running every morning*.

Something large in size, or magnificent to see, is *grand*, such as *a grand building*. But *grand* is not only about manmade objects. The philosophical question of what the universe is and how and why we are here on earth has also been debated through time – the question of *the grand design*. In commonly used American slang, one *grand*, one *g* for short, means 'a thousand dollars'. And it may also used to describe a respected elder – *I shook hands with the grand old man.* On that same note we have the words *grandmother* and *grandfather.* From *grand* we have *grandeur* – *The grandeur of the palace impressed me very much*. But *grandiloquence* refers to pompous, lofty behaviour or talk, and *grandiloquent* is the adjective – *He bored us with a grandiloquent speech that lasted an hour.*

Let's end the chapter with abbreviations. *G* is the short form of *gram*, the unit of weight. We hear of 2*G* or 3*G* or even 4*G* when it comes to technology – the letter stands for *generation*. Earlier a *generation* related only to human beings, broadly 30 years making a *generation*; today technological changes result in a new *generation* technology every few years. The letter *g* is also an abbreviation for *gravity*, that unseen force that makes an apple fall to the ground and prevents us from floating into outer space.

> *Giga* stands for 10 to the power of 9. *Gigahertz* is a billion hertz. A *gigabyte* is a billion bytes; in binary systems, it is 2 to the power of 30, that is, 1,073,741,824, which is rounded off to a billion.

H

H raises a question; is it pronounced 'haitch' or 'aitch'? Stick to the latter and you won't be wrong. It is a letter that does not indicate its sound as you say it. A few words starting with *h* also have a special pronunciation – the opening *h* is silent, for example, in *hour, honour* and *heir*. Earlier in this book we spoke of the use of 'an' and not 'a' before these words.

Have, *has* and the past tense *had* are among some of the most important and widely applied verbs, or parts of a verb, in English. They are used to express a state of activity – *She has done her work*; *They have gone home*; *We have been reading*; *I had been waiting* – all these activities are 'controlled' by *has*, *have* or *had*. On their own, too, the words indicate action or a state of being or experience – *I had my lunch* or *She has pain in her knee.* They also show possession – *I have a book of haiku poetry* or *She has all the Asterix comics*. In a related way, it can be a short reply to a question about some action – *Did you get the news? Yes, I have*. Or – *Have you sent the email? Yes, I have*. There are other specific uses – *I have to go* is to say that it is time for me to go, a soft, ordinary expression; but if *have* is emphasized in speech, the speaker is either late in leaving, or is compelled to go. Any form of *have to* – *I have to eat* or *I have to study* – can have the same emphasis. At times we use *have* and *had* together – *I have had enough of your nonsense* or *I have had to do without his help*. There can also be *had had* together, as something that has already *happened* in the past – *He had had his lunch by the time we arrived*. There are some special uses of the word. *Have it your way* means 'I am forced to agree with your decision or your views'; *had it coming* is 'to deserve', usually with an unfortunate result – *Kumar lost his job, but the way he behaved, I could see he had it coming*.

Hang is usually used to attach something to a hook on a wall – *Hang your coat from that hook*. The past tense is *hung*. But when someone is *hanged* (also a past tense) till he dies, it is one way of executing him – a death sentence handed down by a court in a very rare case of some extremely serious offence. *Hang*, itself, has many related uses – *Time hangs heavy on my hands* means that I have little of interest to do; *The fear of failure hung over him* means that the fear was constantly with him; *She hung on every word of the film star* means that she listened with rapt attention to what the star said. Or *He hung his head in shame*. If you *have a hangdog expression on your face*, you seem to be ashamed or unhappy about something.

There are various other uses of the word *hang*. We say *hang on*, when we want someone to wait – *Hey, hang on, I'm coming*. To continue an effort, to persevere is to *hang in (there)* – *I know it is difficult, but just hang in there and it will be over in ten minutes*. We *hang out* when we are spending time with friends, usually at a popular place – *We hang out every weekend at the corner cafe.* Related to it is *hang around* – *Don't hang around, let me finish my work in peace.* And *hangers on* are those who crowd around at a place doing nothing – *The hangers on at the accident site made rescue operations difficult. Getting the hang of something* is to begin understanding the matter. We know in the computer age of a computer *hanging*; it has a software or hardware problem that stops it from working and one has usually to reboot it to start up again.

Hard means 'tough', and it also means 'difficult'. *These nuts are hard to crack* literally means that they are difficult to break. From that, comes the term *hard nut* – *The cops found the suspect a hard nut to crack, they just could not get him to admit to the crime. These are hard times*, one says, meaning difficult times, usually financially. A *hard-working* person is one who works *hard*! He may or may not be doing a difficult or complicated job, but he puts in a lot of effort to do his job well. But he *hardly* works means just the opposite, the person does not work *hard*! (We say he works *hard*, we cannot say he works 'hardly'!) If a teacher asked her students to find *hard* words in a dictionary, she should actually ask for difficult words, words are not *hard* or soft! But that difference is nowadays not common; *A policeman's job is hard* and *A policeman's job is difficult* – both uses are correct. A *hard taskmaster* is one who pushes his staff unnecessarily at work and makes them work extra *hard*. If someone finds it difficult to hear, he is *hard of hearing*. *Hardy* is the description for anything, especially plants, which can live in difficult conditions.

He is the third person singular pronoun for males. For women the word is *she*. There is a reason for mentioning these two words here. Till a couple of decades ago, referring to any common form of humans, for mankind in general, we used the word *he* – *Every person at this interview thinks he is the best for the job*. Nowadays we have the use of a gender neutral pronoun; some write it as *s/he* or as *she/he* or even as *they* – *Every person thinks she/he is* (or *they are*) *the best for the job*. The social changes that the 20th century brought in, especially to the developed world, included a belief in equality and recognition for women.

He, the personal pronoun, becomes *him* as the object pronoun; 'she' becomes *her*. *Her* is also an adjective along with *his*. Then again, *his* and *hers* are possessive pronouns One would say – *I gave him his clothes and her books*. But there is a tricky use – *He went his way, she went hers*. Here *hers* stands for *her way*. Note that there is no apostrophe. When emphasis is placed, we have *himself* and *herself* – *The principal herself checked the answer sheets*.

H has a number of similar sounding words, let's look at a sample of two such pairs – *hear* and *here*, *herd* and *heard*. *Hear* is an interesting word. A simple use, *hear from*, is about communicating – *Did you hear from your friend* asks if you received any mail or phone call or any other message from your friend. But, *If you don't finish your exam paper, you will hear from the principal* means that you will be given a scolding. *Hear me out* means that I want the other person to listen to the whole story and not interrupt. And *Hear! Hear!* indicates approval by one or more listeners of something said in a speech or a public comment. There is a difference between *hear* and *listen*, the latter implies that one has paid attention to what one has *heard* – *They heard the sound* and *they listened to the speech with rapt attention*. There is no 'to' after *hear*, there generally is a 'to' after 'listen'. The past tense of *hear* is *heard*, which, in turn, is pronounced like *herd*, a group of animals such as a *herd of cattle*. *Herd* is both a noun and a verb; *herded* is the past tense. Have you *heard of* John Keats's 'Ode on a Grecian Urn', one of the great poems of English literature? The poet says – *Heard melodies are sweet, but those unheard are sweeter*.

Here means 'at this place', the opposite of 'there'. Some people wrongly pronounce *here* to rhyme with *hare* or *hair;* actually 'there', the opposite of *here*, rhymes with *hare* and *hair*. And *here* is a joke about the British administration in India. A young Englishman was appearing in an interview for his Hindi proficiency test to join the Indian Civil Service; he was asked, 'How do you say, in Hindi, "come *here*"?' He replied promptly '*Idhar aao*.' 'Very good,' said the examiner, 'How do you say, "go there"?' The candidate, who had forgotten the phrase, replied, 'I shall go there and say, *idhar ao*!' He passed the test!

Have you noticed how many words starting with *h* pertain to the human body? *Hair*, *hand*, *head*, *heart*, *heel*, *heal* and *health*, the word *human* itself. Let us take a look at some of them. The words are so basic that it difficult to explain them, to find meanings and synonyms. *Hand* is a noun – *He took my hand in his* or *The hands of the clock have stopped*. It is also a verb – *Hand me the scissors*. There are many ways to use the word. You may *hand in* your resignation. Charitable organizations give *handouts* as gifts to the poor; the donor would *hand out* these gifts. A judge may *hand down* a verdict in a case. *Hand-me-downs* are clothes of older children given to the younger ones. *Hand in hand* the lovers might walk, but that is the literal meaning, and it can have other uses – *The management and the staff worked hand in hand to improve the productivity of the company.* Using *hand* in the plural we get *hands-on and hands-off – He got hands-on experience when he joined the company* means practical experience or training, but *The company has a hands-off policy* means that the management does not interfere in most work matters. And there is *hands down,* which means 'very easily' – *He won the elections hands down.* An odd-jobs person who is good at repair and maintenance work may be a *handyman.* But *handiwork* – note the *i* – is the work done by someone – *This is his handiwork* is sometimes used in a negative manner.

Head is both a noun and a verb – *He has a calm head on his shoulders* and *He headed the goal in at the last moment. Headed* is the past tense here. There are other uses of *head* or *headed*; to go towards – *He headed home* – or to be at the top – *He heads the list of all-round students. He stands head and shoulders above anyone else in his class* means that he is easily the best in his class. *Head* also is used, in some ways, to denote the person as a whole – *The food will cost us Rs 200 per head.* A *headstrong* person is one who does not listen to others and always wants to have his or her way. Have you been madly – *head over heels* – in love? *Head to toe* indicates the entire body – *He was covered from head to toe with mud.* But *head to head*? It is used for direct comparison – *Head to head, Brazil has won more international football matches than Argentina.* A *heady* mix of cocktails may make you feel 'light' in the *head*, a little fuzzy and not quite in control! And a *headwind* is wind coming at you from the front; the opposite is 'tailwind'.

A significant error many make is in the use of *heartfelt* and *heartiest*. The correct use is *heartfelt condolences* and *heartiest greetings*, not the other way around! The first comes from deep feelings, felt from the *heart*; the second from the word *hearty*, which is a cheerful, happy feeling; you may feel that way when you are *hale and hearty,* or when you eat a good, *hearty* meal. You might also have a *hearty* laugh when you hear a good joke.

What is *history*? It is the record and the study of the past, and covers not only political events but also social and cultural issues, lifestyles and all aspects of living. A well-known book by that name – *What is History?* – written in 1961 by E. H. Carr (1892–1982) discusses not just *history* as we know it commonly, but issues of judgement and interpretation. After all, *history* is what a *historian* tells us; has s/he covered all facts? *Historical* pertains to *history*; *historical novels* are fiction based on past *history* or *historical* characters. *Historic* pertains to *history*, too, used commonly for a time or moment or occasion in *history*, which is memorable, such as India's *historic* win against the mighty West Indies in the 1983 cricket World Cup, which changed the face of the game in India. Such occasions would *go down in history*.

The Greek word *homos* means 'same'. And so we have *homogeneous*, comprising similar elements or components. The opposite is *heterogeneous*, something with dissimilar components or parts. Note the spelling; *e* occurs four times in the word!

Throughout this book we have examples of *homonyms* – consisting of *homophones* and *homographs*; there are also the opposites, *heteronyms* – covering *heterophones* and *heterographs*. This book has them everywhere. Some words can be in more than one category, and that makes the difference even more difficult to understand – so a simple explanation would be best here. We know that *homos* means 'same', *hetero* means 'opposite', 'nym' pertains to 'words', 'phone' pertains to sound and 'graph' pertains to writing. The larger picture begins with *homonyms*, which stands for 'similar words'. The bat you play cricket with and the bat that flies at night are spelt and pronounced the same but have different meanings. Within this larger picture, those words pronounced the same are *homophones*. A few examples, in pairs with different spelling and very different meaning, are – *aisle* and *isle, bow* and *bough, cot* and *caught, die* and *dye, hear* and *here, of* and *off,* and the triple *to, too* and *two.* Then there are *homographs*, words spelt the same way but which have different meanings (and may, though not necessarily, be pronounced differently) – *bow* (*a bow tie, a bow for an arrow*, both rhyming with 'no' and *a bow to a superior*, rhyming with 'now'), or *row* (*a row of cars, the row of a boat*, both rhyming with 'no', and 'row', a quarrel, rhyming with 'now') are two examples.

Heteronyms are words that are spelt the same but are pronounced differently and when they are pronounced differently they have different meanings – again, examples are *bow* (we saw earlier 'a bow to a superior' and 'a bow tie'), *row* ('a quarrel' and 'a row or line of cars'). Another example is *tear* ('a drop of water from the eyes' and 'a tear in a shirt'). These belong to its subgroup *heterophones*, which are words that sound differently in different uses. The other subgroup – *heterographs* – are words that sound the same but have different spellings and obviously mean different things. But doesn't that sound like a *homophone*? It is the same! You can see why the terms *heterophone* and *heterograph* are not commonly used.

It seems all so confusing. But in this very confusion there is a warning; it is easy to make mistakes in spelling or in pronouncing a word. One wonders why, in a language that has such a large vocabulary, there should be such widespread re-use of certain words.

Humans are *homo sapiens*. The Latin word *homo* means 'man' (not the Greek word *homos* we saw earlier); 'sapiens' means 'wise'. *Humans* are the only living creatures with certain higher level brain powers; whether we use them well is quite another matter. There are a number of abstract concepts that derive from *humans*. There is a difference between, say, *humanity* and *humanism*. *Humanity* relates to the *human race* itself – *It was so crowded that it felt as if all humanity had gathered there*; it is also a matter of *human kindness* – *Where is our sense of humanity if we let the poor starve to death*? It would require a *humane* approach on our part to prevent abject poverty. *Humanism* is a philosophical view with – in simple terms – a focus on ethical values.

Hype is an exaggerated impression created about an event, a product or a situation, often a part of a publicity effort or commercial advertising. Sometimes, the media creates a *hype* about something which leads to extra public attention – *The media hype that surrounded the visit of the dignitary was totally disproportionate to the outcome of his visit. Hype* is also used as a verb, with *hyped* in the past tense; *hyping*, too, is used – *He is hyping it up unnecessarily*. *Hype* comes from *hyper*-, a prefix of Greek origin which means 'over'. Thus we have *a hyperactive child* or *hypertension* as a medical term for high blood pressure. The opposite is *hypo-*, again of Greek origin – meaning 'under' or 'below'. A *hypodermic* needle is one that goes under or below the skin. A *hypochondriac* is one who is constantly thinking of imaginary health problems. Think of those who have a problem of either high or low blood sugar – that's *hyperglycemia* or *hypoglycemia*.

We must mention *hyperbole* – pronounced incorrectly by most people; it should sound somewhat like 'high–per–bo–lay'. *My mother cooked for an army* – that is *hyperbole* because she actually cooked a lot of food for a few people. Our visual media is full of it – unnecessary exaggeration in the reporting of a news story, the use of *hyped* up speech, at times making a mountain out of a molehill. Someone is anointed the president of a political party! It should simply be "appointed" – we are not anointing someone as the King or the Pope. The opposite of *hyperbole* is the understatement, which can have the same effect, often in a *humorous* way.

Hobson-Jobson is a dictionary of words taken from Indian words and used by the British during the days of the British Raj. It was compiled by Henry Yule and Arthur C. Burnell and first published in 1886; it is still available and is fun to read. Think of the Hindi/Urdu word *Bilayat* or *Wilayat* meaning 'foreign', referring especially to England (from that we have the slang term for England, old Blighty). *Bilayutee pawnee* or more simply *bilati pani* was the term often used by the British in India for soda-water.

I stands for *I*! That's me! It is the shortest pronoun, and is written as a capital letter, wherever in a sentence we place it, not just at the start. While all proper nouns or names begin with a capital letter, *I* and He, when referring to God, are the only other words that use this form anywhere in a sentence. Many philosophers have dwelt on the meaning and the significance of this human creature that is *I*, of one's place in the universe, of one's self. The seeking of the Self has always been man's quest. Lao Tzu, the Chinese philosopher said, 'Knowing others is wisdom, knowing the Self is enlightenment.'

Four short words – *if*, *in*, *is* and *it*. They are very powerful *in* the formation of sentence structures. *It is* necessary to appreciate their importance *in* English, and, *if* you do, you may be that much wiser! They bring up issues of logic, of philosophy, of abstract concepts. Think, though, of this sentence, which is grammatically correct, but does not make much sense – *if it is in, it is in.*

If is a condition creating word; in case something were to happen, what then? It is used in a condition of uncertainty, where we do not know; *if* we did know, there would be no need for *if*. But the conditions can vary. *If he comes, we will go out* – in case he comes, we will go out. This is very different from *when he comes, we will go out* – the coming is definite, only the time uncertain. *If* is used in various ways. *I asked him if he knew the way* – that is to ask whether he knew the way. *I liked the lecture, even if it was a trifle long* – even though. And there are some common expressions – *His argument is full of ifs and buts* and *I don't like his argument, it is a little iffy*. We have earlier talked of *as if* and the strange slang term which can perhaps be explained by another slang term – 'no way'! In computer software logic, the *what if* query is exactly what it says, what happens next *if* something happens; it provides various scenarios.

In has many grammatical uses. It is mainly a preposition, but it is also an adverb and an adjective. *I put a nail in the wall* – an object is put inside or into another object. It *indicates* boundaries – *My father is walking in the garden*, he is walking within a certain space. In a less visible way, *He is in my circle of friends* or *He spoke in English*. It can be used for time – *Mangoes are in season*; or for systems, styles and other abstract frameworks – *Red is in fashion this year*. *All in all*, *in* is used to *indicate* that something is within something! As an adverb, *in* is commonly used – *Please come in* or *Don't go in*. As an adjective? Well – *The in thing to do these days is to talk in slang*. And *in-* is one of the most important prefixes in the language. In computer terms, as we have said earlier, dot *in* is the *Internet* domain for *India*.

There are various idiomatic uses of *in*. To *do someone in* is to kill that person. To know the *ins and outs* of something is to know it thoroughly. Such a person would certainly be *in the know of* things. To *give in* is to succumb to pressure.

To *drop in* is to visit someone, usually without notice. We all know *check in* – you register at a hotel or you get your boarding pass for your flight at the airport. To *put a finger in the pie* is to get *involved* in something, to meddle in something. We will return to *in* later.

> *Is* is a strange word; it changes its form all the time. *Is* (along with its root 'to be', 'am', 'are', 'was', 'were', 'will be', 'would be' and a whole set of related terms) is one of the most essential and most used verbs in English. This is a very philosophical verb. Without *is*, the basis of existence would be shaky, and English would be nearly impossible to speak. There is a new word in use in Britain these days, 'innit' for 'isn't it'!

The word *it* has many uses. It is the 'starter' for many sentences. If a sentence begins with *it*, it is an abstract use – *It is good of you to come*, or *It is nearly impossible to get through the evening traffic.* Some experts feel that, in writing, '*it*' is a tame start. One of the most well-known lines often quoted as an example of a poor start to a book is from *Paul Clifford* (1830) by Edward Bulwer-Lytton (1803–1873): *It was a dark and stormy night; the rain fell in torrents, except at occasional intervals, when it was checked by a violent gust of wind which swept up the streets (for it is in London that our scene lies), rattling along the housetops, and fiercely agitating the scanty flame of the lamps that struggled against the darkness.* Some feel it is so poor a piece of writing that they take digs at Bulwer Lytton; there is an annual Bulwer-Lytton fiction contest for the worst starting line for a book.[1]

[1] www.bulwer-lytton.com

As a pronoun, *it* also represents a physical object or an animal or even an abstract concept – *This chair has to be replaced, it is broken* or *I love my dog, it is my best friend* or *She has high fever, I hope it will come down by the evening.* In plain grammar, *it* is of neutral gender – he is masculine, she feminine and *it* neutral; 'they' is the plural form.

> The distinction between *its* and *it's* is important, that is, in the use of the apostrophe with *it*. The possessive pronoun *its* – *the cat ate its food quickly* – does not have the apostrophe. The apostrophe is used to contract *it is* – *It is very hot today* becomes *It's very hot today.*

An important term is the *idiom*. One often comes across the term *idiomatic English*. An *idiom* is a set of words, usually a short phrase, which has a special meaning, beyond what the words say. It is the 'figurative' use of language. A very common example is *He kicked the bucket*; he did not actually kick a bucket, he died! Or *He is pulling my leg* – he is making fun of me. Some are more obvious – *a piece of cake*, something as easy as eating a piece of cake. Or *better late than never* – even if something is attended to late, it is better than never attending to it at all; if something is worth doing, do it even if it is late. *Raining cats and dogs* (it is raining very heavily), *a blessing in disguise* (something happens that later turns out to be for the good), *letting the cat out of the bag* (giving away a secret), *washing dirty linen in public* (giving out unfortunate details) – all these and thousands of other *idioms* make English such a rich language.

Many words begin with the letters *in*. Sometimes *in* is a prefix and used to indicate the opposite of something. 'Correct' becomes *incorrect*; 'distinguishable' marks become *indistinguishable*; 'direct' changes to *indirect*. When your municipal corporation does not clear the garbage, you blame the authorities for *inaction* on their part. But not all words beginning with *in* – and there are over 1,500 of them – are antonyms. There is a word in this paragraph itself which is not an antonym – *indicate* does not come from 'dicate'!

India, that is Bharat, is a republic. After *independence* in 1947, the Constituent Assembly adopted the Constitution of *India* on 26 January 1950. The word *India* comes from the river Sindhu, or *Indus*. The *Indus Valley civilization* existed sometime between 3300 BCE and 1300 BCE. A few facts show us the vastness of this land. *India* is the seventh largest country in the world but the second most populous one; the 2011 Census of *India* placed the population at 1.21 billion, which covers 17.5 per cent of the world's population.

Information is data put together to have meaning; it tells you something, about anything. It is an important word in our daily life, for we cannot do anything sensible without *information* – it affects our decision making; indeed, every intelligent decision we make should be based upon accurate *information*. It is possible to interpret *information* wrongly, or to receive insufficient or wrong *information*, but facts are facts! The word *information* is plural; to write 'informations' is wrong! For a single piece of *information*, put together with many pieces of data, we say just that – *a piece of information*, or just *information*.

An *interjection* is the introduction of a word or comment, but it is usually done by cutting into someone else's words or thought; it is an *interruption*. In grammar, it is the use of certain short words usually at the start of something to be said; it indicates that the speaker is about to say something and gives a hint of the nature of what he is to say – *ah, alas, hello, hey, oh, well, wow*, are examples of *interjections* – *Oh! She has already arrived!* Or *Well, I wouldn't do that if I were you. Interjections* are often followed by an exclamation mark in its written form. The element of surprise has the exclamation mark in the first of the two examples here; in the second, the mark is not required because the matter is thought out, and there is no suddenness. The word 'well' is an *interjection* here, but not with an exclamation.

Inter has many related words, but not all of them use *inter-* as a prefix. *Internal* is an example of a word where *inter* is not a prefix – *these are internal family matters.* With a hyphen, *inter-*, that is 'amongst' or 'between', is the opposite of *intra-* which means 'within'. The perspective and range is different – *The inter-university football tournament had 20 universities participating*, while *The intra-university tournament had 20 colleges participating*. There are two *important* related words. *Intermediate* indicates 'between two ends or extremes', in between, such as the Board for *Intermediate* Studies. And an *intermediary* is one who is a 'go between', usually during a process of negotiations between two parties.

Interest has many meanings. *The interest rates for bank deposits are low.* This is a percentage of a principal amount. But *my interest in films* could mean that I see films regularly and know a lot about films. It is a desire to know something or participate in an activity. *Interest* in a certain business or a firm would normally, but not necessarily, be in the plural – *His business interests keep him busy all the time.* Nowadays, we have *interest groups*, which are voluntary groups of people who fight for a cause. *Can I interest you in a cup of coffee?* asks if I can offer you a cup of coffee. *Uninterested* means simply 'not interested'; *disinterested* means 'not having an interest' in either side of a debate or competition.

And now let's turn to the *Internet.* First, note the 'the' before the word, it is always used when the word is used as a noun. One can use it as an adjective – such as *Internet usage* or *Internet service provider* when the definite article may or may not be used, depending on the context. It is a public network to which all have a right of access. Within an organization and therefore not public, one might have an *intranet.* The full technical term for the Internet is the *Internetwork.* Today about a third of the world's population is believed to use or have used the *Internet.*

Inverted commas are the set of single or double commas placed at either end of the lines someone speaks – *He said, 'My name is Rahul.'* The set of dangling commas – ‘’ or “” – are the *inverted commas.* The set that opens the lines spoken is the *open inverted commas*, and the one that closes them is the *closed inverted commas*! You might have two sets of *inverted commas*, one within the other; then the inner set might use only a single comma – *He told me, "When you say 'The sun goes around the earth', you are completely wrong."* In modern publishing often the reverse is followed – single *inverted commas* outside and double ones inside: *'When you say "The sun goes around the earth", you are completely wrong.'*

There are some sets of similar words that we use regularly. One is *immediate* and 'urgent' – the difference is very subtle. Something that is urgent needs attending to very early, but something that needs *immediate* attention cannot be postponed at any cost. *Immediate* is more urgent than 'urgent'.

Another pair is *institution* and 'organization'. The latter is a formal or informal group of people who organize themselves for a common purpose – the Organization of African Unity, for example. An *institution* is a formal body, often with a physical office and other buildings, or an age-old system – the *Institution of Engineers* or *the institution of marriage*. The difference, in a way, is this – you may organize a cricket tournament, but you would *institute* a trophy in someone's name.

The third pair of similar words is *important* and 'significant'. Both words indicate something valuable but not of physical value. One does not say *an important table* or *a significant chair*! *Important* – in thought, in ideas, in effort – indicates that the value is understood; but when something is significant, the value is perhaps not quite clear, it is somewhat hidden, it needs some thinking, and perhaps time, to realize its importance. *The discovery of the Higgs-Boson particle is important; its significance is not yet clear.* In more simple use – *It is important to study history* but *Do you know the significance of 1857 in Indian history*?

What is *irony*? *Irony* is a figure or speech or use of words or an event in which what appears to be the case is very different from what is actually the case, or where the final result is very different from that originally intended. *Ironic* is the adjective, and *ironically* is the adverb. *It was ironic that he was welcomed as the principal of the school from where he had been removed for being a naughty boy!* In Shakespeare's play *Romeo and Juliet*, the dramatic *irony* is that the two noble families, the House of Capulet and the House of Montague in Verona, are bitter enemies, while Juliet, daughter of the Capulets and Romeo, son of the Montagues, fall deeply in love. The visual *irony*, that which the audience is aware of, is that Romeo kills himself thinking that Juliet is dead, when she is not. (And when Juliet learns that Romeo is no more, she kills herself). The difference between sarcasm and *irony* is slight, but needs to be noted. Many people use the sarcastic *great!* as an example of the *ironic* – 'Great! Now you have torn my shirt!' But this is sarcasm.

Italics is the term for letters and words in print that slope from left to right, like the word at the start of this sentence. Why is it used that way? It places an emphasis; one might underline the word, and in handwriting, that is the way to indicate emphasis. *Italics* are also used to refer to the titles of books, journals and so on – Jane Austen wrote *Pride and Prejudice*. In this book, examples are shown in *italics*. If a book is mentioned within an *italicized* line, it would be correct to remove the *italics* for the book – *Jane Austen wrote* Pride and Prejudice.

We use these I-terms often but sometimes forget what they stand for. An *IC* is an integrated circuit, often called a 'chip'. An *ID*, as in an *ID card*, stands for *Identity Document*! *IP* is *Internet Protocol*. *IT* is the short form of *Information Technology*. And *IQ* stands for *Intelligence Quotient*.

J

J is a happy letter, and we'll tell you why. First, let us look at two words that usually make us happy at the dining table.

What is the difference between the *jam* and the *jelly* that we put on our toast? *Jam* is made from full fruit, either cut into pieces or crushed. *Jelly* is made from the juice of the fruit, and therefore does not have pieces of the fruit in it. But both words have other meanings. To *jam* something is to stop it from moving freely – *He jammed the door using an iron rod.* To block is similar – *The crowd jammed the entry.* If you like to play and listen to music, you might go to a *jam session*; often it is an unplanned music session and you obviously like *jamming*. But if you are in trouble, you are *in a jam*! *Jelly*, apart from the fruit product, is the word used for some ointments, such as *petroleum jelly.* And there is a specific use if someone is very scared or in great distress – *He was so scared when he saw the intruder that his legs turned to jelly.*

To *join* is to put together – *You can join the broken pieces with glue.* It also means 'to become a part of' – *He joined the army.* To participate also is to *join* – *He joined in the Diwali celebrations* or *Everyone joined me in congratulating her. Joint* has more than one meaning – a *joint* where bones meet in the body; a large portion of meat for cooking, a roast *joint*; a place, usually a restaurant or a coffee shop to hang around at; in slang, a cigarette with some narcotic drug in it. Shakespeare, who else, uses 'the time is out of *joint*' in *Hamlet*, meaning that circumstances are not all right; if a *joint* is broken, there is pain and distress. A *joint venture* is a business project with more than one person *joining* together to pool in finances or expertise. A *joinder* is a legal term, used when two or more issues are heard together as one matter. A *rejoinder* is a response or reply; it could be, in a legal matter, too, the defendant's reply to the plaintiff's assertions.

Now for the happiest of all three letter words – *joy*. Other words that explain this word are happiness, delight and pleasure and so on. But *joy* is perhaps a little deeper than even happiness, and the other two are somewhat temporary feelings. *Joyous* and *joyful* are similar, but there is a slight difference in usage. The first is an adjective that usually goes with an event or occasion– *A birth in the family is always a joyous occasion.* The second is more a feeling – *The tense atmosphere turned joyful when the baby was born.* A stronger word is *jubilation*, a noun, and the adjective is *jubilant* – complete *joy* – *The jubilant crowd went berserk when India won the* World *Cup.*

There is more – *jolly*, *jocular*, *joke*, *joker*, *jovial*, *joviality*. The *jolly season* is Christmas time. *Jolly* could be a matter of time – *a jolly time was had by all*; or stand for 'very' – *a jolly good idea.* A *jolly* person is one who is cheerful, and fun-loving. A *jolly* person would crack *jokes* and be *jocular* in his or her conversation. S/he is also *jovial*, cheerful, and that *joviality* could spread goodwill and merriment in the company s/he keeps. *Joviality* seems less sharp, less noisy than *jocularity*, perhaps only just.

Telling a good *joke* is not easy. That is why we might say *Passing through two sets of interviews to get that job was no joke.* A *joker* is a professional who makes people laugh in a performance, traditionally in a circus; nowadays we have stand-up comics who perform in auditoria. A *joker* may also be called a *jester*, the *jesters* in the courts of kings, for example. If you say something not meant to be taken seriously, you might speak in *jest*. But why 'crack' a joke? 'Crack' is to split open with a sound; is it used here because the listeners burst into laughter? Finally, take a look at the idiom, *joker in the pack*. It stands for someone or something that changes a likely situation unexpectedly. Literally, the *joker* in a pack of cards, has some special 'powers'; the phrase comes out of that – *In the local elections, the new party turned out to be the joker in the pack.*

Q, *x* and *z* are expectedly the three least used letters in English. *J* comes *just* after these three in usage. *Just* is used here specifically, for accuracy and emphasis – *just after* is 'immediately after'. *She stood just behind me*; we could avoid the *just* if we did not intend to give the girl's position so exactly. *You called just as I was leaving* – that is you called at the very moment I was leaving. It also helps specify numbers – *Who all are coming? Just the two of them.* In some cases, as in the earlier sentence, the word 'only' can be substituted for *just*. Another common use, very much in Indian slang, is – *Why did you go there? Just....* This is a use which actually translates from some Indian languages.

However, *just* also has a noble aspect. A *just* person is one who is fair in his views and *judgement*, who does not wrongly take sides and is righteous, who is *just* in his dealings. In legal matters, a decision must be *just* and correct, that is how *justice* has to be provided. The *judicial system* is the forum for providing *justice*. Justice must be impartial and so the saying, 'Justice is blind'. But sometimes the law itself might be such that *justice* is not provided; that is why the saying 'The law is an ass'.

In any formal society, we need a set of laws to be interpreted in courts of law, through the *judicial* system. The system is called the *judiciary*, which includes the *judges* of the Supreme Court at the apex, the State-level high courts and of the lower *judiciary*, all the civil and criminal courts. In some countries, criminal cases are heard by the *judge* before 12 members of the *jury*, each one called a *juror*, who give their opinion at the end of the hearing as to whether the accused is guilty of the charges or not. To *judge* is not only a legal, *judicial* action; one can be a *judge* at a competition, to decide the winner; the word in all cases implies a correct decision. *Judicious*, from the same origin, means 'reasonable', 'sensible', 'well thought out' – *His speech was a judicious mix of theoretical and practical matters.*

Justification, an abstract noun, is the reasoning given for some thought or action, the grounds for stating or believing that something is correct; it has to be in support of a view or attitude or action. The verb is to *justify*, which, in the past tense, is *justified* – *The police justified the strong action.* The adjective is *justifiable* – *justifiable action* – and the adverb is *justifiably* – *We are justifiably proud of you.*

There is another use of *justification*. The use of margins in printing or typing requires the process of justifying the page or paragraph, or even just the line. In a word-processing software, we have left or right *justification*, or centre or full *justification*, the process of aligning the typed material. In typewriters earlier, we had only the one alignment, the left *justification*.

> *Java* is a general purpose programming language for computers, which was developed in 1995 by James Gosling (1955–). Why this name? It probably takes from *Java* coffee, a type of coffee, supposed to have been popular with the creators of the language. *Java* is the name of a large Indonesian island; the coffee comes from there.

K

K is used in slang in at least two important ways. A *10k* is 10,000, that is, *k* is a thousand. The other is the shortened 'OK' or 'okay', where we lazy human beings just say *k*. The symbol for potassium is *k*. The *K* band is a radio frequency, and so is the *Ku* band.

K is a strange letter, because sometimes it is not sounded at all. *Knave*, *knife*, *knit*, *knitting*, *knight*, *knot*, *know*, *knowledge* – the *k* is silent in all these words. On the other hand, as we know, words starting with *c* followed by *a*, *o* and *u* and many words with the letters *ch* use the *k* sound.

Kind has many meanings. First, it means 'type' – a group – *What kind of books are you reading these days?* There is a certain difficulty is specifying such a group; you cannot count the books in the group easily, even though in theory you may be able to count them. There is the use of an even less countable nature – *This kind of behaviour will not be tolerated.*

Kind is also an adjective that relates to people and their behaviour – *He is a kind person* means that he is a helpful, good-natured person. *Kindness* is the abstract noun; it is a trait that should be easy to come across, but in reality, how many truly *kind* people does one know? Such a person could also be called *kind-hearted*. We can also attribute this quality, say, to the weather – *The weather was kind to us, it did not rain.*

A **kick** is a hit with the foot. To *kick* a ball, in football, is to use the foot to send the ball in the desired direction. The leg movement in swimming is also a *kick*. To *kick the bucket*, as we have mentioned elsewhere, is to die. To *kick a habit* is to give up a bad habit – *He was a heavy smoker, but now he has kicked the habit.* Your unpopular boss may be *kicked upstairs*, if he is promoted to a higher position where he has less chance of doing harm to the office. He should have been *kicked out* of – or removed from – the job; your colleagues had *kicked up* a row about his behaviour. *Kick in* is to start – *The new rules kicked in*; *kick off* is also to start, especially a game of football. To *kick-start* any programme or venture is to give it a push or make a special effort to make it start; this comes from *kicking* a pedal to start a motorcycle. A *kickback* is the term for money received for a favour done in an underhand deal.

We have the word **kin**, one's relatives. *Kinship* is relationship by birth or even by marriage. Normally one's children would be one's *next of kin,* or whoever is the nearest living relative. Then there is *kith and kin* – one's relatives. And we have *kindred* – which pertains to such relationships and is most often used as a positive, friendly adjective; a *kindred spirit* is a person who has the same attitude as you, and thinks as you do.

A **king** is the head of a country, a ruler who usually inherits the *kingdom* as heir to the throne. Great Britain is a *kingdom* though it may be ruled by a queen. *King of Kings* is a term sometimes used in Christianity to refer to God, and the Lord's Prayer, the most significant prayer among Christians, refers to the *kingdom* of God. *Kingdom come*, taken from the Lord's Prayer, is the end of the world; so we have the term *until kingdom come – I may have to wait till kingdom come for him to return the money he owes me. A king's ransom* is an idiom for a large sum of money; it would require a huge amount to secure the release of a king!

In earlier days, European kings had bands of soldiers who were the best in the land, 'special forces' as we might call them today. These were ***knights***, who fought on horseback. In England, in the 6th century, the legendary *King* Arthur had a round table around which sat his *knights*, all equal in importance; these were the *Knights of the Round Table*, whose tales are heard of and read even today – as stories of heroism, loyalty and chivalry. Today, *knighthoods* exist but generally as honorary titles. These have nothing to do with battle, per se, but with excellence in any field of activity, whether in sports or the arts, in literature or science or public life. *A knight in shining armour* is an idiom for a person who comes to the aid of someone, usually a woman, in distress.

To ***knit*** is to make cloth by putting a strand of thread or wool across another, as you *knit* a sweater. The same word is generally used for *a close-knit family* and also for the abstract concept of *knitting together a story*. If you were perturbed, you might *knit your brows* – this means that you would bring the eyebrows closer in a frown. In all these uses, the prime significance is that of bringing or keeping together in a strong bond. *Knit* is used both in the present tense and the past tense (in the present tense, singular, it would be *knits*). *My mother and my aunt knit wonderfully*, as also *Both my mother and my aunt knit me sweaters last year.* The word *knitted* also exists, but usually as an adjective – *This is a knitted sweater.* We do use *knitted* as a verb, but usually with 'have', 'has' or 'had'– *My mother has knitted this sweater* or *My aunt had knitted this sweater* but even here *knit* is preferable. When my mother *knits,* she uses *knitting needles.* But nowadays, we tend to buy readymade, machine-made *knitwear. Knitting* is a pleasurable activity, but Charles Dickens turned it into a gruesome one. In *A Tale of Two Cities*, which deals with the French Revolution at the end of the 18th century, the elite are killed by the revolutionaries using the guillotine, a sharp instrument which drops from a height to chop off a person's head. And as each 'enemy' is executed there is a group of *knitting* women who count the numbers. The effect is chilling.

When you put together two pieces of rope or cloth, without stitching or knitting, it is usually by tying a *knot*, and there are many, many types of *knots*. But when you marry you *tie the knot*. The definite article 'the' makes the difference. A *knot* is also the measurement of speed on water of ships and boats; one *knot* is one nautical mile, or 1.852 km, per hour. It is also a unit of distance used for aeronautical measurements. Interesting that both on sea and in the air, we use the same term for the measurement of speed, but not on ground.

Knowledge is an abstract concept, quite philosophical, and it is difficult to explain its many layered meaning. The verb *know* has *knew* as the past tense, not 'knowed'! *Knowledge*, plainly speaking, is what one has acquired, by obtaining sufficient information about a particular subject or matter – *His knowledge of world history is commendable.* At a more specific level, we can say – *Radhika knows all the sonnets of Shakespeare.* To be able to do something requires *knowledge – He knows how to fix the computer virus*. The term *knowhow* comes from just that, one *knows how* to do something! But *knowledge* does not have to come by study; it can also be by experience – *She knows how to get home* because she was shown the way first by someone and has probably done it in the past on her own.

> In India, we tend to end a letter with the phrase *with kind regards*. The fact is that 'regards' itself shows politeness; *kind* is perhaps used to indicate that the writer feels *kindly* towards the person addressed! Since there cannot be 'unkind regards', this is rather a meaningless use. Nowadays, it is enough to write 'with regards' or 'with best regards'. We also say, *kindly note* or *may kindly see*, especially in government-style writing, a relic of the past; here 'please' can be used in place of *kindly*. We also use *your kind attention* and similar phrases. Actually, attention is not *kind* or unkind; it is just that you should take a *kind* view of the request being made. These are all old-fashioned but still commonly used terms in India to indicate politeness.

L

You are reading this book in the English *language*. A *language* is a system of communicating among humans. A vocabulary of words created from the letters of an alphabet and a grammar that provides the logic for the use of those words, create meaning. In spoken *language*, sounds given to the *letters* and to the words as a whole, and understood by the community, allow for conversation. You don't necessarily need sound; those who are voiceless can use sign *language* and the visually impaired can read using Braille, a system of raised dots, which they touch to make out the words that the set of dots stand for. The word *language*, in English, comes from the Latin *lingua*, meaning 'tongue'. A *lingua franca* is a bridge *language*, which may not be the mother tongue of the people speaking it. In India, English is one of two official *languages*, the other, of course, is Hindi. Across the world, a few thousand *languages* are spoken; the one spoken most widely is English. The scientific study of *languages*, their structure and *logic*, and all related matters, is *linguistics*.

Early in our geography lessons in school, we learnt about *latitudes and longitudes*. *Latitudes* are those imaginary sideways parallel lines across the globe, 360 of them to cover 360 degrees. Taken from the imaginary line of the Equator, they indicate the north or south position of a place on earth. *Longitudes* are imaginary long lines, or meridians, north to south, 360 of them; they indicate the east or west position of a place from the imaginary line of 0 degrees, called the Prime Meridian, that passes through Greenwich (pronounced 'Gren–ich') in England. Obviously at the North and South Poles, the *longitudes* get bunched up. But then, if you stood exactly at either Pole, there would be no East and West. There would be no South at South Pole, and no North at the North Pole.

There is another meaning to *latitude*. Here *latitude* means 'a certain freedom', the scope to do what you wish to do; implicitly, you are given that 'freedom', and it is not necessarily a good thing – *He was given the latitude to do whatever he wished to.*

Lateral comes from the Latin word *lateralis*, pertaining to the side. We can have practical, physical activity – *lateral movement*, as in dance, or by the army; a *lateral pass* in a game like hockey or football; a *lateral shift* in the office, a transfer at the same level at work. There may be mental activity, such as *lateral thinking*, whereby you try to analyse an issue in a new, different way – thinking out of the box, as it were. *Unilateral*, *bilateral* and *multilateral* – a unilateral decision is one taken without consulting anyone; bilateral is something between two parties and multilateral between many. These words are significant in modern international politics. Discussions between, say, India and

Pakistan, would be bilateral negotiations, while the WTO talks are multilateral.

Late, then *later* and after that *latest*. This is the use in a time sequence, when something happens after something – *He always comes late to work, but today I came in later.* The third word, *latest*, is used in many ways, often to bring something up to date – *the latest entrant to the programme; the latest version of the phone; the latest edition of the book*. A person who is no more, who has passed away, is referred to as *late*. In India, where we are required to fill in our father's name in so many forms, we write, if our father is not alive – *XYZ s/o Late Shri (or Mr) ABC*. A *Johnny-come-lately* is one who has just come into a group, but who thinks he knows everything.

And what of *latter*? If two objects, two facts, two ideas, two of anything are mentioned one after the other, the second one is the *latter* one. It is the opposite of 'former'. But if three or more objects, facts and ideas are mentioned, the last of them will not be the *latter*, it will be the *last*! *Latter* is always in comparison with one other – *If you can travel by road or by air, use the latter option.* By the way, *latter* can be used differently in one rare case – *latter-day* – which refers to modern times, that is, present day as compared to earlier days. (We must mention the difference in the pronunciation of two words – *later* is 'lay–ter' while *latter* is 'lat–ter', like 'matter').

Law and its related words are fascinating. *Law* is a set of rules and systems put together by *lawmakers*, that is, our *legislators*, within which framework citizens are expected to behave and act. The breaking of a *law* attracts penal provisions. *Lawyers* are people who have studied *law* formally and appear in court for the *litigants*. But not all *lawyers* can appear in court, only those who are enrolled to do so.

All *laws* are made in the *legislature*. In India, there are two Houses of Parliament, the House of the People, which is the Lok Sabha, the 'lower' House, and the House of the States, the Rajya Sabha, the 'upper' House. The States have their own *legislatures*, but only six of them have two Houses; the others have only one House, the Legislative Assembly. In the *legislature*, the *legislators legislate*, that is they *pass laws*, and create our *legal system*. Anything pertaining to, and following, the *laws*, is *legal*, its opposite is 'illegal'. From here, we have *legitimacy* and the adjective *legitimate*, which means '*legally* valid' – *the legitimate aspirations of the people*. The opposite is *illegitimate*, commonly used for *illegitimate gains* or as in *an illegitimate child* – a child born outside marriage.

There are a few error-prone words to look at. To *lean* on someone or something is to take support – *Please don't lean on me, I cannot take your weight*. The word is also the opposite of bountiful – *The lean months before the harvest are always difficult for small farmers*. If you are thin, you could be called *lean*. In the past tense of the verb, to *lean*, we have two words – *The gymnast leant on her coach as she hobbled out of the arena* or – *Her mother leaned on her more and more after her father passed away.* You would have noticed *leant* and *leaned* in similar use – what then is the difference? Both words are correct and interchangeable And yet, is the latter more used in the context of requiring long-term support?. The way you say the two words, though, is different. *Leant* rhymes with 'went'; *leaned* with 'cleaned'.

Sounding similar to *leant* is lent, the past tense of *lend* – *I had lent him some money, but he refuses to return it.* When you give something, money or any other thing, to someone and expect it to be returned, you *lend*, you give it on *loan.* When you take a *loan* from the bank, you borrow and are expected to return or repay it. There is also *Lent*, with a capital *L*; it is, among Christians, the forty days' period of fasting leading to Easter.

Less is the opposite of 'more'. It is different from 'few' or 'fewer', which are used with countable things. *There is less tree cover in the country today*, but *There are few forests today* or *There are fewer forests today than before*, where the number of forests is countable. It appears technically correct to use the 'comparative' and 'superlative' *lesser* and *least*, but one needs to use *lesser* with caution. It is not quite correct to say 'He had lesser food than her'; since *less* itself is a comparison; it is better to say *He had less food than her.* One can use *lesser* in a limited way, for example – *the lesser of two evils.* Alfred Tennyson (1809–1892) in his famous long poem *Idylls of the King* wrote:

As if some lesser god had made the world
But had not force to shape it as he would...[1]

There is another similar sounding word – *lessor*. It comes from the root word, *lease*. A *lease* is an agreement by which a *lessee* agrees to pay a *lessor* a certain amount of money for the use of the *leased* item, usually property. Written as a *lease deed*, such a document may be registered at the office

[1] https://www.poetryfoundation.org/poems-and-poets/poems/detail/45325

of the registrar, and stands as legal proof of the agreement. A *lease* for the use of a building or such accommodation would be a tenancy, with a tenant who takes the property for a period of time on *lease* from the *landlord.*

Let us look at *let*. At one level, it means 'to permit', it allows us to introduce a topic or thought or action – *let us* (allow ourselves to) *look at let.* And so we have – *let us go, let me speak*, *let it be.* For *let us*, we have the apostrophe for contraction – *let's*, as in *let's go.*

Let may be followed by 'down', 'go', 'in', 'on', 'off', 'out', 'up' – all these create verbal phrases that are widely used. If you *let down* somebody, you disappoint that person who had high expectations of you – *The hockey team let the country down at the Olympics.* To *let go* is to allow someone or something to go free, to release one's hold – *The police let him go as they did not have enough evidence against him*, or – *Before you accelerate, please let go the clutch.* If you allow someone to come in, *you let him or her in*, usually by opening a closed door. But *We let him in on our secret* means that we shared our secret with him. *Let on* is to reveal one's feelings or information, usually used with a negative – *She didn't let on that she was scared* or, in the other sense – *She didn't let on that she knew who the thief was.* To *let off* is to release – *They let off crackers after India won* or – *At the end of the exams the children let off steam.* The opposite sounding, *let up*, is generally used with a 'no' – *there was no let up in his efforts* means that he continued with his efforts. *Let out*, too, has different uses. The opposite of *let in* – *I let myself out of the house* – is one use. To *let out the secret* is to make known the hidden truth; to *let out a scream* is to release a shout; to *let out a house* is to give it out on rent. And so we see notices everywhere – *To Let.*

There is a very important use of the word **letter**, especially for this book – *a letter of the alphabet.* A to Z – each is a *letter*. *There are 26 letters of the alphabet* in English, not 26 'alphabets'. Many people show their lack of understanding of English when they mix up the word 'alphabet' with the '*letters* of the alphabet'. How we understand the letters can be fun! A man from somewhere in East Europe went to his eye doctor. 'Doctor,' he said, 'My eyes are giving trouble, I need a check-up.' The doctor asked him if he could read the last line of the chart, XOHBSZQRTV. 'Read it?' the man said. 'That's my brother's name.'

Letters of another kind? Well, the art of *letter writing* is now lost, after the invention of the telephone and then the Internet revolution. The postman does not come home with *letters* from your friends and relatives; he brings only bills! A *letter* is a message you write to someone; a *love letter* is to your beloved, a *business letter* formally to a business associate. The words 'mail' and 'post', in this context, are similar, but with a slight difference. The post is what comes through the post office. In this sense, mail is the same, but is more commonly used in the USA, where they have mailboxes, not postboxes. But today, if you told your friend, 'I saw your mail,' you would probably have seen it as email, sent from his email ID to your email ID and it would drop into your 'mailbox'.

Liberty is a precious gift; it is freedom, independence from foreign rule or outside control. The phrase, '*liberty*, equality, fraternity' is the motto of the French Republic ('fraternity' means 'brotherhood'). This idealism, of people's rule, finds

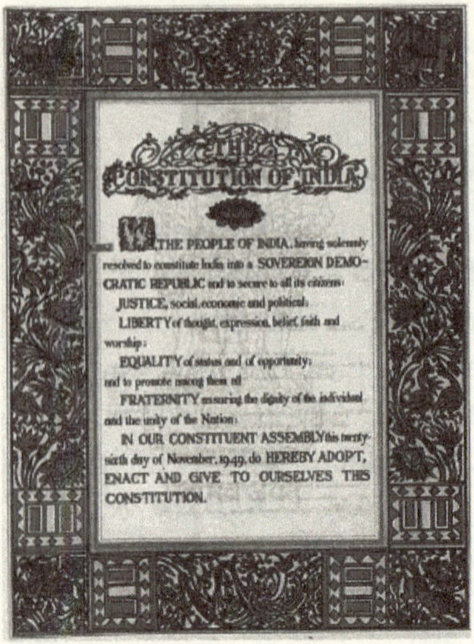
THE CONSTITUTION OF INDIA

WE, THE PEOPLE OF INDIA, having solemnly resolved to constitute India into a SOVEREIGN DEMOCRATIC REPUBLIC and to secure to all its citizens:

JUSTICE, social, economic and political;

LIBERTY of thought, expression, belief, faith and worship;

EQUALITY of status and of opportunity;

and to promote among them all

FRATERNITY assuring the dignity of the individual and the unity of the Nation;

IN OUR CONSTITUENT ASSEMBLY this twenty-sixth day of November, 1949, do HEREBY ADOPT, ENACT AND GIVE TO OURSELVES THIS CONSTITUTION.

its place in the Indian Constitution too, which states, in its Preamble, that 'we, the people' promise ourselves justice, *liberty*, equality and fraternity. Another word, *liberation*, is similar in its meaning. To achieve *liberty*, one has to *liberate* someone or be *liberated* from dependence. That is the process of *liberation*. In common use, too, one may say – *I have given up smoking, I feel liberated!* You do not say 'I feel liberty!' In a plural form, we have the concept of *civil liberties*.

Licence has two opposite meanings. The first is a permit, and yet a way to regulate an activity. Your driving *licence* is an example of such a document; it gives you permission to drive a motor vehicle, and at the same time, it controls all citizens who wish to drive, through motor vehicle rules. Every shop, every trade has a *licence*. The noun is *licence*; the action, that is the verb, is *license*. (But in American English, the spelling for both the noun and the verb is 'license', just as the Americans spell 'defence' as 'defense'.) The other meaning of *licence*, without 'a' before it, is just the opposite as it were; it is a lack of moral behaviour, an immoral attitude. The adjective is more commonly used, *licentious* – *His licentious behaviour upset all the ladies present*. The first licence provides control, the second breaks control.

A *limerick* is a five-line humorous poem, where the first, second and fifth lines rhyme and the third and fourth are shorter lines that rhyme, in the scheme – a,a,b,b,a. The name probably came from the town of *Limerick* in Ireland. Some of the best *limericks* are naughty, but all tell of comic situations. The most famous creator of *limericks* is Edward Lear (1812–1888) whose *A Book of Nonsense* (1845) made the form popular. Here is one of his famous ones:

There was an Old Man with a beard,
Who said, 'It is just as I feared!
Two Owls and a Hen,
Four Larks and a Wren,
Have all built their nests in my beard![1]

What is *literature*? The recorded body of work, the written and oral output, of any *language* is its *literature*. This *literature* is largely, but not entirely, its creative writing – its fiction, which is the aggregate of all novels, short stories, poetry and drama. It also includes non-fiction writing – the work of essayists and of historians who nowadays increasingly write in popular and not academic styles. But is anything we write, say an office letter, *literature*? The answer is an emphatic no. How then do we judge what is *literature*? That is a very difficult question to answer. There is no single, easy definition. All writing meant for and available to the public to read could be the beginning of finding a meaning. But from that mass, one has to take out what is of some quality, writing which is widely read,

[1] http://www.gutenberg.org/files/982/982-h/982-h.htm

appreciated by the readers in general, something out of the ordinary – that perhaps is *literature*. Boris Pasternak (1890–1960), the Russian poet and novelist, has said, '*Literature* is the art of discovering something extraordinary about ordinary people, and saying with ordinary words something extraordinary.'

A very interesting word is *literal*. It is the use of a word or concept without any additional meaning attached. It is the straightforward use of the word, with no exaggeration, a factual use. The opposite of *literal* is 'figurative', 'metaphoric' or 'virtual'. If one were to say – *Climbing the Everest is literally a mind-blowing experience*, surely the blowing of the mind is not a factual matter. The better word might be 'virtually', and yet, modern usage has slowly allowed 'literally' to sneak in and be used where it should not be used. So, *literal* is now also 'figurative'. Strange are the uses of words!

What is *logic*? This is a difficult question to answer. Simply put, it is a manner of reasoning, of setting out, in a *logical* way, the basis for an argument, where argument is not shouting and fighting, but a reasoned thinking. At the end of a debate, you might say – *I could not understand the logic of his argument.*

The word *lot*, used with 'a', means 'a good amount' – *I have a lot of friends*. It can be in the plural – *I have lots of friends*. (It is different from 'allot' – which is to give one's share, to allocate, to indicate one's place.) *Lot*, without the 'a', is also one's share – *My lot in the family property was not very large*, or the result of fate – *It was his lot to go through a life of hardship*. A *lot* is also a term used in the housing industry especially in Britain – *This housing lot is very old and will be torn down soon*. In the plural form, we often end letters or email with *lots of love*, the short form for texting being *LoL*. The term originally stood for 'little old lady'; nowadays it is used most often for 'laughing out loud', which is even more common than *lots of love*. How we have changed.

Two words that create confusion even among persons who know English well are *lose* and *loose*. To *lose* is the opposite of 'to gain' or 'to win'. The noun is *loss* – *India's loss in the hockey tournament was unfortunate, but to lose so badly made it worse*. The past tense is *lost* – *I lost my wallet yesterday* or *I lost my nerves*. This is also an adjective – *I found the lost ball*. The word *loose* can be an adjective; the opposite of 'tight' – *He was wearing a loose shirt which made him look very fat* – or an adverb – *The knot was tied loosely*. The way to check the difference is to ask oneself – can I say 'to lose' or 'to loose'; the first is correct, *lose* is a verb, the second is incorrect, *loose* is not a verb. (You can say 'too loose', but that is a very different 'too'.) From *loose* we have *loosen* – *He tried to loosen his tie* or *The miser decided to loosen his purse strings*.

The word *love* has come up often in the last few paragraphs. *Lovely* is the adjective, or adjectival noun, to describe something beautiful. *Love*, both as a word and as the feeling, is most difficult to define. A mother's *love* for her child, a child's *love* for the parent, a sister's for her brother, a citizen's for his country, *love* between two grown-ups – it is difficult to explain this deep affection, this emotion. Han Suyin (1916–2012) called it a many-splendoured thing in her 1952 novel of the same name.

What is the difference between *luck* and chance? Chance is the probability of something happening. *Luck* pertains to an individual, and can be good or bad. The lower the chance of something happening to someone, and it happens, the *luckier* the person is – provided it is a good thing happening! You wish someone good *luck*, not good chance; his or her chances may or may not be bright.

M

M begins many words in the English language that have to do with *man* and his world – *man*, *male, me*, *my*, *manners*, *mannerisms*, *manufacture*, *management*, *matter*, *mind* and many more. We will talk about some of them. It is also the letter that talks of size – *maximum*, *minimum*, *magnify*, *magnitude*, *meta*, *mega*.

M when doubled to *mm*... expresses something pleasurable. It is supposed to indicate a sound – *Mm..the food smells great*. Otherwise, *mm* is also the short form of *millimetre,* which is one tenth of a centimetre, which, in turn, is one hundredth of a *metre*. And so, 1*m* is one *metre*. A *metre* is 1.094 yards. The speed of light is 299,792,458 *metres* per second. From *metre* we have *metric*, pertaining to a *metre* – *I ran a metric mile today*. *Meter* is the American spelling for *metre*. But it is also the spelling for any type of *measurement* device, an *ammeter*, a *voltmeter*, or, simply, the electricity *meter* which indicates how much electricity you have consumed.

M is important because it is the first letter in all the words we use to address each other by – the common ones are *Mr* (short for *Mister*) which is used for *men*, *Mrs* (pronounced 'Missez') used for *married* women, and *Miss* for unmarried women. In modern times, it was felt that the use of *Mr* for all *men* but *Mrs* for *married* women and *Miss* for unmarried women showed a gender bias; so a new form for all women came about – *Ms* (pronounced Miz). The word gained in popularity after the pro-feminism magazine *Ms* came out in 1971. Interestingly one uses a full stop after *Mr* or *Mrs* in the American style, as they are treated as abbreviations; in Britain, the full stops are not required. All these words come from *Master* or *Mistress*. *Master* was originally used to address one's employer or a socially superior person; the *mistress* was the lady of the house.

Master is also used to typify specialist workmen, like a *master tailor* or a *master craftsman*. The principal of a school is usually called the *headmaster* or *headmistress*. And, when you have *mastered* a subject through a course of study in a university you get a *Master's degree*, perhaps an *MA*, *MSc*, *MCom* or *MCA* in arts, science, commerce or computer applications.

M, as we said, is about *man* – and his world. *Man* is the word for a *male* human being, note the *man* hidden in 'human'! The word is believed to come from the Sanskrit word *manushya* which means 'a human being'. In legal terminology, *man* includes 'woman' – the exact words in the General Clauses Act of the Central Government, which goes back to 1897, are 'In all Central Acts and Regulations, unless there is anything repugnant in the subject or context – words importing the *masculine* gender shall be taken to include females...' What then is *masculine*? It simply is an adjective pertaining to *man* or *men*, the plural of *man*. *Male*, the opposite of 'female', also pertains to *man* or *men*, so the words are often interchangeable.

Mal itself means 'bad' or 'evil' or 'harmful'. So *malevolent* does not deal with *man* but with having a harmful effect or influence (pronounced not 'male–volent' but 'mal–e–volent'). So, too, with words like *malicious*, *malign* and *malignant*. You might have *a malicious worm in your computer*, your enemy might try to *malign your reputation* (pronounced 'mal–ine') or someone might be diagnosed with *a malignant tumour* (pronounced 'mal–ig–nant').

Manufacture originally came from 'making by hand'. But now *machinery* (a number of individual *machines* together is *machinery*) and *mechanical* (the adjective from *machine*) production systems allow most products to be *manufactured* without the touch of human hands. A *manufacturer* is one who *manufactures*. And the *manufacturing* sector plays a very important part in a country's economy.

The word *manuscript* has the same origin. It is usually a document, generally what an author sends to a publisher for publication. The word in its Latin original means 'handwritten', but a typed document or a computer print would also be a *manuscript*; the word 'typescript' is nowadays preferred by some writers, editors and publishers.

Three important words that begin with *man* are *manner*, *manners* and *mannerism*. *Manner*, without the *s*, is a way, a style – *He always speaks in a polite manner.* It might relate to copying a style of writing – *One might write in the manner of Shakespeare*. In a different way – *The manner in which this government is being run, our country will be ruined*. Then there is *in a manner of speaking*, a form of idiomatic speech that *means* 'in a way' or 'in one sense' – *In a manner of speaking, ours is a banana republic, there is no rule of law*. The plural form, *manners*, pertains to behaviour, it is about good or bad *manners* – '*Young man, you have impeccable manners, thank you,*' *the elderly gentleman said*. A *mannerism* is a peculiar or unusual style of behaviour – *He has a strange mannerism of always coughing before he speaks*.

Make, with its past tense *made*, is to create or to construct. Anything, whether built, cooked, sewed – anything that is a physical thing, can be *made* – *Amma, please make me a dosa* or *He made a kite*. But to *make* is certainly not only for physical things; it is also used for abstract *matters* that cannot be physically touched – *She made a sudden appearance on stage* or *He made a lot of mistakes in the exams*. There is a difference in the use of *make* and 'do'. You do your duty, do your homework, do your laundry; there is no sense of creating something new here. With *make*, there is; you *make* jam, *make* a dress, *make* friends. *My Maker* is my God, when someone *meets his Maker*, he has passed away.

A *mark* is a spot or line on a surface, which is seen to be different from the area around it – *a red mark on a white tablecloth* or *a birthmark on my arm*. A *mark* can also be *a punctuation mark* – a comma, a semicolon, inverted commas and so on. It can be a *watermark*, a light design made on certain types of paper to make them special, for example in banknotes or stamp paper. A *trademark* gives a unique, legal status to a commodity or product. A *postmark* is the *mark* made on a stamp on an envelope to cancel its future use and indicating at the same time the date of posting. A *marker* may be a pen that *marks*. It is also a pointer or a condition that helps to categorize and distinguish; an example is a *genetic marker*, which can identify an individual or a species. In athletics, when the 'starter' of a race says, '*on your mark*', s/he tells the runners to get ready at the starting line *marked* on the track.

A *mark* is also an invisible difference, a special something – *He made a mark in the swimming championships with two records*. In *making a mark*, the word is always singular. In a plural sense – and rarely in the singular form – we have *marks* which indicate how well a student has done in his or her examinations. Even if one gets zero *marks*, it still would be *marks*! The singular could be – *Ma'am, if you gave me one grace mark, I would pass!*

Mark can also be a verb. To *mark* is to note with its related use – *Mark my words*. Or – *Mark the date in your calendar.* A manufacturer may *mark up* the prices of his products to increase profits or to cover the increase in raw *material* costs; a shopkeeper might *mark down* the price of some stocks to sell them at a discount.

Me and *my* are among the most commonly used words, both from the personal pronoun 'I' – *He saw me* and *He saw my book*. *My* is of course, the possessive form. But if you wanted to be somewhat sarcastic, you might say – *My, my, look who has come*! Repetition sometimes gives a whole new meaning to a word.

When do you use 'I' and when *me*? If you were to say – *My friend and I saw him,* that would be correct; if you said – 'my friend and me saw him' or 'me and my friend saw him', which is quite popular, it would be wrong. Let us look at another situation. *Hari came to the film with me* – that is correct. But *Hari and I went to the film*, not 'Hari and me went to the film'. If you take out Hari, 'me went to the film' would be wrong! What about this one? *It is not Ahmed and Hari who are going, it is Tom and I*! This is correct because we can add 'who are going' after the 'I'. The 'I' test is to place the verb after 'I' or *me* and see if it fits. *Me* is correct if there is no action and no need for an 'I'. If you say, *He is taller than me*, it would not be wrong, even though one could say 'than I am'. So, if a comparison is made, *me* is correct, and 'I' is also correct if extended by 'am'.

In a rare context, either *me* or *my* can be used– *I hope you don't mind my coming to the show* is the same as *I hope you don't mind me coming to the show*. From *my*, you also get *mine*. *This is my book* can become *This book is mine*. The difference between *my* and *mine* in a practical sense is this – *my* needs a noun after it ('this book is my' is wrong, only *This is my book* is right) while *mine* does not need a noun after it, the noun 'book' has already been mentioned. You do not normally use *mine* for human beings, you say *This is my brother*, not 'this brother is mine'! You could, no doubt, show your affection with *mine* – *How are you, brother mine* or *Meet this brother of mine* (note the 'of' when you are talking of your brother in the third person).

What distinguishes *may* from *might*? First, we have the completely different uses of the two words. *May*, with a capital *M*, is the fifth month of the English calendar. *May Day* is the first day of *May*, a day of celebration of the spring season and also the International Workers' Day. *Mayday*, the two words together, is a signal of distress in radio communication – it has nothing to do with the *month*, but comes from the French term *m'aider*, which roughly means 'please help me'. *Might* is a matter of strength – *He hit the intruder with all his might*. The old adage that *might is right* goes back to the view that one can do whatever one wants to if one is strong. *How the mighty have fallen* is a phrase that refers to someone of high status who is now seeing bad days.

But *may* and *might* are both in the realm of uncertainty. *May* indicates the possibility of something happening or not happening in the future – *He may come; She may go; It may be cold; I may not get the job*. There is also an element of the past – *She may have gone home.* It implies uncertainty – a certain lack of definite knowledge about an action or situation that *may* have already occurred. What then is the difference with *might*? Both are generally used interchangeably. And yet, when do we say *It might be cold* or *She might have gone home*, not *may*? One basic way is in the use of *might* in reporting – *She said it might be cold.* Or, *Her boss said that she might have gone home.* Of course, without the reporting, one could write either *I don't know where she is, she may have gone home* or *I don't know where she is, she might have gone home.* Both would be grammatically correct. The subtle difference, if any, is in the timing of her going home, *might* implies some time back, *may* is approximately in the present context. There is also, for *might*, the possibility of something that could have happened, but did not – *I might have come first in class had I not fallen ill.*

Two more aspects of the correct use of *may*. *May* seeks permission – *May I come in*? This is the correct form, not 'Can I come in?'; you can come in because you have the physical ability to enter, but you *may not* come in without permission! (Even here, *might* is possible as an extra 'polite' request – *Might I go home now?*) And the other rule is that in a sentence where uncertainty is already established, *may* should change to *will*. Here is an example of a wrong use of *may* made by a TV channel; its reporter said, 'It is not likely that the high court may give a decision today.' The correct sentence should be *It is not likely that the high court will give a decision today*. The uncertainty has already come in with 'not likely'; you do not need it again with *may*!

Matter is physical stuff as well as abstraction. In common terms, *matter* is something that has weight and volume (and volume is three-dimensional – with height, length and breadth). Weight comes from the pull of gravity on earth; if there were no gravity, there would be no weight and we would be floating in space! This weight is technically called *mass,* which, in scientific terms, is the resistance to acceleration. But both *mass* and *matter* have other *meanings*. *Mass*, with a capital *M*, is a church service, especially for Catholics; you *might* on special occasions go to *a midnight Mass*. Interestingly, physical *mass* is singular – *Both objects have mass*. A plural form, *masses,* exists only to refer to the people, the general public – *The masses rose in revolt against the dictator's rule*. The word *massive* indicates a very large size – *a massive structure*.

Einstein showed us that *matter* can be converted to energy, a 'non-physical' entity, giving us his famous equation $E = mc^2$ (remember Chapter E?). In common language, *matter* can be used for conceptual issues. *What is the matter*, we might ask. *It is a very complicated matter* could be the answer. Or one could say – *It doesn't matter.* If one is depressed one *might* feel that *nothing matters any more*. Or – *Thank you for your good wishes, they matter a great deal to me*. In all these uses, *matter* is an issue, a problem, a thought, a situation, an impact – all abstract, non-physical concepts. If you said something in a *matter of fact* manner, you would be saying it without emotion. There is another related meaning, which is the stating of a fact but with an emphasis – *He is not just another relative; as a matter of fact, he is my brother.* There is a similar phrase – *the fact of the matter*, which means the truth – *The fact of the matter is that we are a very large country.* There is also *the heart of the matter* – the core issue.

Maximum is the highest and *minimum* is the lowest value or number in a set of values, or numbers. We have the *maximum* and *minimum* temperatures, or *maximum* mileage, or the *minimum* distance to travel. There is a difference between *maximum* and 'optimum' – if the first means the 'highest' amount, the other means the 'right' amount – *The maximum students are in this class – 50 – but the optimum number should be 40.* There is also *maxim*, from the same root, which means a well-known saying. Do you know of the word *minim*? It is, in varying ways, a certain half note in music, a certain quantity of fluid, and a short downward, vertical stroke in handwriting.

An interesting word is *mean*; it has many meanings. The first is as a part of a trio of words – *mean, mode* and *median*. In simple arithmetic, *mean* is an average – *the mean sea level* or *The mean age of the group of three students aged 10, 11and 12 is 11. Mode* is the number that appears the most number of times in a set of numbers; in 3, 5, 2, 3, 5, 3 and 3, the mode is 3. And the *median* is the middle one of a set of numbers – if there are five numbers 2, 5, 7, 8 and 9, the third one, 7, would be the *median*. This simple explanation is not a substitute for a course in *mathematics*! *Mode* is also used for system or type – *The most popular mode of transport in our city is the underground metro.* A *median* is the road divider on our roads, especially on highways. *But mean* has many other *meanings*! One is an intention – *I mean to study mathematics today*. Another is what you find throughout this book, *this means such and such*; it explains a word or a sentence, an idea or a concept. From this we have *meaning*

– *If there is a hidden meaning to what you are saying, I don't understand it! Mean* is also the word used to describe someone who is ungenerous, or who is not likeable – *He is a horrible, mean person.* It could also be used as an adverb – *Don't be mean.* But *modern* slang has *mean* as an adjective for 'excellent' – *He cooks a mean biryani.* The past tense of the verb *mean* is *meant* (pronounced 'ment' like 'went') – *I meant to go to work today, but I was too ill to go.*

An important word beginning with *m* is *media*. Let us first look at the word in the singular – *medium*. It has many meanings. *Medium*, usually as an adjective for size, is the *middle* size, between large and small – *He always buys medium-size clothes,* or *He is of medium height.* It is also a substance or system through which something is done or communicated – *The medium of instruction is English,* or – *She paints using oil as her medium.* You could ask, at a restaurant, for a *medium steak*, in between a rare steak, which is not grilled much, and a well-done one! But the most interesting *meaning* of *medium*, perhaps, is a person who is a *medium* and supposedly communicates with spirits.

Media is a plural word, but it is a singular form; some would say 'the media are...' but, in common use, we say 'the media is...'. What indeed is *media*? Today it stands for the totality of news processing and communicating, as a system and as an industry – it stands, in a sense, for the fourth estate, the fourth pillar of democracy. *When the story broke, the media went overboard in trying to get her version.* Earlier, the usual word was the 'press', which comprised the *print media*; today television, online and social *media* have expanded the range.

Television reporting is still young in India, and it is worth making a brief mention here of the poor quality of

English used by some English news channels. Many of those who report live on these channels, or those who write the ticker headlines are often deficient in their English. Some actually speak grammatically incorrect English. There is a terrible use of hyperbole, often wrongly – 'a letter bomb' meaning a very important or tricky letter! Phrases like 'this very moment' (instead of 'now'), 'this particular incident' (not 'this incident'), 'tell us exactly what happened' (simply, 'what happened') are all part of the *media's* use of exaggeration. There is the use of 'really' or 'truly' or 'absolutely' half a dozen times in a story to emphasize its supposed accuracy and veracity. Then there is the misuse of aphorisms – 'The ball is in the Supreme Court's court' – or a translation from Hindi – 'It is on the police now to take action' (instead of 'up to'). Some channels are forever airing exclusive interviews. Obviously, every interview in unique, but it is exclusive only if the person interviewed does not give an interview to any other channel.

It is difficult to keep track of errors committed by the visual *media* as we don't sit down deliberately to wait for them, but a few short gems, taken over just a few days, are given here – '(She) has been one of the more vocal faces of the (party)'; or 'For 52 years the family has been lying in wait to get land promised to a martyr'. And then the weather – 'The temperature is down and under' and 'The southwest monsoons have given way to umbrellas'. It is better to use simple English than to be laughed at for the use of wrong English.

To ***meet*** is to get together, either by earlier appointment, or by accident,unexpectedly. *Met* is the past tense of *meet* – *I met him at office this morning*. A *meet* is also a gathering, such as *an inter-college meet*. Formal *meetings* are related to work or other similar activity, but *meetings* can be informal, too, and you might tell your friend, *I'll meet you downstairs in 10 minutes*. The other common use is – *Let's meet up tomorrow*; it is possible to do without the 'up', but it gives an impression of bonding, and possibly of a *meeting* after some time. To *meet with* is an Americanism. The other *meat* is the flesh of birds or animals, eaten by those who are not vegetarians. We use the term non-vegetarian for *meat-eaters*.

Meta, from its Greek origin, stands for 'after', 'beyond' or 'higher'. An example is *metaphysics*, which is beyond the laws of physics, at a higher plane – *The discussion was about metaphysical, spiritual issues*. *Metadata* is data about data, a level beyond the original. A common use of the prefix is in *metamorphosis*. To *morph* is to change, and *metamorphosis* often implies a drastic, significant change.

What is the difference between *meta* and *mega*? *Meta*, we have noticed, pertains to more non-physical *matters* – going beyond. *Mega* is large, gigantic, generally in a physical sense – a *mega mart*, a *mega constellation*. A *megaton* is one *million* tons; it is a force of explosion equal to one *million* tons of TNT. *Megalomania* is the delusion of grandeur and a *megalomaniac* is one who thinks he is all-powerful and great.

A *metaphor* is a figure of speech; it is a way of describing something, where a concept or object is used to describe another unrelated concept or object. A simple example – *Despite my bad day at the office, my boss's encouragement was music to my ears*. There is a difference between a *metaphor* and a simile, which also does the same job, but slightly differently. *My love is like a red, red rose*, said the poet Robert Burns (1759–96). That is a simile. Had he said – 'My love is a red, red rose', it would have been a *metaphor*.

Sometimes we get mixed up in our cleverness, and that's when we end up using *mixed metaphors*. Perhaps the most quoted example of a *mixed metaphor* is one that goes back over two hundred years. A certain Sir Boyle Roche is believed to have stated, towards the end of the 18th century, in the British Parliament, 'Mr Speaker, I smell a rat; I see him forming in the air and darkening the sky; but I'll nip him in the bud.'

Apparently, this worthy gentleman was also well known for *malapropisms*. The word comes from *mal* – which we know is 'bad' or 'wrong' – and apropos – 'relating to' or 'pertaining to'. The word comes from Mrs Malaprop, a comic character in the play *The Rivals* (1775) by Richard Brinsley Sheridan (1751–1816), who goes around using a wrong word for a similar sounding correct word. One such use is 'a nice derangement of epitaphs' when she means 'a nice arrangement of epithets'!

A rather unusual figure of speech is the *metonym*. It is the substitution of a word, or phrase, by another to *mean* the original, and the substitute word or phrase is the *metonym*. If we say that the Rashtrapati Bhavan issued a clarification, it refers to the office of the President of India. The building itself did not do anything.

Metre is a *measure* for distance, as we have said, but it is not just that; it is also the rhythm in poetry. Often, the *metre* in a line of poetry is tetrameter (four *metres*) or trimeter (three *metres*). A sonnet, one of the most well-known forms of poetry in English, uses pentameter (five metres). Each metre in poetry usually has two or three syllables or beats. Interestingly, though the word in British English is *metre*, the common spelling for pentameter, tetrameter, trimeter and so on has 'er', not 're'.

The *mind* is that part of the human being that allows us to think, to feel, to imagine, to recall, to recognize, to consider and judge. While the brain is the physical part of the body that enables us to think, the *mind*, which is not physical, uses the brain to have a particular thought or a certain feeling. Perhaps the brain and the *mind* could be considered as the hardware and the software of human beings. In the *Mahabharata*, in reply to a question from a spirit, a *yakshi*, 'What is faster than the wind?', Yudhishthira replies, 'The *mind*.' *Mindlessness* is 'without thinking', unfeeling – *a mindless act of cruelty. Mindfulness* is being aware of what is happening around a person – *He was mindful of the difficulties that lay before him.*

Mind can also mean 'be careful with'. *Mind your* manners means 'behave politely'. An idiomatic use of this care with good manners is *mind your p's and q's*. This comes from the early printing press where a page was made up of letters in a frame; since *p* and *q* looked alike if seen from the wrong side, it was necessary to be careful in placing the two letters correctly. *Mind Your Language* was a popular comedy serial on BBC Television; the phrase is common, and means that you should be careful of what you say. To someone who is being inquisitive about something you do not wish to discuss or share with him, you might say – *Mind your own business.*

From *mind*, the noun, we have *mental*, the adjective. The adverb is *mentally* – *He was mentally prepared for the tough assignment* or *He is mentally unstable and requires constant caring*. The word *mentality* indicates a way of thinking, an attitude. Sometimes we follow without thinking what others say or do; that is a *herd mentality*, the term comes from the way sheep follow the leader without any apparent reason. The phrase *mind over matter* is used to indicate that the spiritual side of *man* is more important than his physical body. Mark Twain once said – 'Age is an issue of *mind* over *matter*. If you do not *mind*, it does not *matter*.'

The word *minor* relates to children who are not yet legally adults – *He is certainly a minor, he can't be more than twelve years old*. The same word, as the noun *minority*, is used also to denote less than half in terms of a population, or a small part of a whole set of people – *They belong to a minority community* or *A small minority opposed the proposal*. There is another *meaning* of *minor*, which is 'small' – *There is a minor error in the report*. The opposite word for *minor* is *major*, for those above a certain age – in India, and in many other countries, that age is 18 years. There is yet another use; when you study a subject as a main subject with other subjects as 'subsidiary', you would *major* in that subject; the usage is *majored* – *I majored in English*. The *Major* in the army, with a capital *M*, is a junior-level officer. (And this is another capitonym.)

Mis, with one *s*, implies the opposite of something when it is used as a prefix – *misdeed* is a wrong deed or action, *mistrust* is the opposite of trust, *misdemeanour* is bad demeanour or behaviour. *Misadventure* is an unfortunate incident, an adventure gone wrong; it is also a *mishap* ('hap' is from 'happening'). Just because a word starts with *mis*, though, we cannot assume that the word is an opposite of another word. *Miserable*, or wretched, does not have 'erable' as an opposite word.

In modern grammar, we have the term *modifier*. A *modifier modifies* a sentence, but it can be removed from the sentence without changing the basic structure or thought. Usually adjectives and adverbs, together with adjectival and adverbial clauses would be called *modifiers*. *I have this great wish to learn English* – 'great', the adjective, is a *modifier* of 'wish'. Or, *come quickly*, where the adverb 'quickly' is the *modifier*. This term makes grammar that much simpler.

What is a *myth*? We have through the book *mentioned myths* and *mythical* creatures, but what is a *myth*? It covers, in a few words, the vast lore of beliefs and stories about gods, goddesses and demons that are found in all countries, in all cultures, which tell of the creation and existence of the universe in general and our earth in particular. *Myths* together make *mythology*. A unicorn – a horse with a horn on its forehead – is a *mythical* creature. Today, in *modern* terms, a *myth* may be that which is not real, or not true – *The myth that the sun goes around the earth was proved false by Galileo.*

Among the many common errors we Indians make in speaking English, two may be mentioned here. Someone called Ashok Kumar might introduce himself as 'Myself Ashok'; it should be *I am Ashok*. And someone might call him or introduce him as 'Mr Ashok'; it should either be *Ashok* or *Mr Kumar*.

n

N is important for representing an unknown *number* and *nth* represents the last, the largest, of an unlimited series – that is *x* (any number) to the power of *n*, written as $(x)^n$ or *x* to the *nth* degree. This is a remarkable thought, this limitlessness. You may have come across *N.B.* in documents – it stands for the original Latin *nota bene*, '*note* well', or 'take careful *note* of'. In grammar, *n* could be the short form of *noun*.

A *nation* is a country, a political and geographical entity, which has its own government, and its own legal and administrative system. Most nations are represented at the *United Nations* (UN) as member-states. There are presently 193 member-states in the UN. When you travel abroad, the immigration authorities check your *nationality*, expressed through your passport. Incidentally, anything to do with the *nation* is *national* – like the *national* anthem, the *national* flag, *national* holidays. The difference between *nation* and *notion* is enormous, and so the correct spelling is important. A *notion* is an idea, perhaps a fanciful concept – *He has a strange notion that the earth is flat!* And *notional* means 'theoretical', 'ideal' or 'speculative' – *The chairman of the company receives a notional salary of one rupee annually.* If you own a house valued at millions of rupees, that value would only be *notional* if you were never to place it in the market. And the face value of a financial instrument, such as a bond, is its *notional value.*

News is a collective *noun*, and therefore used with a singular verb – *The news is broadcast every hour.* There is a story of an editor who, in the place of East, West, *North* and South – E, W, N and S – which is the common use of the four corners, brought *North* forward by mistake and created this acronym. A *newspaper* is a regular, time-bound publication of *news*, now as much online as in print. The first modern day *newspapers* came from Germany, in the early 17th century, and the first paper in English was the *Oxford Gazette* of 1665. Not unexpectedly, thanks to the presence of the British in Calcutta (now Kolkata), the earliest *newspapers* in India came from that city; the first of these was *Hickey's Bengal Gazette*, which ran for about two years from 1780.

Nine is the last of the single-digit numbers. If one multiplies *nine* by any number, and adds the digits of the answer until it is just a single digit, the result would be *nine*: 9*1= 9, 9*2 = 18 (1+8 = 9) and so on. Numerous mathematical patterns can be formed with 9. If a *number* is divided by the same number of 9's as there are digits in the number, the answer is a continued repetition as a decimal of the number; for example, 123/999 equals 0.123123123 and so on. The number *nine* is significant for the *nine* muses of European culture and for the *navarasas* of Indian dance and theatre (the *nine* emotions evoked amongst the audience). It is also important for the *Navaratnas*, the *nine* 'jewels', or wise ministers, in the courts of King Vikramaditya and Emperor Akbar.

N is the letter that leads to *negative* thinking if you think in English, with *no*, *not*, *never*, *none* and *nothing*. Let us begin with the double *negative*. As with mathematics, in English too, the logic is that two *negatives* make a positive. When it is correctly and intentionally used, one might say – *What I said wasn't quite unintended*, meaning that it was quite intended. An example of the wrong use of the *double negative* is – *The election result will not be final till the decision of the high court has not come*; the *not* after 'the high court' must be removed. This is a common error among many Indians because we tend to translate from Hindi.

No is the opposite of 'yes'. *Did you go to work today? No.* This short one word reply includes a longer answer which is understood as given – *I did not.* So the complete answer is – *No, I did not.* There are a couple of other ways in which *no* and *not* are used together. The first is *no, not... – Did you break the vase? No, not I.* Another is *I will not take no for an answer!* One could also join 'can' and *not* to say – *You cannot go*; this is the one instance when *not* can be attached to another word to make a single, unabbreviated word.

Never is *not* ever; one might say – *Never do that again*! Then there is *none*, as in *no* one – *None of us knew how to swim.* Put it differently – *No one admitted to the theft, none was to be blamed. None* is a singular pronoun. You could also have *none other – None other than the MD himself led the discussions.* And there is *nonetheless*, a less common version of *nevertheless*; both mean 'however' or 'even then' – *He had failed in maths, nonetheless the principal gave him another chance and promoted him.*

Nothing is 'no thing', the absence of any thing. There is an ancient Greek philosophical concept that the world could not have come from *nothing* – *Nothing shall come out of nothing.*

Like *nothing*, we have *nowhere* – *not* anywhere. *He had nowhere to go, so he sat on the park bench till it was lunchtime.* One can also be *in the middle of nowhere*, that is, far away from habitation or in a desolate place. Or *I am nowhere near the end of the book,* that is, I have a long way to go before I finish reading it. The opening lines of a famous song, *Nowhere Man*, by The Beatles, are:

He's a real nowhere man,
Sitting in his Nowhere Land,
Making all his nowhere plans
for nobody.

Non- is a prefix, added at the start of some words to indicate the opposite; sometimes used with a hyphen – *His venture was a non-starter right from the beginning*. We mentioned our use of *non-vegetarian* earlier; one could also have a *non-alcoholic* drink. You might also use *non* without the hyphen – as in *nonviolence, nonentity* or *nonsense*. A *nonentity* is an unimportant person, unknown in society. *Nonviolence* was the hallmark of Mahatma Gandhi's movement for India's independence, his philosophy of ahimsa.

We read of Edward Lear and his limericks earlier. That was *nonsense poetry*. But there are others equally famous – Lewis Carroll (1832–98) for example. Lewis Carroll, who gave us the immortal *Alice in Wonderland* (1865) and its sequel, *Through the Looking-Glass* (1871), both masterpieces of literature for children, wrote his famous *nonsense* poem

'Jabberwocky' in *Through the Looking-Glass*. We quote the opening lines here; you will see how sounds can give life to unreal creatures and words, in *nonsense* form:

'Twas brillig, and the slithy toves
Did gyre and gimble in the wabe;
All mimsy were the borogoves,
And the mome raths outgrabe.

'Beware the Jabberwock, my son!
The jaws that bite, the claws that catch!
Beware the Jubjub bird, and shun
The frumious Bandersnatch!'[1]

North, represented by *N*, is one of the four cardinal, that is principal, directions. In a map on a wall, it is the upper part, and in political terms tends to signify the rich countries of the world. In modern business jargon, too, *north* represents going up, as in a graph; so in the economy, or sales, or profits, or anything else, going *north* means that the situation is getting better. *Northern* pertains to the *north* – the *northern* wind is a cold wind from the *north*. The *northern lights* are the Aurora Borealis, a phenomenon of coloured light in the sky in the extreme *northern regions* of the *northern hemisphere*. Aurora is the Roman goddess of dawn, and Boreas the Greek god of the *north wind*.

There would be no language without *nouns*. A *noun* is a unit of grammar, a word that stands for a person, place or thing; we learnt that in school! Add to that an idea or thought, abstract though it may be. In fact, if you were to say – *A*

[1] http://www.jabberwocky.com/carroll/jabber/jabberwocky.html

thought came to me last night, the word 'thought' would be a *noun*, as would *night*, both abstractions that are not physical bodies. *Rajat told a bunch of friends that he had a great idea at night while in bed* – the first *noun* 'Rajat' is a *proper noun*, the second 'bunch' is a *collective noun*, the third and fourth *nouns* 'ideas' and 'night' are *abstract nouns* and the last, 'bed', a *common noun*! There is also a *pronoun*, 'he', which stands for a *noun*! There are strange subgroups of nouns, such as the *count nouns* and the *mass nouns*; three men can be counted, even all men can be counted, but mankind cannot be counted, it is a *mass noun*. – a singular form. *Count nouns* can have the plural form. 'Innings' and 'news' are commonly used *singular nouns*, even with the *s* ending. There are also *collective nouns* – 'staff', 'group', 'flock', 'herd' and so on.

Anything *novel* is new; it is generally used as an adjective for something that did not exist before – *a novel idea*. The abstract noun, *novelty*, is used to describe a new feeling or emotion – *The novelty of travelling abroad excited him immensely.* A *novelty* item is a trinket or a gift item usually of low quality or little value, found in *novelty shops*.

More importantly, as a noun, a *novel* is a story in prose which is not a short story; an average *novel* would be about 80,000 words. One of the longest *novels* originally written in English is also one of the first written in the language – *Clarissa or the History of a Young Lady*, by Samuel Richardson (1689–1761); the book was written in 1748, and is about a million words! In those days, reading in dim candlelight was one of the few forms of entertainment that people had. A *novella* is a short *novel*; there is no hard and fast rule about the size, but it could be between 20,000 and 50,000 words. One example of a *novel* entirely in verse is Vikram Seth's (1952–) *The Golden Gate* (1986).

Number – that is another important word beginning with *n. Numbers* allow us to keep count and do mathematical actions, perhaps as important as our need to communicate with words. One commonly says that the *numbers* are 1 to 9, but 0 is also a *number. Even numbers* are those that can be divided by 2, the others are *odd numbers*. A *prime number* is a *number* that cannot be divided except by 1 or by itself; the largest known *prime number* has nearly 13 million digits! A full stop after 'no' gives us the short form of *number* – *this is house no. 64*; the hash sign also stands for *number* – *door # 64*. The adjective is *numerical* (pronounced 'new–merical'). Here is a puzzle – which is the only *number* which, when written as a word, has the letters of the word in alphabetical order? Forty!

One, two three, four, etc., are *cardinal numbers*. When these are reworded to indicate the order in which a *number* occurs – first, second, third, fourth, etc. – they are called ordinals, and 'st', 'nd', 'rd' and 'th' are ordinal indicators. Interestingly, the words 'first' and 'second' do not come from the words 'one' and 'two'. 'First' comes from 'foremost' in old English; indeed we have the phrase 'first and foremost'. 'Second' is from the Latin *secundus*, which means 'next', or 'following'. Incidentally, 'three' is from old English 'thri', so similar to the Sanskrit 'tri'. The ordinal numbers are adjectives – *This is my first job* or *This is my second day at work*. Add 'ly' after the ordinals, and they become firstly, secondly and so on, usually as numbers for some points of an argument; *I have three reasons – firstly ..., secondly ..., thirdly....* In modern speech, 'firstly' 'secondly' and 'thirdly' are not always used; indeed, first, second, third and so on is fine. And while 'first of all' is sufficient emphasis, there is no 'second of all' or 'third of all', just second, third and so on.

Most of us have learned this rhyme as children:

One, two
Buckle my shoe;
Three, four
Shut the door;
Five, six
Pick up sticks;
Seven, eight
Lay them straight;
Nine, ten
A big fat hen.

That is a *nursery* rhyme to teach *numbers* to children. *Nursery rhymes* are what we all learnt as toddlers in *nursery school*. 'Jack and Jill', 'Twinkle, Twinkle, Little Star' and 'Baa, Baa, Black Sheep' – these are *nursery rhymes*, short songs with simple lyrics to amuse little children. But many of them reflect the times they were first sung, and are not really 'pretty' songs for children. 'Baa, Baa Black Sheep' is believed to be about the slave trade, 'Jack and Jill' about the French King Louise the XVI, who 'lost his crown', and Marie Antionette, who 'came tumbling after'.

Alfred Nobel (1833–96) – note the difference in spelling from *noble* – was a Swedish engineer and chemist who invented dynamite and forever changed the way explosives would be used. One newspaper called him a 'merchant of death'. And yet he left behind a legacy, creating, in 1895, the most acknowledged international awards, known by his name, including one for peace.

O

O, the full circle letter, is sometimes used to mean 'zero', or 0; a first-year course numbered 101 is generally called *one o one*. Shakespeare, in his play *Henry V*, speaks of *this wooden* O, referring to the stage, which in those days was often in a circular auditorium. *O*, by itself, has an old style usage for hailing or addressing someone – *O King*, the courtier would have said, speaking to the king; *O Lord*, we still say in prayer. It is also used as an exclamation. The usual form is the exclamation *oh*! It is an expression of surprise – *Oh, it's you*; of addressing someone – *Oh, my darling*; of irritation – *Oh! Get out*; of anguish – *oh, no*! And we all know the new lingo – *OMG, Oh my God!* Add another *o* to *oh* and we have *ooh*, generally an exclamation of pleasure.

In even more common use is *okay* – *How are you? I'm okay*. 'All right', 'well', 'fine', 'agreed', 'accepted' – all these words can be substituted in context by *OK* or *okay*. It also describes a mediocre person or effort – *He was okay, nothing much really.* The origin of the word is not clear and there are many stories about it. According to the Oxford English Dictionary, it could be an abbreviation of 'orl korrekt', a fun misspelling of 'all correct' in the US in the 1830s. It is today one of the most versatile words in English and probably one of the most used words across the world.

An *object* is something you can see and touch, and can hold if it is not too heavy. As a verb, one may *object* to, that is disagree with, something; one might even protest – *I object to your use of foul language* or *Residents objected to the garbage piling up in their neighbourhood*. The difference is important because, as a noun, one stresses the first syllable, 'ob'; as a verb, the stress is on 'ject'. The noun for this verb is *objection*, but the stress is on the second syllable! In traditional grammar, a sentence like *I bought a book* has a subject 'I', a verb 'bought' and an *object* 'a book'. *Objective* has many shades of meaning, especially 'intention' or 'goal'. *My first objective is to get a good job*. But if I examine a report *objectively*, I do that without any prejudice or bias – with *objectivity*.

O creates some of the most important prepositions in English – *of*, *off*, *on*, *over*, *out*. *Of* indicates possession or relationship, it pertains to someone or something. There are different aspects of the word. *The first line of the song* – the line pertains to the song; *this book of mine* – the book belongs to me; *the end of the tunnel* – indicates the location; *the source of his anger* – the cause *of* something; *a citizen of India* – a matter *of* representation.

Off is, in a sense, the opposite of *on*. What then is *on*? We'll come to that! *Off* is an example of one word representing many grammatical terms; it can function as a noun, verb, adverb, adjective or, most commonly, as a preposition. As a noun, it is not very common but *playing to the off* is a cricket term. As a verb we have *Off with you* meaning 'go away', or *Off with their heads*, as the Queen of Hearts says in *Alice in Wonderland*, using *off with* for 'cut *off*'. These are special uses. As an adverb we might have an announcement – *Please switch off your mobile phones*. As an adjective *off* is quite common – *She wore an off-shoulder gown* or *She sang off-key*. And *off* is a very common preposition – *Please keep off the grass*. In this use, the preposition *off* means 'away from' and relates to space or distance; *off the main road* is a little away from the main road. *The plate fell off the table* – here, too, the plate has changed its position. Indeed, *off* (along with *on*) indicates place and location.

Off is a common term in sports. In cricket, the *off side* is the area to the right of a right-handed batsman facing the bowler. (The side to the batsman's left, is the *on* or leg side.) We have the *off-break* ball coming from the right of the right-handed batsman into him, it is bowled by an *off-spinner*; an *off-cutter* is a faster ball by a pace bowler, which brings the ball into the batsman from the *off* after it pitches on the wicket. The batsman might hit the ball as an *off drive*. In football, a player is *offside* and commits a foul when he is in play between the ball and the opposition goal, with no player from the other side between him and the goal. In hockey, to make an already speedy game even more fast-paced, the rule makers have removed the *offside* rule.

Sometimes *off* adds a verb after it and creates a noun. One's *offspring* is one's children. *Offtake* is usually the quantity that is taken from a wholesale point to a retail point – *The offtake of foodgrains from the Food Corporation has increased*. It could be used for the distribution of bank credit, or the spread of a resource. *Offbeat* is something that is different in style, like *an offbeat film*, it is *off* the beaten path. Something that branches out of something is an *offshoot* of the *original* – *The offshoot of the entire discussion was that our working hours were increased! Offline* is a very popular word today – you may work on your computer either connected to the Internet or not, you are then either *online* or *offline*. *Offshore* basically means 'in the sea', away from the shore, away from land. It has led to a very significant business model, that of *offshoring*, or removing a part of a company's business activity to another country. This is done if, in present-day international business, a firm feels that its costs in the country of origin would be higher than in a country where the *offshoring* is done.

Off added to the end of a verb can also create nouns, sometimes used with a hyphen but not always – *The space vehicle's lift-off was perfect,* or *The plane's takeoff was smooth*. Then *face-off*; when 'face' and *off* are joined to mean 'confrontation' – *The face-off between the presidential candidates on TV was widely viewed.* And a *trade-off* is, in making a choice, to give up something to accept something else – *The trade-off was between balancing the budget and making larger investments in infrastructure.*

Off and on means 'intermittently' or 'at times' – *he comes off and on to our place*. A comment made *off the cuff* would be made without thinking, without considering its impact on the listener.

Be careful about using the right word – *of* or *off*. When in doubt remember, *of* pertains broadly to something belonging to something, about people or things; *off* is about action or space and distance. *Of course* means, 'yes, certainly'; *off course* is 'away from the correct way'. By the way, do you 'dispose of' or 'dispose off' something? The first is correct; 'off' is incorrect and would seem like you wanted to throw things away violently!

The prefix **omni** signifies all; it means 'every' or 'all encompassing'. We say God is *omnipresent*, present everywhere; *omniscient*, all-seeing and all-knowing; and *omnipotent*, all-powerful. *Omnifarious*, a word rarely used, means 'various', including 'all types' – *His omnifarious duties keep him busy till late at night*. In more common matters, an *omnibus* is a largish bus. But it is also a book which has a variety of writing – such as *a Dickens omnibus* which would include a number of Charles Dickens' novels, or *a poetry omnibus*, a large collection of poetry.

On is generally a preposition – it indicates that something is on top of something else. *The cat is on the mat.* That is a nursery school way of explaining *on.* But someone being *put on the mat* has a less obvious meaning; that person has been warned or punished by a person in authority – *His boss put him on the mat for coming late to work very frequently. On and on* is the phrase for something continuous – *He goes on and on about the good old days*; but *on and off* is just the opposite, it stands for something intermittent, not continuous – *The driver kept switching the engine on and off*. If you say *I am on my way*, you have left your point of origin for your destination. If something is *on the blink*, it is out of order or not working – *My TV set is on the blink, I need to have it fixed.* A person who is always active and positive and wanting to do something is said to be *on the go*, but is there a touch of the ambitious in it? If there is a steady increase, say, of crime in the city, one might say *crime is on* *the rise*. A person may be *on duty*, at work – *The bus driver is on duty till midnight*. Or s/he may be *on call*, ready to go to work if called – *The police are always on call, ready for an emergency*.

On is not just a preposition. It may be an adverb. *The lights are on; The meeting is on; They marched on*. There are also many words where *on* is prefixed to a verb – *the onrushing waters*, *the ongoing debate*, *the oncoming traffic*. There are words beginning with *on* that are nouns or adjectives, or adverbs, too – *onlooker*, *online* or *onward*. As with *off*, we use *on* and *onside* frequently in sports terminology.

One stands for the first numerical digit, the singular, unity. The number 1 is unique; it is the basic unit of counting and is the first number (after zero). So, too, in the use of language; anything that is *number one* is first, the best or at the very top in rank – *This book is number one on the bestseller chart*. A special position is given with the use of terms like *one in a million* or *one of a kind*.

Significantly, *one* stands for 'I', in an unusual way, distancing personal feeling into a kind of common thought. Instead of saying, *I must go to the exhibition*, I might say, *one must go to the exhibition*. Is there a difference? Yes, indeed, even if not too much. *One* attempts to make it inclusive of *others* in the group. But *one* could also be used for 'you' or 'we'. *One should go home now* could be a polite way of saying *You should go home now*. At many places in this book, you would find *one might say...* or *one may say...*; it is a way of making speech less personal. But at times, the use of the word can become complicated. *One learns to live with the traffic on our roads* is fine, but if you were to say *one must have one's wits about one when one is driving*, it remains technically correct but very awkward. A somewhat odd use is *on one's own* – *In today's world there is little family support; one has to learn to live on one's own.*

One is used in many ways. *One by one* means a series, 'in single file' – *They entered one by one. One after another* or *one at a time* mean the same. *One and all* covers everyone – *The minister was available every afternoon to one and all.* By itself, *one* can imply a random point in a long phase of time – *One day, he came to see me* or *One of these days I must go and see him.* It can show a choice – *Either one will do.* Have you heard of *one-upmanship* – the 'art' of doing one better than others, of outdoing competitors all the time with style?

From *one*, we get that favourite word of storytellers – *once*! Just like *one day*, many stories for children begin with *once upon a time* to indicate the starting point of the story in time. *I have been to his house once*, means 'I have gone there *on one occasion*.' A remarkable fantasy based book, published in 1958, about King Arthur and his Knights of the Round Table is *The Once and Future King* by T. H. White (1906–64); the title is from the supposed engraving on Arthur's tombstone – 'Here lies Arthur, King once, King in future'.

One has to be careful with the use of words and their correct spelling and pronunciation. '*On* us' are two short words, but joined together they become *onus*, responsibility – *The onus is on the Indian batsmen to do well in the forthcoming Test series.* You would have a neat pun if you said *the onus is on us*. Be careful with the pronunciation, too. *On* is like 'awn' but *onus* is 'own–us'. *Onion*, by the way, is pronounced 'un–yun', not 'o–nyun' or 'awn–yun'!

A word we tend to use wrongly is *only*. It is mainly an adjective or an adverb, and usually means that there is no other or better – *In our office only Aditya understands this technology* or *Only the president has the powers to dissolve Parliament.* Let us take the second example. If we shift the *only* and place it before 'the powers' it would mean that the president has no other powers, and that is laughable. If we were to place it before 'to dissolve', we would get the same silly result, (but *only* would then be qualifying a verb and it becomes an adverb). If we have *only* before Parliament; then the president cannot dissolve anything other than Parliament – which is certainly not what is intended to be said. The positioning of *only* is important.

Indian English has this typical use – 'I am going home only', as if I cannot go anywhere else! In this sentence, *only* is not needed, or it should come before 'going'. Otherwise, *only*, in such cases, would usually be followed by some activity – *I am going home only to play football*, for example, or *I am going home only because I need to have a bath*. In Indian languages, a word can often be placed in any order and yet make sense, but in English, words must be placed correctly in a sentence.

Two interesting words are *onomatopoeia* and *oxymoron*. The first, *onomatopoeia*, is quite unique. It has four *o*'s in the word and has four vowels together, only *u* is missing. It is used for words that indicate a sound – *aah, crack, hiss, plop, shhh, thud, wham*. An *oxymoron* is not a silly cow or an idiot from Oxford! It is a figure of speech where two opposite, contradictory conditions are brought together – *act naturally, genuine imitation, found missing, good grief, same difference, almost exactly, alone together, small crowd, front end*. But

[*oxymoron* itself is an *oxymoron*, because in its Latin root it means 'sharply stupid'. As they say, common sense is most uncommon.]

Opera is a form of theatre, with music and songs, largely in a Western classical mould, interspersed with dramatic action. Nowadays, in the usual way that the IT sector has 'borrowed' from other ideas, *Opera* is a browser software, first introduced in 1995. The word *opera* comes from 'work' in Latin. It has the same origin as *operate*, *operation*, *operator*, *operative* and *opus*.

To *operate* is to handle and use a machine for any work – *He operates the harvesting machine very deftly*; this person is an *operator* and his action is *a harvesting operation*. A doctor who performs surgery on a patient – a surgeon – also performs an *operation* – *The six-hour operation was successful* – but we do not call him an *operator*! In fact, it is better to use the word 'surgery' than *operation*, though in India we generally do not use that word. Actually, the word *operator* can have a somewhat negative implication – *He is an operator* or *He is a smooth operator*, can imply a cunning person who has a way with words to get what he wants and can get out of any tricky situation. But what about *operative*? It is used in two ways; first, as pertaining to an *operation*, such as *post-operative care*, and second, in a very different way, usually a term for an agent, such as an *intelligence operative* or a *terrorist operative*. *Opus* is a rather significant composition: an artistic work, especially one on a large scale – *a magnum opus*.

Open is the opposite of 'shut', 'closed' or 'covered'. *Open* is one of those words which can be an adverb, an adjective or a verb. Or even a noun as in the *Indian Open* or the

US Open – a tournament with no basic entry restrictions – but note the capital O. As an adverb we might say– *The road is open to traffic*; as an adjective – *We have an open sky policy in aviation*; as a verb – *Please open the door.* If one does not shut a door, it is *open*; but then what is *open and shut*? The phrase is used, generally without hyphens, to indicate something very obvious – *The evidence is very clear, it is an open and shut case.* The meaning is in the words – a case that can be closed as quickly as it is opened. *The only course open* means 'the *only* way available'. *She is open to the idea* means that she is willing to consider the idea. If she has *an open face*, she appears to be honest and has nothing to hide. *Open*, in that sense, also means 'frank', 'candid' or 'public' – *There was an open debate on the new traffic systems for the city.* An *opening night* of a play or the *opening show* of a film is the first performance of a continuous run; but *opening* may be used as a noun – *the show had a gala opening. Open source* software is one which gives the user the access to the source code, the programme used to create the software.

Opportunity and *opportunism* – these are two words with the same root but different meanings. *Opportunity* is a time or situation, a chance, for doing something – *I had a great opportunity to score a goal, but I messed up the chance.* From this we have *opportune*, the adjective, as in *an opportune moment*, a suitable or correct time for some activity – *He waited for an opportune moment to reveal the truth. Opportunism* is the ability to take advantage of a situation for one's benefit, without necessarily considering the correctness of that action. An *opportunist* is a person who would do just that. A person conveniently switching political loyalty to his advantage would be a *political opportunist.*

Or is a conjunction, very commonly used with 'either', to provide a choice – *either you should go, or I.* But it can be used in simple comparison – *a or an*; *Arun's shirt or Anup's shirt.* It can also mean 'in other words' –'*Go' is a verb, or an action word.* In this chapter alone, *or* has been used over 75 times. One may not notice how *or* is slipped in so often in our use of the language.

Yet another short but significant word is *out*, the *opposite* of *in*. The word as a prefix creates many words – an *outfit* is a dress for an occasion or a uniform – *The outfit for the parade was in blue.* It is also a group of people undertaking a particular activity together – *He is the lead guitarist in the new jazz outfit. Outrage* is widespread anger – *There was outrage over the death of the child in the accident. Outreach* is the extent one can reach out, generally in a scheme or programme – *The outreach of social advertisement through TV is vast.* All these words have many variations in their meaning.

Let us take a look at two multidimensional words, *outright* and *outward. Outright* means 'immediate' – *The seller wanted to reach an outright settlement today itself*; 'unconditional' – *I was not sure if the seller had outright ownership of the property*; 'total' or 'clear' – *Our team's outright defeat in every match was extremely humiliating*; 'entirely' – *He rejected the accusation outright.*

The other word, *outward*, has movement in it, going away from somewhere – *The outward journey was very tedious.* To move out from a centre is also *outward* – *Strong shock waves moved outward from the epicentre of the earthquake.* But it is also a visual, matter – with its related meaning, a matter of pretence – *Outward appearances are deceptive* or *His outward behaviour did not show that he was actually very unhappy.* Here the word could have the suffix 'ly' and become *outwardly – He behaved outwardly as if he was happy.*

There are many words in which *out* simply means 'better' or 'more' – to *outrun* someone is to run longer or faster than him or her, to *outdo* someone is to do better than him or her, to *outshine* is to shine brighter, but it actually is to perform better, usually in exams or sports. *Outer*, is a comparative adjective as the *opposite* of 'inner', which means 'further away from the centre' – *Please use the outer road to avoid traffic* or *The outer dimensions are three feet by two feet.* The common word *outside*, the opposite of inside, indicates anything *out* of, or away from, a certain space or position – *outside the house* or *outside the box* or *outside his hearing.* To think *out of the box*, though, means 'to think differently', to find a new, unusual, possibly unique solution. *Out and out* means 'completely' – *He is out and out a scoundrel.* If you are not feeling too well, you would be *out of sorts.* Something *out of this world* is something wonderful or fantastic.

Over is another preposition like *on.* It has a hint of movement and space about it. When a cat jumps *over* a mat, it jumps across it, from one side to another. *Over* implies being above, not under. In that sense, it can also be a cover and not moving – *the sky over us* – but there is a sense of space between the two objects, the sky and us. It is used as a prefix with another word – *The overworked employee resigned* or *The overjoyed supporters ran to meet the players.* In cricket, an *over* is a set of six balls bowled by a bowler to a batsman.

As a prefix, *over* forms many words – *overcome, overrun, overreach, overturn, override, overthrow, overgrown, overwhelm, overwrite* and so on. Of these, some are particularly interesting. *Overreach* and *overthrow* are not literally to reach *over*, or throw *over*. To *overreach* is to attempt more than one's capacity, and has a touch of ambition to it; to *overthrow* is to change a government or system, often by violence, and a peaceful change through the ballot is rarely called an *overthrow*. In cricket, when a ball is to be returned by a fielder to the bowler or the wicketkeeper, but is thrown inaccurately, allowing the batsmen one or more extra runs, the runs are the result of an *overthrow*! What contrasting uses of the same word! 'Whelm' is to completely cover, to submerge, but it is rarely used by itself; the common use is of *overwhelm*, mainly as a high degree of emotion – *I was overwhelmed by his kindness.* (There is an 'underwhelmed', which is now gaining in use). To *overcome* is to conquer some difficulty, not come *over*, which is fine on its own! The theme song of the American civil rights movement of the late 1950s and early 1960s – to remove discrimination against the black population of the USA – was 'We Shall Overcome'. The song, now sung all over the world, in English and in translation, represents the voice of the oppressed.

Orange, the fruit, is pronounced 'aw–renj'. There is no word in English that rhymes with orange. Orange, apart from 'peach', is perhaps the only colour named after a fruit. It is believed that the fruit went from India to Europe and then to the Americas. Before the word was used for the colour in early 16th century, the word commonly used for the purpose was the Old English 'geulohread' meaning 'yellow-red'. The word 'orange' may have originated from the Sanskrit *naranga*, which itself may have come from *narthangai* in Tamil.

P

P is perhaps the most significant letter for English grammar and literature. There are many terms that begin with *p* – *paragraph*, *parts (of speech)*, *person (first, second or third)*, *phonetics*, *phrase*, *plural*, *poetry*, *poem*, *poesy*, *poetics*, *prose*, *prosody*, *present and past participles*, *predicate*, *prefix*, *preposition*, *pronoun*, *pronunciation*, *punctuation*; all of them are absolutely essential to our understanding and appreciation of the language.

Before we get to these words, we must remember that, along with *g* and *k*, *p* also has the strange role of being at the start of many words without any sound and without any use. Like 'gnat' and 'gnaw' and 'knife' and 'knight', we also have *pneumonia*, *pneumatic*, *psoriasis*, *psephology*, *psychiatry*, *psychology* – all big words with no use of the *p*. P. G. Wodehouse (1881–1975), the British humorist, had a character in some of his work called Psmith, with the *P* silent!

Let us go through some abbreviations. *P* is the short for *pence*, the British coin; a 100*p* makes £1, one *pound*. *P* is a *page* – *Please see p. 500 for example*; *pp* is the short form for *pages* – a book may be *500pp*. But *pps* stands for *papers*, especially in government file noting. In business circles, a *P.O.* could mean a *purchase order* but *P.O. box* would be a *post office box*. *P.S.* is *post script*, an addition after a main letter is ended and signed. The *PT* teacher in a school is the *physical training* teacher. *PR* is *public relations*; many organizations have a *PRO*, the *public relations officer*, who is today often called the customer relations officer.

A large *part* of this chapter pertains to matters of grammar and language. *Part* is not the whole, only a *portion* of the whole – *What you have said is only a part of the whole story*. But it has other meanings – *He has been given a part in a play* means that he has been given a role to act in the play; to say *He is taking part in a play* could mean that he is *participating* in a play, but possibly for offstage, or backstage, work. But if you are a *participant* at a meeting, in a debate or at an athletics meet, you are *participating* in that event or *taking part*. You can also *partake* of a feast, joining in the special occasion.

However, *to part* is also a breaking away – *She was sad to part from her friends when she went abroad for higher studies*. *Part* is also an aspect of some situation or condition – *These troubles are a part of life*, or *Leaving home is a part of growing up*. *For the most part* means 'largely' or 'mainly' – *For the most part, your notes are not understandable*. *Part and parcel* is a basic component – *Friendships are a part and parcel of a happy life*. A strange word, *part*; it brings together and it breaks up. Then again, think of the similarity and differences between *a part* and *apart*.

From *part*, we have *partial* (pronounced 'par–shul' to rhyme with 'dull') – *His recovery has been only partial* – and *partially* – *He has recovered only partially*. But there is also another meaning – to be *partial* is to be biased, to favour, to prefer – *The teacher was obviously partial to that boy* or *He is partial towards mangoes*. There is the abstract noun *partiality*. From the same origin, we also have *particle*, a tiny entity, a speck, but which has volume and mass. In very simplistic terms, *particle physics* is the study of the smallest *parts* of matter. And there is *particular* – something specific – a word Indian media is very fond of using – *this particular incident* – when it is not at all required.

And now let us get to the grammar and language of English. We begin with *paragraph*. In this book there are hundreds of *paragraphs* – often called 'paras' in short, but somewhat incorrectly (like 'photos' for *photographs*). Generally the writer of a work which is not *poetry* breaks up the work into *paragraphs* for two reasons. First, there are different thoughts or issues addressed, or, in a story, different events described, and each of these deserves to be given its due position through a separate *paragraph*. Second, the reader gets a chance to separate the issues visually, as run-on lines would be very confusing, and boring, after a point.

There are eight *parts of speech* in traditional grammar – the noun, verb, adjective, adverb, pronoun, preposition, conjunction and interjection. These eight form the basis of English grammar. A combination of these forms the structure of a sentence and provides the grammar of the language. Some include the 'article' or, nowadays, the 'determiner' as a *part of speech*.

What is a *participle*? The two main ones are the *present participle* and the *past participle*. It is a form of a verb, or part of a verb phrase, which acts as an adjective to help describe something. Let us look at the simple verb 'to go'.

The going rate for houses in this area is very high. Note the 'ing' form of the present participle. As a phrase we might have – *Who is the boy going down the road?* But *participles* are also used for indicating the *past* or the *present* timing of an action. In *I am going* or *I was going*, the word *going* is a *present participle*, while *gone* in *I have gone* or *I had gone* is a *past participle*. There is also the *perfect participle*, *having gone* – *Having gone home early, I had a good nap*. There is immense variety in the use of participles, and only a small sample has been given here.

Phonetics and 'phone' are two words that come from the same root – the Greek word for 'sound' or 'voice'; both deal with sounds that we understand. *Phonetics* is the study of sounds made to create human speech. It is no use making sounds that another person will not understand, so these sounds must combine to produce syllables and words in a particular language, and must have meaning.

A *phrase* is a part of a full sentence. It is a group of words that is without a verb and therefore does not have complete meaning in itself (as compared to a clause). In the first sentence of this paragraph, *a part of a full sentence* would be a *phrase* – it makes only partial sense!

Plural is more than one. A boy is one, it is in the singular; two or more boys is *plural*. But some words are always *plural* – binoculars, forceps, glasses, pliers, scissors, tongs, pants, jeans, trousers and so on. There are two equal parts or halves to each of these implements or pieces of clothing; indeed the correct usage for scissors is in saying – *Please get me a pair of scissors*. If you did not use *pair* it would have to be 'the scissors' – *Please get me the scissors* (not 'a scissors'). *Antics*, *heroics* and *hysterics* are other examples of plural words. In societal terms, *pluralism* is the living together of multiple groups in relative social harmony; we might say India is a *pluralistic* society.

Read this, about the *plural* form, the first lines of a long *poem* whose origin is not known:

We'll begin with a box, and the plural is boxes,
But the plural of ox becomes oxen, not oxes.
One fowl is a goose, but two are called geese,
Yet the plural of moose should never be meese.[1]

The difference between *poetry* and *prose* is at once very simple and very complex. At a simple level, *poetry* is the totality of *poems*; a *poem* has 'broken' lines, which may or may not have rhyme. Unless it is a very short *poem*, it is usually broken up into stanzas, also commonly called verses, though strictly 'verse' has a broader use, and stands for *poetry* itself. An example of a very simple, beautiful *poem* is one by Christina Rossetti (1830-1894):

Who has seen the wind?
Neither I nor you:
But when the leaves hang trembling,
The wind is passing through.

Who has seen the wind?
Neither you nor I:
But when the trees bow down their heads,
The wind is passing by.[2]

[1] http://www.worldwidewords.org/articles/ar-eng1.htm; This traces the poem to 1896, and even earlier versions, but with no name of the poet.

[2] https://www.poemhunter.com/poem/who-has-seen-the-wind/

But there are *poems* with no rhyme at all, or very irregular rhyme, and even if there is rhythm, it may not be simple. Much of this is *modern poetry*, which can be said to have started in early 20th century. Here are the opening lines of a *poem* by Ted Hughes (1930–98), *The Thought-Fox*, which is about the writing of *poetry*:

I imagine this midnight moment's forest:
Something else is alive
Beside the clock's loneliness
And this blank page where my fingers move.[1]

What then is *poetry*? According to William Wordsworth (1770–1850), one of the great English *poets*, 'Good *poetry* is the spontaneous overflow of powerful feelings.' Ultimately, *poetry* must make us feel a little uplifted, a little happy to find a thought or an expression that is superior to, and certainly different from, ordinary *prose*. *Poetic* is the adjective. But *poetics* is the theory of literary forms, the study of such theory, which would especially include *poetry*. The *Poetics* of the Greek philosopher Aristotle (384–322 BCE) is the earliest known Western treatise on *poetry* and drama. In Indian literature, the *Natyashastra* of the sage Bharata is the most well-known work on Indian *poetics*; its age is not very certain but could be even older than Aristotle's work. *Poesy* is an uncommon, old-fashioned word for *poetic* 'feeling', or the creative process involved in writing *poetry*.

Prose is writing that does not have any of the requirements, and controls, of *poetry*. It is what can be called 'run-on'

[1] Oscar Williams, ed., *A Pocket Book of Modern Verse*; Washington Square Press; p. 628

writing, in creative writing or fiction such as novels and short stories, in non-fiction such as essays and biographies; indeed any form of words used to say something other than poetry is *prose*. *Prosaic* comes from *prose*, which means 'ordinary' or 'dull' expression lacking the beauty of *poetry*. But *prose* can be very *poetic* too, and bad *poetry* not *poetic* at all. *Prosody* is not about *prose*, it takes us back to *poetry* – it is the study of rhythm and structure in *poetry*.

Pre- means 'before', and *post-* 'after'. Many a word in English begins with these two *prefixes*. A *prefix* is a grammatical term for a word or a set of letters fixed at the start of a word to create another word, at times its opposite, at times an extension or for emphasis, at other times simply a new word altogether. Starting with the simple 'a' there are many *prefixes*; here are a few of them – *anti-*, *bi-*, *counter-*, *de-*, *dis-*, *en-*, *extra-*, *hyper-*, *inter-*, *intra-*, *non-*, *over-*, *pan-*, *pre-* (the *pre* in *prefix* is itself a *prefix*), *post-*, *pro-*, *step-*, *sub-*, *super-*, *supra-*, *ultra-*, *un-*, *under-*. We have come across many of them already. Not all these groups of letters used as *prefixes* actually act as *prefixes* every time. What appears to be a *prefix* may not necessarily be one. *A-* is a *prefix*, but not all words starting with *a* use the letter as a *prefix*; *a* is not a *prefix* in 'as' or 'antenna' or 'attention'!

The term *predicate* has come earlier. It is that part of a sentence which follows a subject. In *The boy stood on the burning deck*, the subject is 'the boy' while the rest is the *predicate*. *Predicate* also means 'the basis of something', and has a sense of dependence, with 'on' or 'upon' after the word – *The decision of the government is predicated upon the availability of sufficient data for a correct analysis.*

A *preposition* is a word that is positioned or placed before another word or phrase or clause and joins two parts of a sentence – 'to', 'by', 'in', 'on', 'over', 'under', and a whole range of such words. 'To' is a *preposition* in *She went to the market*; 'by' in *He stood by the roadside*; 'in' in *The toy is in the box*; 'on' in *The boy stood on the burning deck*; 'over' in *The cow jumped over the moon*; 'under' in *under the bridges of Paris*. In all these examples, the *preposition* indicates place or direction, and comes before a noun or a noun phrase or clause.

Pronouns are important; they stand for nouns – *I, you, he, she, it, we, they*. These are *personal pronouns*, they all pertain to persons. In grammar there are three '*persons*' – the *first person singular* – I – and its *plural* – we; the *second person singular* and *plural* – you; the *third person singular* – he, she, it – and *plural* – they. When these words do the action, they are 'subjects' that come before a verb, and so they are *subjective pronouns*. But when something is done to them, they become 'objects' that come after the verb, and then they are *objective pronouns* – *me, you, us, her, him, it, them*. Interestingly, *you* and *it* are both 'subjects' and 'objects' – *If you call me, I will call you back*; or – *That dog, it played with my shoes till I had to shoo it away.* The *possessive pronouns* are *mine, ours, yours, hers, his* and *yours*. (*Me* becomes *mine, us* becomes *ours* and so on.) There are other *pronouns*, too. An *interrogative pronoun* asks the questions 'who', 'what' – *Who is that* or *What is this?* But these are also *relative pronouns* – *He is a man who doesn't know manners* or *I am not sure what she wants*.

How does one *pronounce*, or say, words? The noun is *pronunciation* – the *o* is removed! Correct *pronunciation* is yet another strange aspect of English. Different groups of speakers have different ways of *pronouncing* a word. This has much to do with accents, and might depend on the way one speaks one's own language at home. But, that apart, there are certain inherent difficulties in *pronunciation.* In English, as we have seen, the way a word is spelt does not always explain the way it is to be said. There is a world of difference in *pronouncing* each of these words that end in 'ough' – *tough, bough, cough, dough, through* and *thorough.* On the other hand, the same vowel sound is produced by many differing sets of letters – *say, weigh, they* and so on.

There are other complex aspects of *pronunciation.* As one example, the letter *s* has a variety of sounds. Between *princes* and *princess*, for example, the difference is mainly in the way the *s* is pronounced; in the first word, the *s* is somewhat like *z*; in the second, it is a clear *s*. Are there any rules to correct *pronunciation*? There are many tiny ones, but there are so many exceptions that generalizing is nearly impossible. We have looked at dual *c* and *g* sounds earlier and the missing sound in *k*, *g* and *p* in some words. *E* at the end of a word is silent, except in a few cases such as *apostrophe* and *extempore*. The *t* in '...tion' is pronounced 'sh'; one exception is *bastion* (somewhat like 'bass–ti–un') and another is *question* (like 'ques–chn').

The difference between a verb and a noun is sometimes reflected in the *pronunciation* of the word. Many words beginning with 'pro' and 'con' have this special way of differentiation. Words such as 'project' ('praw–ject' is the noun and 'pro–ject' the verb), 'process' (the emphasis is on 'pro' for the noun and on 'cess' for the verb') and 'produce' ('praw–duce' and 'pro–duce') are examples with 'pro'. And *conduct, content* and *convict* are examples with 'con' where, as a noun, 'con' is stressed, but as a verb the stress is more on the latter half.

A not so well-known example of the weirdness of English pronunciation is 'ghoti'. This strange word is attributed to George Bernard Shaw, but it is actually believed to have been first constructed by one William Ollier Jr. The word *ghoti* – 'gh' as in 'rough', 'o' as in 'women' and 'ti' as in 'nation' – is the same as 'fish'. This is obviously quite stretched and far-fetched, but in a funny way it exemplifies the problems of English pronunciation. There are certain limitations in the English language, because it has fewer letters than, say, most Indian languages. There are only five vowels; most Indian languages have many more. In English, the same vowel and the same consonant create many sounds. But English is not embarrassed by its limitations; it is a self-confident language.

Punctuation is the use of the comma, the full stop, the semicolon, the colon, the exclamation mark, the question mark, the dash, the hyphen, inverted commas and brackets. These have been discussed in their appropriate chapters. Nowadays, we have those creatures called the emoticons, like this one ☺, or ☹, but they are not *punctuation* marks. Lynn Truss (1955–) wrote a very interesting book in 2003 titled *Eats, Shoots & Leaves: The Zero Tolerance Approach to Punctuation*. The title is taken from a joke about a panda bear that walks into a café, eats a sandwich and then, as he leaves, shoots in the air. When asked why he did that, the panda shows a manual which says, 'Panda. Large black-and-white bear-like mammal, native to China. Eats, shoots and leaves.' As you can see, a comma in the wrong place, after 'eats', makes a big difference.

It is the difference between 'Let's see, Amma' and 'Let's see Amma'.

A number of words starting with *p* are similar; they often cause confusion and are wrongly used. Let us begin with a simple pair – *principal* and *principle*. The person in charge of the running of a school or college or any other academic institution is its *principal*. A *principle* is a belief, a viewpoint – *I agree with you in principle, but have some issues with the details*. The word is often used in the *plural* form – *He is a man of strong principles*.

The error in the use of the next pair of words is committed even by *people* who know English quite well. *Purposely* means 'intentionally' – *He purposely did not go to the meeting to avoid being questioned*. But *purposefully* means 'determinedly' – *He strode purposefully to the meeting to answer all questions*.

There are many homophone words beginning with *p*; these include *pail* and *pale*, *pair* and *pare*, *peal* and *peel*, *peek* and *peak*, *pane* and *pain*, *peer* and *pier*, *pore* and *pour, pray* and *prey*, *plain* and *plane*. Let us look at a couple of these *pairs*.

A *pail* is a bucket – *Jack and Jill fetched a pail of water*. *Pale* is a light shade of colour, the opposite of dark or colourful – *He is looking pale* or *The shirt was of a pale grey colour*. But it also implies something inferior or less appealing – *This is a pale imitation of the original* or *In the presence of the expert, our own knowledge paled into insignificance*. A *pale* also is an enclosed area, a *paling* is what encloses it; *beyond the pale* usually indicates going outside the norm – *His shouting went beyond the pale of good behaviour*.

A *pair* is a set of two – *a pair of socks*. To *pair off* is to put two together – *The tallest and the shortest were paired off*. An *au pair* is a domestic live-in help. To *pare* is to remove skin, as when one *pares an apple or a potato with a paring knife*. And you might *pare* a *pear*; that is the third word with the same *pronunciation*.

There are also many homographs – *part*, *past*, *peer*, *pore*, *post*, *plant*, *premise* and *present*, for instance. Some of these have been mentioned earlier. Let's look at one example here.

Post is the 'snail mail' that you receive from the *post office*, and to send a letter by *post* would require that you *post* it. To *post* a notice on the notice board is to put it up. And you could *post* it to your friends' group on the Internet. *Keep me posted*, one might say, which means 'keep me informed'. A *post* is also a *position*, and in government one may be *posted* to a *post*, that comes through a *posting order*. A *post* is also a *pillar* or *pole* – *The horse was tied to the post.* It is also a *pole* to indicate the start or end of a race, especially in horse racing – we have the phrase *first past the post.*

Post also means 'after' – *Post the coup, the country plunged into chaos*. But *post* is not often used that way, it is more often a prefix – *post-operative care in a hospital* or *the post-lunch session in a cricket match*. A *post-mortem* is an examination of a body to understand the cause of death. *Ex post facto*, is with retrospective effect, *post facto* meaning 'after the fact' – *His chairman approved his actions ex post facto*. And to go *post haste* is to go as quickly as possible. But what of *postpone*, to put off or delay? Here *post* is part of the whole verb *postpone* and not a *prefix*. Indeed, a new word *prepone*, to bring forward, is an Indian creation; when it first appeared in somewhat common use in the 1980s, some sticklers for grammar were not happy because *pone* by itself has no meaning in this context (In fact, it is a kind of bread!).

A premise is a supposition – *His entire theory is based on a wrong premise. Premises*, usually in the plural, can be a building and the land on which it is built – *There are three families living on the same premises.*

Let us look at other words that cause confusion. *Prescribe* and *proscribe*, *perspective* and *prospective*. To *prescribe* is to recommend, as when a medical practitioner, a doctor, *prescribes* medicines for a sick person. He issues a *prescription*. But one could also *prescribe* a non-medical regimen, such as a fitness programme, or a textbook, even a whole syllabus for the university. To *proscribe* is to ban, usually used for *proscribing* a book; the noun is *proscription*.

Perspective is an existing view – *Try to look at the problem from his perspective. Prospective* is in the future – *They were looking for a prospective bride for their son.* The noun is *prospect* or *prospects*; a view – *The prospect from his window was bleak* – or a possibility or likelihood – *His prospects in his job were bright.* As a verb, it is a search, usually for minerals – *prospecting for gold*, for example.

A *pro* is the short form of a *professional*, one who is paid for his work, the opposite of 'amateur' who does something without seeking payment, for the love of it. But to be *pro* something (not a *pro*) is to be in favour of that, usually an opinion or a movement. *Pros and cons* is the arguments for and against an issue – *What are the pros and cons of India removing the death penalty?* The 'con' here comes from 'contra', the opposite.

The importance of *p* is not only that, in terms of grammar, it allows man to communicate in English; *p* is relevant to the life of man on earth. The words vary from matters of the individual, the *private* and *personal*, to those of the community, pertaining to the *people*, the *public*.

The private world of man begins with his *physical* appearance, his body, his *physique*, but also covers his *personality*, which involves his mind, the *psychological* aspects of the human being. Indeed, *psychology* (the *p* is silent) is the scientific study of mental activity and behaviour. An expert in this field is called a *psychologist*. A person's *personality* is, in very basic terms, the way he thinks, behaves and reacts to outer influences. The word comes from the Latin *persona*, which, most unexpectedly, means 'a mask'.

The *psyche* is the human mind, the conscious and the unconscious thought. The word is derived from its Greek origin which means the soul, that part of the human being no one seems to understand. *Psychiatry* is the study and treatment of mental disorders and a *psychiatrist* is the doctor for these disorders. In all these words, the *p* is silent! There is a joke about this – an elderly lady wrote to an adviser, 'My son has been paying a psychiatrist 100 dollars every week for the last three years. He must be crazy!'

From the inner recesses of the mind, we soar to larger thinking, to *philosophical* issues. *Philosophy* is a difficult matter to explain. Briefly, it is an approach to life, to our very existence, our beliefs and values; in ancient Greek it was the desire for wisdom. In Sanskrit, *philosophy* is *darshan*, sight or seeing, a *philosopher* is one who 'sees', and from there we have the word seer – a spiritually evolved person.

Our *public* world begins with *people*, a plural word. (There is a use for *peoples*, when many groups of people are referred to, but that is not a common term). When there are many *persons* together, we use the word *people* – they *populate* the earth. All the *people* living on earth make the earth's *population*.

The need for the right policy for governing ourselves is crucial. But for some reason, *politicians* do not seem to understand this. *Politics* has a Greek origin; it means *pertaining* to, or about, citizens, that is the *public*. The important thing is the way, in a democratic system, the people choose their *political* leaders, those who make and manage *public policy*. A *policy* is a principle, a reasoned decision that lays down a certain way to do things. A corporate body could have a *purchase policy* or a *staff policy*. A government is likely to have a *population policy*, a *health policy*, a *foreign policy*; these lay down the approach that a government has in various sectors of governance. These are meant for the good of the people and if the *policy* does not help achieve that, it is a *poor policy*.

The word poor has two meanings. A *poor* person is one who is not financially well off, he or she lives in *poverty*. As an economic group, about a third of Indians are *poor*, and the term used for them is *the poor*. But if the *policies* of the government are *poor*, then *poverty* cannot be reduced. So the word *poor* is used both in financial and qualitative terms.

After these serious matters, let us look at a few figures of speech for fun with words. What is a *panagram*? You would all know the famous line *The quick brown fox jumps over a lazy dog*. This is a *panagram*, in 33 letters, practised by those wishing to improve their typing skills; it contains all the letters of the English alphabet. But there are other, shorter, sentences that also have all the letters and make perfect sense – *Pack my box with five dozen liquor jugs* (thirty-two letters), and *The five boxing wizards jump quickly* (thirty-one letters). There are others that have even fewer, but are not as easy on logic.

The *palindrome* is a set of letters, words of even numbers that can be read left to right or right to left. There are clever uses of *palindromes* of different kinds. A simple example is *Malayalam*. *Madam* – which reads the same backwards is more interesting in *Madam I'm Adam*, which is a *palindrome* in a sentence; *Dennis sinned* is another short example. Longer examples are the famous lines supposed to have been said by Napoleon – *Able was I ere I saw Elba*, and *A man, a plan, a canal: Panama*. But the most interesting *palindromes* are *perhaps* those where a shifting of the first letter of a word to the end gives back the same word in reverse – *assess, banana, dresser, grammar, potato, revive, uneven*.

The next word is *pleonasm*, the use of unnecessary words to express something. A very common example is *actual facts*; since facts are facts, which are always correct and true, there is no need for the word 'actual'; that is also the case for *true facts*. Another is *advance warning* – all warnings have to be in advance, otherwise they are not warnings! One more, again so much in use, is *terms and conditions*.

Let's sneak in *proverbs* here. *Proverbs* have nothing to do with verbs. They are short statements, commonly known, which state a 'home truth' and give advice. There are hundreds of them in English; we mention only two here. *A bad carpenter blames his tools* – one should admit one's mistakes and not blame others or one's circumstances. *A friend in need is a friend indeed* – someone who is helpful when you are in difficulty is a true friend. But is it 'in deed' or 'indeed'? This is a visual *pun*.

A **pun** is fun with *p* in the place of *f*! It is the use of two words that sound the same, or are very similar, but have different meanings, a funny 'play' on words. In Chapter B, we had 'bare necessities' sung by a bear. And in 'O', we had the visual pun, 'the onus is on us'. To catch a pun requires a good grasp of the language, but once you catch on, it is truly funny – *A thief who stole a calendar got twelve months.* Or – *With her marriage she got a new name and a dress.* Then, the old one – *Can February March? No, but April May.* Indeed, *I once wrote a play using puns; it was a play on words! I was called a pundit.*

The silent *p* again. *A* **pseudonym** is a name adopted by a person to hide his or her actual name. This is often done by actors who use stage or screen names that they, or their agents, feel would be more interesting than their real name. Marilyn Monroe (1926–62), the Hollywood star, was Norma Jeane Mortenson; Michael Caine (1933–) was born Maurice Joseph Micklewhite. Mumtaz Begum Jehan Dehlavi was the name of the famous Hindi film star Madhubala. Writers sometimes use pen-names. Charlotte, Emily and Anne Brontë, the three novelist sisters, first wrote a book of poems as Currer, Ellis and Acton Bell. Joseph Conrad, the British novelist of Czech origin, was Jozef Teodor Konrad Korzeniowski. Recently, a detective novel, *The Cuckoo's Calling*, written by a certain Robert Galbraith, turned out to be the work of J.K. Rowling (1965–), the creator of the Harry Potter series.

Q

Q has the longest word starting with a letter but also pronounced like it. *B* is like bee, *p* is like pea, but *q* is pronounced *queue* – such an unusual looking word. *Q* is one letter that is almost always linked with another, and that is ***u***.

Q has a number of words related to the number four. *Quad* is a simple word, usually used as a short form of *quadrangle*, usually a square open area in a campus. The word comes from the Latin *quadri*, or four; here it is an area with four angles. *Quadrilateral*, in geometry, is a figure with four sides (*latus* in Latin means 'side'). And there are *quadratic* functions or equations in mathematics.

If *quadri* is for four, *quint* is for five. *Quintile* is therefore one-fifth of the whole. A *quadrillion* is 1 followed by 15 zeroes, while a *quintillion* is 1,000 followed by 15 zeroes.

Quarter is one fourth, 25 per cent, of one – *a quarter kg of sugar* or *a quarter of an hour*. A *quarter* is also a coin in the US currency; it is a nickel, a *quarter* of a dollar. *Quarters*, in plural form, are a place to stay – *My quarters are far away*. The verb, to *quarter*, is to cut up into four parts. There is also the *quarterback*, a very important position in American football. A *quart* is a quantity, a unit of volume – a *quarter* of a gallon. And there is the printing page size *quarto*, being a *quarter* of a full sheet, and therefore with eight pages of printed text.

A *quartet* is usually a group of four musicians; it is also a piece written for four musicians, say, a *string quartet* written for four string instruments. But anything in four parts could be a *quartet*. T. S. Eliot's famous *Four Quartets* is a set of four long poems exploring man's relationship with God. A *quintet* is a group of five singers or musicians, for example a *jazz quintet*, or a piece of music written for five instruments. So much for numerical matters.

Let us look at *quality* and *quantity*. In speaking of an amount, the word is *quantity* – *He consumed an enormous quantity of food*. The trick is to differentiate between 'number', 'amount' and *quantity*. 'Number' is for countable things – *He bought a number of books*. The word *quantity* is used for things that can be measured – *He ate a large quantity of rice*; each grain of rice cannot be easily counted, but whether someone eats a hundred grams or half a kilogram is measurable and can be weighed. And yet we speak of the number of stars in the sky, not the 'quantity of stars', even though the stars cannot be counted. And 'amount' is usually for an approximate, uncountable, abstract quantity – *No amount of effort could make him pass his maths papers*. You could also say – *He ate a large amount of rice*, but you might prefer to use *quantity* here, which is a little more specific than 'amount'. There are subtle differences, and the correct use comes out of regular practice. In modern grammar, the term is *quantifiers*; they help in keeping up with numbers, they respond to questions such as 'how much' or 'how many' – *(a) few*, *(a) lot*, *much'*, *many* are *some* examples.

Quality is also something that cannot be counted, it cannot be touched; it is a standard for judging whether something is of 'good' *quality* or 'bad' *quality*. We ask for good *quality* rice at the grocery store, and complain about the *quality* of mobile phone reception. How does one judge *quality* then? We can judge whether our *quality of life* is good only by proxy measures. According to the Human Development Index 2015, created by the United Nations Development Programme, India was in the 130th position out of 188 countries.[1] What then is the *quality of life* of the average Indian? You be the judge.

Despite the scope of 'good' and 'bad' *quality*, the word on its own implies something better than the average – *He is a quality batsman*. To reach a certain standard, and attain a certain position, therefore, you may have to *qualify* for that position – *She missed the qualifying marks for the Olympics* or *The teacher was not qualified to become the headmistress of the school because she did not have the necessary qualifications*. To ask for one's *qualifications* at a job interview is usually to ask how much he or she has studied.

A *qualifier* in grammar *qualifies* or modifies an adjective or adverb; it raises or lowers the degree of that *quality* – *a very good book* (where 'very' is the *qualifier*) or *he sang rather badly* (where 'rather' is the *qualifier*). *Almost, a bit, fairly, a little, much, most, quite, somewhat* – these are a few *qualifiers*. But what about adjectives and adverbs themselves? They may also be considered to be *qualifiers*,

[1] http://hdr.undp.org/en/composite/HDI

they do *qualify*, as in *a beautifully orchestrated piece* where 'beautifully' is a *qualifier*.

A few five-letter words – *quick*, *quest*, *queer*, *quiet* and *quite*. *Quick* is 'fast' or 'speedy', as an adverb it is *quickly* – *He is a quick runner* and so *He runs quickly*. A student could be a *quick learner*. Someone who is *quick* in thinking and finding solutions is a *quick thinker*. But if he gets angry easily, he is *quick tempered*.

A *quest* is a search, but more; it is a difficult search that takes time and much effort, an expedition perhaps – such as the *quest for truth*, as we say philosophically. The related word *question* is difficult; how do you explain it? That is a *question*, with a *question mark* at the end. A *question* asks and expects a reply. A *rhetorical question*, though, does not expect a reply; it makes a comment or statement in a question form – *What is the use of teaching you? You will never learn.* Or *Do you think you can sleep all day?* A related word is *query* – a *question* – nowadays very commonly used in searching on the Internet. But it is also commonly used in commercial correspondence, for an enquiry about some product or service.

Queer is a tricky word, it has undergone change in its use in recent years. It means 'strange', 'unusual', a little uncomfortably so – *I have a queer feeling that we are being watched.* To use a cricket term, *queering the pitch* is making something difficult or tricky – *As it is things were going wrong, but he queered the pitch further by deliberately blaming her for the mess.* The word is now also used for a homosexual person; till a few years ago it was used in a derogatory way, but now, thanks to a change in attitudes, and an increased legal and social acceptance, it is now used to describe the community of same-sex people. It is necessary that the word is used correctly, in its present form, with respect for all people.

An extremely common and irritating error is the mix-up between *quiet* and *quite*. The first is a noun or an adjective meaning 'an absence of noise' – *The quiet of the house after the boys left was wonderful* or *I was surprised to see the usually quiet child crying loudly.* As an adverb, the word is usually *quietly* – *The children were studying quietly.* But it could by itself be used – *Be quiet!* The other word, *quite*, is a strange qualifier; it can mean either 'entirely' or 'somewhat'. *I quite agree with you* means I entirely agree with you. But *The food was quite good* implies that it was not bad, only somewhat good. There cannot be any word like 'quitely' and that is the trick of checking the correct use. To a *question* – *Are you all right?*, if one were to say *Quite!*, it would mean 'yes'; if the reply was *Quiet!* one would be asking the speaker not to talk! There is indeed a difference in pronunciation, too.

Quid is slang for a pound sterling in England. But *quid pro quo* is a Latin phrase, one of those very few in common use; it means 'one for another', a deal – *He lent me the money as a quid pro quo for help with his studies.* Another word is *quit*, to give up – *He quit smoking last year* or *He quit his job*. The significance of the word in modern India history is in the *Quit India* movement of 1942, the civil disobedience movement that Mahatma Gandhi launched against British rule, and which began the final push towards India's independence.

Quotation marks are the inverted commas that enclose the words of some person, as she or he spoke or wrote them. What they enclose is a *quote*. Often one *quotes* a well-known person to strengthen a point one is trying to make. Famous *quotations* are themselves a pleasure to read, and a number of websites provide us a dip into the words of great men and women.

Most words with *q* have a *u* attached, but there are a few that don't. These are not generally of English origin. *Qi*, a life force in Chinese, *qazi*, an Islamic priest and *qawwali*, a kind of song in Urdu, are examples. The use of *u* with *q* comes from old English, when 'qu' was 'cw'. The word *queen*, for example, was earlier spelt 'cwen'!

A very interesting word is *quintessential*. It refers to something or someone typical, which represents a norm or style – *He is the quintessential Englishman* means that he represents all that is very typically English, and the very best of it. Or – *The use of the word 'rather' is quintessentially British*. *Quint* pertains to five and 'essential' relates to the elemental, the core. The five elements are earth, air, fire, water and ether. So we have all the five elements in *quintessential*.

A modern word of daily use, with *q* but no *u*, is *qwerty*. It represents the six keys from left to right on the upper row of letters in an alphanumeric keyboard, the *qwerty* keyboard. It exists from the days of the old typewriter and is not a computer innovation; it was first used in Remington typewriters in the 1870s. The designing of the keyboard was such that the letters should not jam the type bars as they pressed up; it depended a great deal on the frequency of use of each letter. Even today, no one has found a better format.

R

R is onomatopoeic – roll it around, like rrrrr, and you would get the sound of a dog's growl. In fact in olden times, it was often called the dog letter; Shakespeare uses the term in *Romeo and Juliet*; the Nurse who looks after Juliet says, '...that's the dog's name..'

There are seven letters of the English alphabet that take an *h* after themselves to form natural English words – *c, g, p, r, s, t* and *w*. (Others like *d* for 'dhobi' or 'dhow', for example, use only words imported from other languages.) Of these, six change their character with the *h*, only *r* remains pronounced as if the *h* does not exist – a few examples of words in common use are *rhinoceros*, *rhododendron*, *rhombus* and *rheumatism*.

R can stand for *right*, or *radius*; in a car gear shift, it would stand for *reverse*. *R*, usually with a circle around it (®) in documents and products, stands for 'registered'. *RF* is *radio frequency*. *RFID* or *radio frequency identification device*, is the system by which *radio frequency* waves are used to tag data on objects to identify them from a relatively short distance. This helps in keeping track of an object, a part in an assembly line perhaps, or a product on a store shelf. In today's texting lingo, *r* is 'are'!

Two important 'words'; they are actually acronyms common in the IT sector, but some readers might not know the full terminology – RAM and ROM. *RAM* is *random access memory* and *ROM* is *read only memory*. *RAM* is data stored in a *random* manner, which is not in sequence and can be accessed *randomly*; if all data had to be reached sequentially, say alphabetically or chronologically, think of the time one might take to reach a file on Zoology! *ROM* is also data, stored in a way that it cannot be easily altered, it can be read but not edited. There is also *REM* – short for *rapid eye movement*, a phase in a sleep cycle.

RIP is commonly used after the name of a person who has just passed away; it is to pay respect and to wish him or her peace in the other world. Though it does happen to mean *rest in peace*, the origin is Latin – *requiescat in pace* (pronounced 'paache'). In Internet terminology, *RIP* is *routing information protocol*, without which there might not be any limits to the number of loops of a path from a source to a destination. The common use of *rip*, with no capital letters, is to tear off – *He ripped off a sheet from his notebook to write a letter.* Note the additional *p* in the past tense and that there is invariably an 'off' along with the verb. To *rip off* is also a slang phrase, to cheat – *He ripped me off when he sold me that cheap pen for fifty bucks!* Something too expensive for its actual worth is a *rip-off* – *The buffet lunch was a total rip-off.*

If you receive an invitation with *RSVP* written somewhere at the bottom, it asks you to let the person inviting you know if you accept the invitation or not. *Repondez sil vous plait* is a French phrase that says *respond if you please.* Nowadays, one often sees the invitation say *RSVP (regrets only)*, so if you are going you need not reply. But it is poor etiquette to not reply to an *RSVP*.

Re is very common in use today; it is used for *regarding*, about, in the matter of. In a business letter one might begin with *Re: the supply of 100 qwerty keyboards*. The other abbreviation is *ref*, short for *refer* or *with reference to*; at the start of that business letter one might also say – *Ref: your enquiry letter number 1234 of 1st April regarding the supply of 100 qwerty keyboards*. One might use *reg*. for 'with regard to', but never 'with regards to', a very common error. *With regards* is used only to end a letter. *Re* also happens to be the short form for one rupee – *Re* 1 – and *Rs* for more than one rupee. Some of us tend to convert the written word into speech to say *Give me rupees two hundred*; it should be *Please give me two hundred rupees*.

> *R* has a number of words which are homonyms, spelt or pronounced similarly, and one must be careful about their spelling or meaning. *Red* and *read* is a very common example. *Red* is the colour, *read* is the past tense of, yes, *read*! In the present tense, *read* rhymes with *reed*, while in the past tense it rhymes with *red*.

A word often used is *rather*. It has its special uses. It is used in comparing choices, an adverb showing preference – *I would rather read this book than go to see a film*. Or *I rather like this book*. It can be an adjective, a qualifier – *This is a rather grim book*. And it is also an exclamation in reply to a question – *Did you like the book? Rather!* To use *rather* for comparing (with a 'than') it must have 'would' before it, not 'will' – *I would rather you studied law than medicine*. But one might use 'should'; it is then a matter of doing the right thing – *I should rather see you in my office than at home*. Another use is of *rather than*, the two words together – *I preferred to see the film rather than read the original book*. There is a slight difference between 'a rather' and 'rather a' – *This is a rather difficult way* explains the degree of difficulty; *this is rather a difficult way* tends to politely hint that the choice of the route was wrong. All in all, *rather* implies a limitation – somewhat, up to a point. It tones down the description; not very, just *rather*. As we have said earlier, the word is quintessentially British!

Ration, *rations*, *rational*, *rationale*, *rationality*. They all derive from the Latin word *ratio*, which stands for logic or *reason* or calculation. We still use it in legal parlance; if a judge asks the legal counsel what the *ratio* of his arguments is, he is asking the lawyer for the legal basis of that argument. *Ratio* is generally used today to show a proportion – *The ratio of boys to girls in our college is very high; it's 5:1 (five to one)*.

Ration is a fixed, calculated amount, such as a stock of things but generally used in the plural – *The ration shop is open every afternoon from 4 p.m. for you to buy your rations*. It is also used slightly differently – *There was strict rationing during the war. Rational* is very different, the other aspect of the original *ratio*. *Rational* is logical, something that can be *reasoned* out, *reasonable*; the opposite is 'irrational'. *Man is a rational animal* is the well-known saying, which differentiates man from other animals. But is there a *rationale* for it? *Rationale* with the *e* at the end and pronounced 'ration–aal', is the logic or *reasoning* for any viewpoint or thought or opinion. *Rationality* is the state of being *rational*.

Ratify is a word in common use in international relations and in contractual matters. To *ratify* a treaty or any understanding is for the agreement to be approved formally after it has been reached by negotiators. *Ratification* of such an agreement is done by the principal authority and only then does it formally come into effect. To *rectify*, on the other hand, is to correct, as in the *rectification* of a defect in any document.

To *realize* is to understand – *He realized that he was making a noise only when the waiter pointed it out.* But it is also to *reach*, to succeed in – *He wanted to realize his dream of becoming a mountaineer*. The noun is *realization* – *Realization dawned on him. Reality* is the state of actual existence. Just remove one letter from *reality*, and you get *realty*, which is to do with *real estate*, land and housing and all immoveable property.

The most important use of *re* is as a prefix for 'again'. To *redo* is to do again; to *renew* is to activate again, like *renewing* a book at the library! But not all words with *re* mean something 'again'. *Redress* is not to dress again, it is to set right, such as a grievance; *refuse* is not to fuse again, it is to decline, to say 'no' (when pronounced like 'ref–use' it also means garbage).

A few more uses of *re* as a prefix. *Recall* is to call again but generally in the mind, that is to remember – *My grandfather would recall his childhood days when there was no electricity.* There is a new commercial meaning to *recall*; *recalling a product* is to take it back from buyers because of some manufacturing defect.

To *refund* is to return money or a payment for a sale or an activity that was meant to happen but did not; the noun is also *refund* – *We were given a refund of our ticket money when the show was cancelled.* As a verb it would be *They refunded our money. Refund* is interesting, it does not exactly mean 'fund again', but to put back into the fund that had been depleted of money.

To *return* is to turn again, it is to turn back. We use it wrongly when we use the phrase 'return back', a very common mistake. Since *returning* itself is going back or coming back, the use of 'back' is unnecessary – a pleonasm. The correct use is *let us turn back* or *let us return*, depending on the context. *Return fare* is the cost of a journey both ways, since one *returns* to the place of departure. *Return* is also to get back to an original line of thinking or idea; a speaker might move away from the main point of discussion, and then *return* to the original issue, saying – *to return to the main point....* There is another important use of the word *return* in a democracy. At the end of an election process, after the votes are counted, the winner is *returned* to the legislature by the *Returning Officer*, who declares the results.

Let us move to financial matters. When you pay taxes on your income you file your tax *return* to state your income and tax liability. When you make an investment, you earn a dividend on that investment; that earning is the *return on investment*. The term is not used for interest earnings from bank deposits, but from investments such as in bonds, stocks, shares, proprietary business; these earnings are the *r.o.i.*, the *return on investment* When you look for the best *returns* possible, you look at the *r.o.r.*, the *rate of return.*

Returning to the past is often a very emotional matter. 'Old' music, for example, seems to be very popular; the slang term is 'oldies', and as a genre, this is *retro* music. There is also *retro* fashion, or even *retro* art. It comes from the Latin *retro* meaning 'the past'. *Retrospective* is what you see of the past, the opposite of prospective. A festival of films by Satyajit Ray today might be called a Ray *retrospective*. *Retro* is also used in modern technology. When a *rocket* engine in a spacecraft is used to produce a thrust in the direction opposite to the direction of the spacecraft, it is a *retrorocket*. Small *retrorockets* are often fired to nudge a spacecraft into its orbit, or to reduce its speed while landing on a planet. And *retrofitting* is the improvement to an existing factory by adding some new equipment so that there can be better use of existing equipment.

Let's look at two significant words – *respect* and *respective*. The first word is not easy to explain; it is the regard you might have for someone you hold in high esteem. To such a person you would show *respect* and be *respectful* to him or her; you would *respect* his or her views. When s/he, or anyone else for that matter, passes away you would pay your *last respects*. But *respective* is different. It pertains to more than one person or things, in a differentiating, comparative sense – *The respective merits of each candidate were discussed in detail* or *Ram and Hari gave us their respective views*. If used as *respectively*, there is sequencing; *Ram and Hari respectively gave us their views* implies that Ram spoke first.

In official 'lingo', and corporate jargon, you might come across the word *revert*; in reply to your letter you might hear from the office – *We shall revert to you shortly*. What is meant is that the concerned person or department would get back to you shortly. The error that occurs in the usage of this word is that the reply stops with *we shall revert* though 'to you/him/her (or whoever) should be added. *Revert* is actually to return to a previous condition or position, so the office jargon is a strange use of the word.

Riddles are word puzzles, a statement or a question, sometimes in rhyme, which are to be solved. One example, at a junior schoolboy level:

They call me a man, but I'll never have a wife,
I was given a body, but not given life,
They made me a mouth, but didn't give me breath,
Water gives me life, but the sun brings me death.
What am I?

Answer: *A snowman.*

And one more, perhaps right for this book. Question: *Which comes first, the chicken or the egg?* Answer: *Chicken of course; haven't you heard of a dictionary?*

Let us look at *right*, a very interesting word. It is used in multiple ways; there is a philosophical way, it has also a political approach and it actually provides both direction and emphasis. In a moral and philosophical context, *right* is the opposite of 'wrong'. Perhaps the ultimate duty of any person, socially and spiritually, is to do the *right* thing. There is a concept of *righteousness*; a *righteous* person is one who does what is moral, what is correct, what is *right*. We say *He is a right thinking person.*

But *right* is used also without any moral tone, only to denote something correct – *This is the right answer* or *The boy got all his answers right*. The word is also the opposite of 'left'; it is a direction, a side – *the right half of the body* or *the right side of the road*. We often say – *The left hand does not know what the right hand is doing*. Politically, as we know, the 'left' and the *right* are opposed to each other; the 'left wing' believes that the *right wing* rejects the approach of social and economic equality. The term came about when in the French parliament, in the days of the French Revolution, the *rightists* sat to the *right* of the chair of the parliamentary president (today's Speaker in many parliaments), while the leftists sat to his left. The government of the day, in many countries, continues to sit to the *right* of the Speaker, with the Opposition to the left. There is *rightly* – including *quite rightly* or *rightly so* – to indicate correctness, but no 'leftly' at all!

In England, *Rt. Hon.*, or *Right Honourable*, is a title by which people call the prime minister, and some lords and officials. Some Commonwealth countries such as Canada, Australia and New Zealand have a similar practice. The *Rt.* here is probably more to do with 'very' or 'completely', to indicate a great degree, than any other interpretation. (This is similar to *right up my sleeve*, which implies that something is very much within my capacity). *Rt. Rev.* or *Right Reverend* is used for Anglican bishops (who are to be *revered*!). *Right* can be a noun – *He went to the right,* an adverb – *Go right,* and an adjective – *Take the right turn.* It can also be a verb – *to right a wrong.* There is also the emphasis that *right* provides. It indicates immediacy – *Come here right now*; accuracy – *The accident happened right here*; totality – *He went right down the road, but could not find the house.* And then the emphasis – *right* with an exclamation mark is 'okay' or 'yes' – *Right! Let's go!*

R has some interesting words that are the same as both a noun and a verb – *record* and *report* are two important examples. *Record*, the noun, is a document, which exists because someone has *recorded* something or kept a note of something. This is much required for legal and official reasons. As a verb, *The election officer must record the votes polled by each candidate before announcing the results* or *Every judge records his or her reasons in writing before he or she pronounces judgment.* Samuel Pepys (1633–1703) *recorded* the events of the 1660s London in his diary; that document is today well known as a *record* of the social history of England of his times. A *record* is a mark set (clearly written down somewhere), which is the best achievement in that field of human endeavour – *He set the world record in the high jump*. It also is the music-playing device, now making a feeble comeback, a gramophone record, usually made of vinyl. The verb *record*, in this case, is to put on a track or store the music or other sounds that are to be maintained for future listening – *We recorded the entire proceedings of the meeting.*

The other word *report* is similar. It also deals with *recording* something, but usually written down as a document, and generally tells someone in formal terms of something that has happened or has been heard of. It is also the result of some action taken or the final information about the action taken, such as a *police report*. The police, incidentally, begin their investigations only after they have received an FIR, a *first information report*. But a *report* need not always be in writing; the teacher may tell a difficult child, *I will report you to the Principal*. In a very different way, a *report* is also a loud sound, like *the report of a gun*.

Four words – *root*, *rout*, *route*, *router*. The first, *root*, has a number of meanings. It is usually in plural because there are many *roots* at the lower end of a plant or tree, which is attached to the soil; the *roots* draw water and nourishment from the soil and send it to the other parts of the plant – *Strong roots are necessary for strong trees.* It is also what attaches your hair to your scalp or your teeth to your gums. And thus, we have the cause, the origin of a condition – as the saying goes, *Money is the root of all evil.* If money is *the root cause* or the basic reason for corruption, how does one *root out* or eliminate corruption? One's family or cultural *roots* go back centuries. In the study of language, in linguistics to be precise, one looks at the origin of words. In English most words derive from their Latin *root.* Some retain their old English *root.* In mathematics, too, we use the word. The *square root* of 4 is 2; if 2, the *root* number, is multiplied by itself, that is squared, the answer is 4. And to *root* for someone is to cheer for that person, it could be for a team or a group too – *We all rooted for the Indian team.*

To defeat comprehensively is to *rout*, whether it be an army or the rival team in football – *We were routed 10-nil in the finals of the football tournament.* It is pronounced like 'rowt' to rhyme with 'clout', 'flout'and 'stout'. Add an *e* and we have *route*, spoken like 'root', which means a way, the way to take – *This is the shortest route from Bengaluru to Chennai* or *There was brisk trade between ancient Asia and Europe on the old silk route.* We also have the word as a verb, to channelize – *Please route your application through your boss.*

A *router* is a device which channelizes and sends packets of data between computer devices, it *routes* the data. The problem is in the way we say the word. As with most technological things, the American style is in vogue. Instead of *route* being pronounced like 'root', the Americans say it as 'rowt'. And so a *router* is now increasingly pronounced 'rowter'.

Do you remember the *three r's*, without which you would not have passed through school, or been *reading* this book? The three r's are *reading, 'riting and 'rithmetic*, the basic tools for education. (Note how an apostrophe is used at the start of a word, here to stand for *w* and *a* respectively.) In modern environmental management, there are *three r's* too – *reduce, reuse, recycle.*

S

S is doubly remarkable. Among all the letters of the English alphabet, the largest number of words in English start with this letter. But it is most important not when it begins a word, but when it ends it, because that *s* gives the plural form of most nouns – *boy* and *boys, girl* and *girls, town* and *towns, village* and *villages.*

Singular words are 'news' (not a plural of 'new' which is not a noun in any case), 'information', 'data' and 'dialogue'. Information is always *singular* – *The information we have is that the train has met with an accident.* If there is more than one piece of information, it is used just that way – *We have put together various pieces of information.* It could also be *bits of information*, but never, never 'informations'! Data is plural, the original Latin word being *datum*, but it is a *singular* noun. There is no word like 'datas' and no one says 'the data are'... No one uses *datum* per se, and the word is now obsolete; as a single piece of data makes little sense, we always say – *The data indicates that there have been 110 accidents in the last one year.* How do you think of a noun as *singular* or plural? Check the verb it uses. An error that many film persons, including reviewers, make is in their use of the word 'dialogues'. The word 'dialogue' is a conversation between two persons, as different from monologue, which are lines only by one person. The entire dialogue of a film is just that, its dialogue. The reviewer should write – *The dialogue is outstanding*, not 'the dialogues are outstanding'; that would be poor English. But over the past few years the plural form has gained ground.

S also gives the present tense of most verbs. In this *sentence* itself, 'gives' is the present tense of 'give'. The present tense is important, when you describe an event or a book, play or film. You can tell the story in the past tense, but it is often more immediate if you tell it in the present tense. *So the hero went to the girl's house...* or *So the hero goes to the girl's house...* Which creates the suspense better? There is a terrible Indian habit of using the future tense, 'So the hero will go to the girl's house...' This is totally wrong!

Recall, from Chapter A, that if you end a word with *s* but have that apostrophe after it, you get the possessive. As you know, the apostrophe before the *s* removes the possibility of the plural form. But there is a catch there. For words which are abbreviations with capital letters, like DVD, PhD et al., the earlier way of showing the plural was DVD's, PhD's; this is even now correct, but increasingly, DVDs or PhDs, without any apostrophe, is being used. For numbers, too, the current way is to write 100s or 1990s.

Another aspect of the *singular* is that an organization, though a collective of people, is used in the *singular* – the government, the company, the Cabinet, the office, all these use 'has' or 'is' or any other verb in the *singular*. There is a tendency to use the plural form also – *The government have formulated rules* – but when you apply the rule of 'it' versus 'they', to judge whether it is a *singular* noun or a plural noun, you end up with the use of 'it' and with that 'is' not 'are'. One does not say – 'The government are not stable, they are likely to fall'; the correct use – *The government is not stable, it is likely to fall.*

Singular has another special, unique use; it comes from the concept that there is no second of its kind to make it possible to use the plural form. *The Supreme Court gave a singular judgment on our fundamental rights in the Keshavananda Bharti case. Singular*, after all, comes from *single*, an adjective from 'one' – no other.

S is the common abbreviation for *south* – 10^0 *s* – or for *seconds* – *2hr 10m 20s*. *Sr*. is for *senior* – Lyndon Johnson, *Sr*; *St* is for *saint*, like *St Peter*, or for *street* – *4th st.*; *sq*. is for *square*, as in *sq. metres*. At times *sp* is used for *spelling*.

A *second*, we all know, is 1/60th of a minute, generally the *shortest span* of time that is counted; only when modern stopwatches came into existence, did time-keeping go into microseconds and now into nanoseconds, one billionth of a *second*. Think of Usain Bolt running the 100 metres in 9.58 seconds; the *second* fastest is 9.69 seconds, a mere 0.11 *seconds* slower. But it is still the *second* fastest.

Let us look at this other meaning of *second*. It is, as we know, the ordinal form of the number two, which comes after one, *second* after the first – *He was always second in class, he just could not come first*. There is a verb *to second*, which is to support a proposal or a thought, again from being the *second* after someone has first made a proposal; in all formal meetings, any resolution that is passed will need a proposer and a *seconder*. There is also *secondment*, the placing of *someone* for a temporary period in a position other than his original position – *He was seconded from the university to the government for a year; the secondment will end next month*.

To *see* is to be able to view, to be able to look, through the eyes. The past tense is *saw*, the participle is *seen*. A *saw* is also an instrument to cut wood; *sawed* is the past tense for that word, and *sawn* the participle. A *See*, with a capital *S* to avoid a mix up, is the jurisdiction of a bishop in the church. The word *see* is used in many ways; it does not have only a literal meaning. To *see* is to understand – *I see what you mean*; to consider – *I shall see what I can do*; to look to the future – *I see India rising*; to look to the past – *I see him still, after all these years*; to examine – *Let us see what to do next*; to experience, to work – *The old man saw service in the Second World War*; to meet – *She saw him for dinner at the club*; to permit – *The principal will see you now*; to escort – *They saw her home after dinner*. If you use it as *He has been seeing her*, it means that he is dating her; he obviously likes to spend a lot of time with her.

To *see off* has two meanings, to *send* off – *We saw her off at the gate*, and to pass through a challenge – *He saw the shine off the new ball before he attacked the bowling*. To *see through* also has two meanings, to discover the true nature of a person or a situation – *She saw through the plot*, or to complete – *My mother saw me through college with her meagre pension*. To *see to* is to attend to – *Will you see to the arrangements, please?* But *see to it* can be a bit of a threat – *She saw to it that the arrangements had been made* is fine, but *I will see to it that you do not get a promotion* is a threat. A *seesaw* is a plank for children to sit on; it has a pivot at the centre so that when one side goes up the other side comes down. When you go up, you *see*, when you come down you *saw*!

An important difference between to *see* and to look is this – you *see* something, but you look at it, there is a definite focus. Also, *she looked after me* is correct, not *she saw after me*.

Seen is the participle of *see* – I *have seen* or I *had seen* – but *scene* is a little more difficult to explain. It is what one *sees* as a place – *a village scene* or *the scene of the crime* – or a *situation* – *When the teacher entered the class it was a scene of complete chaos*. In slang you might ask, *What's the scene like*, to find out what the *situation* is. But a *scene* is also a part of a film – *The last scene of the film was very moving*. In plays, we might have a set of *scenes* that together make the play, which are acted out on stage, and earlier painted *scenes* were used as the backdrop; so backstage work is literally *behind the scenes*. That is also used for anything done in *secret* – *The government's behind-the-scene effort with the opposition parties to push through the legislation was not successful*. With *scene*, we have a slight sense of a short time visual impact. The longer, larger vision is *scenery* – *The scenery changed as we drove farther north. The place was of exquisite scenic beauty* – an adjective here. *Scenario* is the whole picture, as in a storyline, but often the situation in real life.

Sever and *severe*. Do note the spelling and the pronunciation – like 'se–vur' and 'si–veer'. To *sever* is to break or cut off – *She severed all links with her family*. It could be physical too – *The severed hand was found by the railway track*. An employee may be paid a *severance* amount, a financial package, when s/he leaves an organization. But *severe* is 'harsh' or 'extreme' – *He was given a severe punishment for his misbehaviour.* Or – *The severe winter lasts a long time in the Scandinavian countries.* There is also *several*; it means 'many' – *He had several options to choose from.* An unusual use is *they went their several ways.* This is the old use of the word, meaning 'separate', not together; in Elizabethan drama – the actors might enter or exit *severally.*

We have talked of *Shakespeare* earlier. What is it that makes him so widely read and performed, centuries after his times? What makes him immortal? It is not that his tales were original; in fact many of his plays use stories or biographies written earlier. But in all his work *Shakespeare* transformed the originals with his insights into human nature, his immense control over language and his remarkable sense of the dramatic form. In our daily lives, we quote *Shakespeare* all the time, without realizing that he is the origin. These are not just literary quotations, but phrases that are in daily use – What's in a name? (*Romeo and Juliet*); a sea change (*The Tempest*); fair play (*The Tempest*); it was Greek to me (*Julius Caesar*); milk of human kindness (*Macbeth*); give the devil his due (*Henry IV, Part I*); salad days (*Antony and Cleopatra*); too much of a good thing (*As You Like It*). These and many, many other common phrases are *Shakespeare's* contribution to the English language.

Let us look in-depth at how a word is used in multiple ways, with the example of *short*. There is a whole cluster of words and phrases around the word. It is a measure, both in size and time, and is less than the optimum or the whole. He is a *short* boy, but why is he *short*? It is because he is *shorter* than an average height. There is a process of judgment, and of analysis, involved in determining this. This can be exact, if there is a specific number in mind. we may have *a 10 per cent shortfall in wheat production.*

Shortage, on the other hand, is used for a lower amount of something than is required – *a food shortage during drought*, or a *water shortage every summer.* At such times, food or water may be *in short supply.*

Short, as we see, is itself a relative term, though grammatically, we have the comparative form, *shorter*; it is used if *one person is shorter than another*, or *His pencil is shorter than mine*. *Short* pants, or *shorts, in short*, (pun intended), are *shorter* than trousers, though they could be of various lengths. In the context of size and shape, we might have *short hair*, *short tops* and *short skirts* – all possibly stylish. But *short* is also used with time. It denotes a time before a particular time – *It was 10 minutes short of midnight*. Or we may make *a short trip* and have *a short holiday.* It can also mean 'soon', in a little while – *The boss will see you shortly*. The word can be used with a dual purpose – *a short flight* would be both in terms of distance and time, as would *a short story*, which is not only *shorter* in the number of words than a novel but also takes less time to read.

Short is also associated with behaviour and attitude. *He gave me short shrift* means 'he paid me little or no attention'. *He shortchanged me* means 'he cheated me', strictly speaking by returning me less than he ought to have done. *The teacher was short with him*, that is, she was somewhat impatient, even angry, with him. *He has a short memory* means that he does not remember things easily. A *short-tempered person* is one who gets angry and loses his temper, very quickly and often. And he has his *shortcomings*, that is, he has his faults, his flaws. A *short-sighted* person is literally one who cannot see far; in idiomatic use, he is one who does not think of consequences or of the results of his actions.

There are a number of idiomatic and also somewhat literal uses of *short*. To *cut short* is to reduce in time – *We cut short our stay and rushed home.* But to *fall short* is to be not up to the mark – *He fell short of their expectations.* A gist, a description that highlights a matter is *the long and the short of the matter.* Though *in short* is similar, it is not quite the same – *He was an ignoramus, a bird-brained, moronic, nothing-in-the-head, foolish imbecile – in short, an idiot.* To be brief and not long-winded is a good thing and so *It is good to keep a conversation short and sweet. For short* is to have a *short* form – *His name was Padmanabhan, but we called him Paddy for short.* To *stop short* is literally that, not to go too far – *His boss stopped short of dismissing him from service.* But to *stop someone short* is to rudely ask him to stop – *He stopped me short as I was explaining the problem. Short of* means 'other than' or 'except' – *Nothing short of a jail term will make him understand the consequences of his action.* A *shortcut* is to take a short way, both literally – *I took a shortcut to his house and saved at least ten minutes* – and metaphorically – *He always takes shortcuts at work, some day he will have to pay for it.*

In modern day finance, *short* is often used to indicate the nature of financial instruments such as bonds. In a bank, one might have *short-term* deposits, usually 90 days to one year; there are *short-term* bonds, which may be for, say, one year. Financially, one can be *short* of funds – *He was caught short when he needed to return the loan.* To *sell short* commonly means getting lower return on a sale than the expected or the original value. A *short run* could be used for a stretch of a few days when the stock market is rising or falling continuously. (We keep watching the BSE SENSEX; it is the *short form* for Bombay Stock Exchange

Sensitivity Index.) *In the short term*, this would reflect the market trend.

The use of *short* in sports, especially cricket, needs mention. If you have not practised enough for the tournament, you might be *short of practice*. And if you are not physically fit, you might be *short of breath* as you run for the ball. In cricket there are a number of fielding positions, all indicating distance from the batsman – *short square leg, short fine leg, short leg, short mid wicket, short third man* and so on; all are closer to the bat than the conventional positions. A bowler bowls a ball further away from the bat than the 'good length' ball; it is *short of length*, and if the ball is from a fast bowler and rises high, it is *short pitched*. If while taking a second run, the batsman has not touched the crease at the end of the first run, the umpire would call it *one short*; it is used for any run not completed.

Interestingly, the kitchen and food also comes into the uses of *short*. Solid fat, such as margarine, which is used to make certain kinds of pastry, is *shortening*. *Short dough* is crumbly – dough is what bread and pastries are made of. From this we get *shortbread*, and other such baked food; *shortcrust pastry* is that type which does not rise, being used for tarts for example, because the pastry *shortens* or shrinks during baking. Since western style baking is becoming popular in India, it is good to know these terms.

Two numbers, *six* and *seven*. *Six* is *hexa* in Greek and so a hexagon is a *six*-sided figure. A honeycomb in a beehive is hexagonal. *Six* is important in many ways; to the four cardinal directions of east, west, north and south, we add 'up' and 'down' to get the third dimension. The five senses are hearing, smell, sight, taste and touch. There is also a sixth *sense*, extra-sensory perception; this is the special mental faculty of *sensing* something not physical, which some scientists believe exists. A common belief is of *six degrees of separation*; this theory propounded originally by Frigyes Karinthy (1887–1938) is that all humans are linked to one another through common connections, which are at the most *six* removed in a chain.

Seven, the fourth prime number, has much significance. *Seven* days make a week. The *seven* colours of the rainbow are violet, indigo, blue, green, yellow, orange and red – the vibgyor. In music, we have *seven* notes, both in Western and in Indian music – do, re, me, fa, so, la, ti and sa, re, ga, ma, pa, dha, ni. In Hindu marriages, an important ritual is the *seven steps* around the sacred fire by the bride and the groom, the *saptapadi*. In ancient times, we had the *Seven* Wonders of the World, of which the Great Pyramid of Giza, believed to have been completed more than 2,500 years before the birth of Christ, still exists – truly a wonder. In literature, *seven* is important. Fairy tales include *Snow White and the Seven Dwarfs*; the *Secret Seven* are a group of child detectives created by Enid Blyton (1897–1968). *Seven Pillars of Wisdom* is an autobiographical work, by T.E. Lawrence (1888–1935), popularly known as Lawrence of Arabia; the reference is to the Proverbs in the Bible – *Wisdom has built her house; she has hewn out her seven pillars.* Shakespeare in *As You Like It* refers to the *seven* ages of man.

There is some idiomatic use of the two numbers. We have *six of one and half a dozen of the other* – both are the same and so it means that two alternative choices are actually the same, there is no difference. *Six* feet is the depth at which a coffin is usually placed underground; so *he is six feet under* means that he is dead and buried. To be *in seventh heaven* is to be in a state of great happiness; it comes from the ancient belief that there were *seven* heavens and the farthest was where the angels and such creatures resided. Here is a crossword clue for those who try their hand at them; *Bliss after six? Seventh heaven!* But if I am *at sixes and sevens*, I am in a state of confusion or in a quandary and not sure of what to do.

Slang is a set of informal words, and their use is not 'standard'. These are words that have come into common use but only among those who would understand them. The *slang* word may not be understood by all speakers of English. *Don't get aggro* for 'don't be aggressive with me'; *He has gone bananas* for 'he has gone mad'; *He is a geek* for 'he is bright but his social skills are poor' – these are some ways *slang* is used. A *slanging match* is a quarrel with both sides shouting at each other.

Society is the living together of human beings, of differing economic status and yet with a common culture, a housing *society*, a cooperative *society* or a larger human *society* as a whole. *Social* is the adjective, pertaining to *society*. *Man is by nature a social animal*, Aristotle said. The economic differences between the rich and the poor in *society* create *social divisions*; we have phrases like *high society*, used for the rich and famous. A *socialite* is one who is or tries to be a member of the *high society*. Those who do charitable work for the poor, or for those disadvantaged in other ways, do *social service*. *Sociology* is the study of *society*, *social work* as a course of study is somewhat more practical. If someone is a *sociable* person, she is friendly. The difference between *social* and *societal* is very minor, but it exists. *Social* is seen from the perspective of the individual in *society*, whether as a *social* person or in the context of his or her place in *society*. *Societal* has a broader definition, pertaining to *society* as a whole, concerning the structure of *society* or its larger, academic issues.

A new concept that has come to stay is *social networking* and the related *social media*. A network is a structure or an arrangement. Leaving out the theoretical stuff on *social networks*, let us just say that *social networking* commonly refers to the use of technology to be a part of a *social* circle. It allows friends, colleagues and acquaintances to communicate with each other in a group, and comment on any aspect of our lives. The strange aspect of such distant networking is that we sometimes forget how to interact face to face! The use of the Internet for web journalism has created *social media*, and includes all web-based journals, magazines, Facebook, Twitter, et al.

South is one of the four cardinal directions. In a map of the world, it would be that part below the Equator; it happens to indicate that part of the world which is relatively poor, parts of Asia, Africa and South America. In present-day world politics therefore we have North-*South* dialogue for economic parity, or *South-South* cooperation. *South Asia* covers the countries *south* of the Himalayas – India, Pakistan, Bangladesh, Bhutan, Sri Lanka, Maldives, Afghanistan and Nepal. There are countries, like Myanmar for example, that could be considered to be part of *South Asia*, but the countries named earlier form the *SAARC* – the *South Asian Association for Regional Cooperation*.

Spelling, like pronunciation, is tricky in English. It is not based on the letters as placed, it is not phonetic, which means it is not based on sound, and there is no single, all-powerful rule. Short words and long words are pronounced the same – cot and caught, rot and wrought, wait and weight. What does one do? Well, as in the case of pronunciation, one places the word in context. Obviously, one does not sleep on a 'caught'. There are some tricks, though, but only a few can be covered here. *I* comes before *e* – *view*, *tier* – when they are placed together, except after *c* as in *receive*. To this, the exception is with words that have an 'ay' sound – *eight, freight, foreign, neigh, neighbour, reign, sleigh, sleight, weigh, weight*; all these words also have 'gn' or 'gh' after the 'ei'. Some other exceptions are *feint, feisty, heist, rein, seize, their, vein* and *weird*.

Singular words ending with *y* become 'ies' in the plural form, or in some verb forms – *study* becomes *studies*; in the past tense, *y* becomes 'ied', *study* changes to *studied*. If a single-syllable word ends with a consonant preceded by one vowel, that consonant generally gets repeated – *bed* becomes *bedded* or *bedding*, *put* becomes *putting*, and *set* becomes *setting* but *pout* (with two vowels) becomes *pouting*; *stop* becomes *stopped*, but *stoop* (with two vowels) becomes *stooped*. But be careful, *stamp*, though with one vowel, becomes *stamped* because there are two consonants, not one, at the end.

Before we move on, we must remember that there are other meanings of *spell*. *A spell of rain* or a *spell of bad weather* is about a period of time. It is also a set of words that is believed to have a magical effect on or for the person who chants it. A *spell* is sometimes cast with an evil intention, as in the old witches' tales, but that is not always true. A beautiful view, or a fine piece of music, can cast a *spell* on you, and a person you love could do that, too.

Spoonerism has nothing to do with *spoons*. Reverend William Archibald *Spooner* (1844–1930) was well known for switching certain letters, or sounds, of words as he spoke and so created a very different set of words; this has become well known as *spoonerism*, and creates lots of laughs. This is similar to but not the same as a malapropism. *Caught a ball* becomes *bought a call* or *the missing history book* could be *the hissing mystery book*. The letters are not important, the sound is. Rev. Spooner is attributed with many; one of his best is 'queer old dean' instead of the 'dear old queen' Victoria!

Step is like 'short'; there is whole range of meanings in the use of the word. Placing one foot ahead of the other is to take a *step*. A *step* is also one level in a staircase. *One step at a time* is to be cautious, and *step by step*, a careful process. To *mind your step* or to *watch your step* is to be careful. To *step* into *someone's* shoes is to take over the responsibilities of that person. To be *in step* is to march properly in line, such as soldiers do at parades; *in step* with the times is not to be old fashioned, to be up to date, as it were; and an *instep* as one word is the inner curved area of your foot. *Step* as a prefix indicates a relationship in a family not by direct marriage but because a second marriage of a member of the family – a *stepfather*, a *stepmother*, a *stepbrother* or a *stepsister*.

Then we have *step* with those common adverbs – 'up', 'down', 'in', 'out', 'back', 'forward'. *Step up* is to increase – *The Opposition stepped up the pressure on the government to resign* or *His pay was stepped up;* to *step down* is to resign, to give up a position – *The prime minister stepped down after the government lost the vote in parliament*; *step back* is literally that, to *take a step back*, but it is used to indicate a reconsideration, a rethinking – *He changed his investment plans at the last minute and stepped back from certain ruin. Step forward* is also just that, but it is usually to volunteer, whether singly or in a group – *They all stepped forward to help at the time of the disaster*; *step out* is to leave or go out for a while – *She has stepped out for lunch*; *step in* is to help at a difficult moment – *He stepped in at the last moment to act in the play when the lead actor fell ill.*

There is a difference between *State* and *state*. Another capitonym! A *State*, with a capital *S*, is a province. In India, we have 29 States, such as the *State* of Karnataka or the *State* of Assam. The *State*, with 'the', stands for the government, the entire administrative system that governs the people. To *state something*, without the capital *S*, is to *say something*, to make a point, often in a formal way – *The witness stated on oath that he had seen the murderer* or *She stated the facts as she knew them.* The noun is *statement* – political leaders are always making *statements* about their party's position on every issue, but formally the government has to make a *statement in the legislature* from time to time to explain its policy in various matters. And *state* is also 'condition' – *his state of affairs* or *the state of my health*.

In grammar, a *suffix* is a set of letters added at the end of a word which changes the function of the word. For example, 'ly' is a *suffix* added to the adjective *slow* to create an adverb *slowly*. Some common suffixes are *-ed, -en, -fy, -ish, -ism, -ness, -less, -ly, -tion.*

Syntax is the structure of sentences, formed by the position of words and phrases, to provide grammatical logic. There is a certain logic of a language, and each language has its own *syntax*. The words are placed in a particular sequence. To give an example, in Indian languages, the verb can often be placed either before or after the noun; in English, this is not possible. In Hindi we say *ghar jao* or *jao ghar*, both meaning 'go home'; in English the verb 'go' has to come before the object 'home'. Look at another example – *He had read my five books* and *He had read five of my books* – the meaning is very different. In the first phrase, there are only five books to be read, in the second there are many but of them five have been read. That is the logic used to structure the language. *Syntax* is what makes computer programming so accurate, and errors will not allow a programme to run. *Syntactical* errors, one would have earlier said, but now *syntax* itself can be used as an adjective!

> *Syzygy* is a most unusual word with its three *y*'s and no vowel. It has a variety of meanings. One among them, from astronomy, is the straight-line configuration of three celestial bodies; if the sun, moon and earth are in straight line, they are in syzygy! Carl Jung (1875–1961), the founder of analytical psychology, used the term for the union of opposites.

T

The letter *t* begins some of the most commonly used words in English, the 'pointers'– *that, this, those, these, then, there*. It also makes much use of a double sound, two *t*'s *together* or close to each other – *titter, tatter, tattoo, twitter, toot, tout, tart, tort, trot*.... The word 'letter' itself has a double *t*! And of course all those other words ending in 'tter'. List them?

T is the abbreviation for *ton* or *tonne*. A *T-shirt*, which we all wear, is called that because of the shape; its two sleeves stretched out is the top line of the *T* and the body is the lower part of the *T*. If it fits you well, perfectly, it *fits you to a T*; that phrase is for all fittings, not just of *T-shirts*! A *T-junction* is where a road ends with a turn to the right and to the left. A *T-bone* is one that ends like a *T*. *TT* is the short form of table tennis. *Tr.* is the abbreviation for *translation* or *translated*. *TNT*, the explosive material, is *trinitrotoluene*.

Like many other letters, *t* has its share of homophones and homographs. *To*, *two* and *too* – these are three short words which sound the same and so one understands them through their use. A significant use of the letter *t* is with the infinitive form *to* – *to go home, to do my work, to travel by bus*. It could explain an action *to* be done – *I have to go home*; an action already done – *I had to go home*; an action desired or expected – *I wish to go home.*

But *to* is not used only in an infinitive form attached to an action. It can point, and point *to* a noun – *This is the way to my home*. Or – *Please get to the point, you have taken ten minutes already.*

Two – 2 – is the second number, after one. It is the only even prime number, and any number is an even number if it can be divided by *two*. *Two* makes a pair; when you multiply a number by *two*, you double it, or if you break something, you might break it in *two*. On the other hand if you *put two and two together* (which makes a simple addition with the result 'four'), you are making an easy and obvious inference. *Two times*, as we all know, is *twice*.

The third word *too* means 'also' or 'very' or 'even', depending where the word is placed, and in what context. *I too went to the concert* – I also went. *The grass was too wet for us to sit on it* – it indicates a condition; how wet was the grass? *He is too short to reach the top of the table* – it explains how short he is. There is a sense of comparison, though not directly. But as soon as we use *too* we need to explain – *He is very short* is enough, but 'he is too short' has to be put in perspective. *He too was unable to reach the top of the table* – he also was unable to reach the top. *Too* seems to require a relationship.

Three, the *third* number in counting from one, is an interesting number. This is the first odd prime number after one itself. It takes a minimum of *three* straight lines to enclose a space – a *triangle*. *Tri* is a very common prefix – a *tricycle* (a cycle with three wheels), a *triathlon* (a marathon with three sports – running, swimming and cycling), a *trimester* (an academic term covering one *third* of an academic year or a term of *three* months in a pregnancy). A *triad* is a group of *three*, used in various contexts. In philosophy, for instance, thesis, antithesis and synthesis form the basis of debate, for seeking answers to all questions. *Three* is important in religious thought. Brahma, Vishnu and Maheshwar, the *three* deities of Hinduism broadly denoting birth, life and death, are the *trimurti*, the *triad* of the creator, the preserver and the destroyer. Note the common *tri* in Sanskrit and in Greek and Latin, only the pronunciation is different. The Father, the Son and the Holy Spirit in Christianity are called the *Trinity*.

A *triumvirate* is a group of *three* powerful persons controlling a government system, such as the Roman triumvirate of Caesar, Pompey and Marcus Crassus. In modern terms, a group of *three* such persons might be called a *troika*. A grouping of *three* is also a *trio*; in music, for example, one might have a piano *trio*, usually a piano, violin and cello, or a string *trio* of *three* string instruments played by a group of *three* musicians. And in art, one might come across a *triptych*, a set of *three* panels held together, which form a whole work of art. Remember that if you multiply a number by *three*, you *triple* that number, such as a *triple* century, a single batsman scoring 300 runs in an innings in cricket. And so a *triplet*, a set of *three* babies born together to the same mother. Instead of *three*, if there were *two* born, they would be *twins*.

Thrice is *three times*, a number multiplied by *three* would be *thrice* the original number. But *trice* is a quick moment – *The magician vanished in a trice.* Actually the magician probably did a *trick* to 'vanish'. A *trick* is also a set of four cards played in games such as bridge. A hat-*trick* is what one comes across in football or hockey, when one player scores *three* goals in a row for his team. In cricket, a bowler does a hat-trick when he gets *three* wickets in *three* consecutive balls. But why the hat? H.H. Stephenson (1833–96), an English cricketer, took *three* wickets in *three* consecutive balls in a match in 1853; a hat was passed around and the collection was used to buy a hat, which was presented to him.

There are two ways of pronouncing the word *tear*, and it depends on its meaning. *Tear* to rhyme with 'ear', is the drop of water that flows down one's cheek when that person is crying; it is often used in plural form – *She could not hold back her tears.* The word is a noun. But *to tear* something is a verb and it rhymes with 'fare'; it is to make something into two or more parts, usually something like paper or cloth. You can't quite *tear* up, say, a sheet of steel or a brick! The past tense is *torn*, not *teared*! But to *tear away* is to pull oneself away – *He had to tear himself away halfway through the match as he had to go for a meeting. Tare* is the weight of a vehicle or any receptacle that is meant to hold something. The *tare weight* of a goods vehicle, for example, is its weight without any load. And to rhyme with the first *tear*, there is *tier*, a level – *The stadium had 10 tiers of seats.* We are all used to the *tiers* in railway compartments – we ask for *two-tier* or *three-tier* sleeper accommodation.

T has a very large range of words with *h* riding on its back. Other letters such as *p, s* and *w* also have *h* riding on them at times, but there is only one sound they then produce. With 'ch', as we have seen in Chapter C, there are two sounds, and so too here, with 'th'. In the case of 'th', these words are pronounced with a softer sound as in the Hindi *thali* – *thank*, *thin*, *think*, *thought*, *thick*, *thud*, *thumb*, *throw* – or with a *d* as in the Hindi *dum* – *than*, *then*, *that*, *there*, *these*, *those*.

The most important aspect of grammar with *t* is *tense*, the written or spoken indication of the time when something happens – past, present and future. All verbs have a range of *tenses*. Time is basic to our existence; all events in this universe have happened in the past, are happening right now in the present or may happen in future. And so we have the *past tense*, the *present tense* and the *future tense* – *I was, I am, I shall be* or *I went, I go, I shall go*. In a continuous way, we have the past continuous, the present continuous and even the future continuous – *I was going, I am going, I shall be going*. There is also the *'perfect' tense* – *I had gone, I have gone, I shall have gone, I should have gone, I will have gone, I would have gone*. But why the word *tense*? It is from the French *tens* – *time* – and the Latin word *tempus*, also *time*.

An interesting aspect of the *future tense* is the use of 'will' and 'shall'. Traditionally the word used with *I* and 'we' is 'shall' – *I/we shall visit him tomorrow. Will* is the normal use for the second person you and the third person he/she/it/they – *You will get your money tomorrow* or *He will study for his exams now*. But earlier, *will* used to give an emphasis with I and *shall* an emphasis with he/she/it – *I will call you tomorrow, most certainly* or *Whatever happens, you shall have your money tomorrow.* That emphasis is nowadays not much in use – *I will* is generally used, not *I shall*.

Often a verb in the present *tense* only needs *d* or 'ed' to change it into the past *tense* – *add* becomes *added*, *change* becomes *changed*, *need* becomes *needed*. Out of these examples, change already has an *e* at the end, and so only *d* is added. With many verbs, however, the present and past *tense* can be very different from each other. These are irregular verbs. Let's look at a few examples of verbs in their present and past *tense*, along with the *'perfect' tense* (where have/has/had is added before the main verb) – *bid/bade/bid, bring/brought/brought, do/did/done, draw/drew/drawn, go/went/gone, see/saw/seen, write/wrote/written.* Each set is very different from the others. A whole list can be found in a book of grammar or on various websites.

The most important word with *th*, indeed of all words beginning with *t*, is *the*. It is *the* most common word in English. It is *the* definite article, *the* book, *the* specific book not any book. In its use, though, *the* also becomes the opening word of many sentences; *the* word is often used to automatically pertain to a person, place or thing – *The day was hot* or *The sun set over the mountains.* In most cases, *the* may not create a special emphasis, but one knows which day or which mountain is referred to. As for *the* sun and *the* moon, these two being unique, we would always use *the*, except when we talk specially of a red sun or a pale moon, to describe a special condition. *The* comes softly, unobtrusively, into our speaking or writing. It is used six times, without our realizing it, in *the* four opening lines of a poem by Thomas Gray (1716–71), *Elegy Written in a Country Churchyard*, which *the* poet begins by describing *the* evening village scene:

The curfew tolls the knell of parting day,
The lowing herd winds slowly o'er the lea,
The ploughman homeward plods his weary way,
And leaves the world to darkness and to me.[1]

The is not used with proper names, except to pinpoint and indicate. We do not say *the* Ram, *the* Rukmini, *the* Mr Thomas, unless we need to confirm that person – *The Ram you mention is not a friend of mine* or *Is this the Mr Thomas you referred to?* But for well-known persons or unique objects, or special reference, as we said of *the* sun and *the* moon, we might use *the* word – *the* Queen of England, *the* Kohinoor diamond, *the* Vatican. *The game of cricket* and 'a game of cricket' – the second one is for a specific game. These special references go against the common rule for the use of the word *a* and *the; the* indefinite and definite articles. There are also special times when *the* is repeated, to explain an urgency in *the sooner the better*; or quantity in *the more the merrier.*

Like 'a' or 'an', *the* too has its special logic. Look at *three* phrases – 'in case of murder', 'in *the* case of murder', and 'in *the* case of *the* murder'. *The* first is used as possibility with *the* word *if* – if there happens to be any murder (it is very theoretical); *the* second covers a type of crime – in *the* case of murder and not dacoity; *the* third is about a specific murder that has been committed.

Than is a comparative word. It is used only to compare – *I am taller than he is*, or – *She is shorter than her friend.* There is 'er' just before *than* where the matter under comparison

[1] Edward Leeson, ed; *The New Golden Treasury of English Verse*; Pan Books, 1980; p 243.

takes the 'er' form; *tall* becomes *taller*, *short* is *shorter*. If the word does not take 'er' there would have to be a 'more' or a 'less' – *He is more irritating than she is* or *She is less interested in music than her friend.*

Thanks is a short cut to saying *thank you*, which itself is the short form of *I thank you.* You could have *many thanks*, *thanks a million* or *thanks much* or some such phrase as alternatives. But what is the reply? Earlier, the British would respond with *not at all* or *don't mention it*, with an *old chap* thrown in for good measure; then the Americans came in with *you're welcome*; now the usual response is *no problem* or *no issues.* But the last is a response to *sorry* as well, and so is somewhat convenient. A slang way is to say, *sure* – why, we do not know! Among friends a common and easy way to respond is with an *anytime*. The use of *thanks to*, other than in a literal sense of giving *thanks*, is a little strange; it means 'because of' and can be used without meaning any *thanks* – *Thanks to the traffic jam, we got to the airport late.* Shortcuts in the texting age – *Tx, Tks,* even *TkU.*

Then indicates time, a point in time – *I was then 10 years old* or *It was then that the accident happened.* It explains sequence, always after another event – *I went to the market, and then I went home. Then* can also stand for 'in which case' or 'if so' – *Then tell me, why have you come? Thence* is not a word in common use now; it means 'from there'. *Then and there* means immediately – the professor explained the complex problem *then and there*. *There*, of course, indicates a place – directing attention to that location. But *thereafter* also goes back to sequence, it is simply 'after that'. *Then* also has another use. It stands for 'in that case' or *therefore* – *Do you feel, then, that we are doing the right thing? Therefore* means 'so' or 'as a result', or, as was just used, it can also be replaced by *then* under certain circumstances.

This, *that*, *these* and *those* point, specifically, the first two to singular nouns and the other two to plural nouns – *this bat, that ball, these bats, those balls. This* and *these* indicate nearness and *that* and *those*, a greater distance. *These* are determiners, *they* indicate and determine which balls or bats we are talking of. But we do not need them only ahead of nouns, they can be pronouns themselves – *This is my friend*; *These are the issues I mentioned to you*; *That means you do not agree with me. These* words are also used for comparison, or creating a relationship, but using distance – *this book* (which is nearer) *is better than that book* (which is further away). The phrase *this and that* means 'one thing or another' – *We spoke about this and that over a cup of tea* – indicating very general things, nothing specific. The other phrase is *this, that and the other*; quite the same meaning as *this and that.*

That has an additional task, it explains a relationship – *the house that Jack built.* Here 'which' could replace *that*; the use of *that* is nowadays somewhat flexible. *That* has another important role, it is a conjunction that joins two parts of a sentence – *I said that I would come* or *He thought that the garden was very beautiful.* What I said or what he *thought* is explained through the use of *that*. Here, *that* allows direct speech to change to indirect speech. *I said, 'I will come'* is direct speech; *I said that I would come* is indirect speech, being reported. Note how 'will' changes to 'would'. In reporting, we can do without *that* – *I said I would come.* And, sometimes, we can do without it elsewhere too – *the house Jack built.*

Though and 'although' are the same; they are conjunctions that actually compare two states or conditions – *Though she had to work to pay her college fees, she came first in the university.* In some ways, they stand for 'however' or 'but'– *She came first, though I don't know how* could be – *She came first, but I don't know how*. And yet, we cannot have – 'Though she came first, but I don't know how'. This is a common error. 'Even' can be added for emphasis before *though*, but never before 'although'.

Thought is a difficult word to explain, it is an idea that comes to the mind through *thinking*; then what is *thinking*? *Thought* also happens to be the past tense of *think*. But, as a concept, it is a process of the mind, to allow the mind to consciously evolve ideas, to reach decisions. Man *thinks*, without *thought* we would not be human; it can be said that it is the human brain with its *thinking* process that has brought us to our present stage of evolution. The philosophical position was stated by Rene Descartes (1596–1650), the French philosopher – *Cogito, ergo sum*; in English it means *I think, therefore I am*. It can have its moral tone; Shakespeare, that master of *thought*, says in *Hamlet* – *Nothing is either good or bad, only thinking makes it so*.

Think and *thought* are words used in many ways. A *thinking person* is one who is rational and *thinks through* an issue to find a solution. He may or may not be *a thoughtful person*. Such a person may have many *thoughts* and may *therefore* be unaware of what is happening around him or her, but *thoughtful* more correctly relates to a person who is aware of the needs of other people around him or her and of *their* well being, a helpful person. *Think of* is to *think* about, to have an opinion – *If you think of the corruption in our country, you will wonder where our democracy is going.* To *think through* is to find a final opinion after *thinking* deeply about a matter – *He thought through the problem and came to an unusual solution.* To *think up* is similar, but not the same; it is to cleverly devise a solution – *Can you think up an excuse for not going to school today?* To *think fit* is to consider something appropriate – *Send him this mail, if you think fit.* To *think better of* is to change one's mind, actually after *thinking* through the pros and cons – *She thought the better of telling him her decision.* One might say – *Think twice before you tell him*; that means that the implication of telling him should be considered in depth. But *She thought nothing of telling him* means that she did not find it anything out of the ordinary to tell him, it was not something that needed deep *thinking*.

To ***twist*** something is to bend it, or distort its shape. One could *twist* a piece of wire, or *twist* facts to tell something false. To *twist someone's arm* – *arm-twisting* tactics – may not just cause pain, but it would force that person to agree to something he or she does not want to agree to. A well-known *tongue twister* by Carolyn Wells (1862–1942) is this limerick:

A tutor who tooted the flute
Tried to teach two tooters to toot.
Said the two to the tutor,
'Is it harder to toot, or
To tutor two tooters to toot?'[1]

Like most such concepts, it is easier to explain *truth* as the opposite of falsehood. A *truth* is a fact. A fact has *to* be *true.*

[1] The Jingle Book, Carolyn Wells (Macmillan, New York), 1899, page 86

The noun *truth* becomes the adjective *true*, or *truthful* – *a true story* (which is a contradiction, an oxymoron), *a truthful boy* (one who *tells the truth*, he speaks *truthfully*). There are many theories about what is *truth*, but, in a philosophical sense, the *Truth* is what, in all religions, one seeks to reach as the ultimate attribute of God. A *truism*, though, is an oft stated fact which is obviously a fact, a cliché – *The sun rises in the east, my boy. Truly* is the way you might end a letter – *yours truly*; it is now old-fashioned and generally restricted to ending a letter to the editor of a newspaper.

Which seven letter word in English has ten words hidden in it without rearranging the letters? Answer: *Therein*. The words are therein, the, there, he, her, here, herein, ere, rein, in.

U

The last vowel in the English alphabet is *U*. It is tricky as it can be pronounced in three ways – as in 'but', rhyming with 'cut', then as in 'put' to rhyme with 'foot', and, third, as in 'unit', the *u* to rhyme with 'dew'! There are a few other sounds, but this would need a phonetics lesson.

U is used to indicate *universal* in the film certification system, to indicate that a film can be *universally* seen, by viewers of all ages. It is the chemical symbol for *uranium*, and the short form for various words – *Union* (*UT* for *Union* Territory); *United* (Man *U* for Manchester *United*); *University* (*U* of XYZ for *University* of XYZ). In modern lingo, *u* is used for 'you' – *how r u*?

There are well over 3,500 words that begin with *un*, a vast number of them using *un* as a prefix. *Un*- as a prefix means the opposite of the word. *Untrue* is the opposite of 'true', *unseen* is the opposite of 'seen', *undo* the opposite of 'do'; *unfortunate* is the opposite of 'fortunate' and *unlucky* that of 'lucky'. A*n unending stream of visitors* is a continuous, seemingly endless stream. But *un* before a word does not always mean the exact, direct opposite; *untoward* is not the opposite of 'toward', there is only a slight connection. Toward means 'in the direction of' while *untoward* means 'inappropriate' or *unfortunate* – *His boss's untoward remarks about his work left him extremely upset.*

Some rules of pronunciation are useful here. *Un-*, when used as the prefix to mean 'opposite', is pronounced as in 'sun' – *unaided, unassuming, uninhibited, unborn* and *untrue*. On the other hand, *un* at the start of words without being a prefix but with an *i* after it, may be pronounced like 'eun', as in *unite, union* and *universal*. This rule of *u* and *i* with one consonant in between is true of other vowels and other consonants too, words like *ubiquitous, urology, use, utility* and *utopia*; Words where the *un* is not a prefix but there is no vowel after the *un*, continue to use *un* to rhyme with 'sun' – *uncle, under, unless* and *until.*

Under is a strange word. It may indicate a level below – *She is sitting under a tree*, (because the branches are above her), or below the surface – *He is swimming under water*, or at the bottom of – *The book is under all that junk*. It is less than – *He ran the mile in under four minutes*, or lower than – *She was not able to vote as she was under 18*. An area may also be explained by *under* – *The area under wheat is more than under rice*. It also indicates control and jurisdiction – *After her parents died suddenly she was under the care of her aunt* or *The people suffered under a tyrant king*. From this comes the question of rank – *They worked under a difficult boss*. Then there is a matter of law – *This is a crime under the law*. When a categorization is done, we have – *This is a crime under the Penal Code*. But the category need not be only for law – in a list, you might look for an entry *under* a particular category. It could be a condition or circumstance – *He was under tremendous stress* or *He was under pressure to do well.*

Under, by itself, is a preposition, but as a combination with other words it forms adjectives or verbs. There are many examples. *Underhand* means something secretive – *They made an underhand deal to cheat the old woman of all her money.* Such a deal would likely be made by persons from the *underworld*, those who are crooks and criminals, part of the *underworld* mafia. The police detectives who would *uncover* such a deal might be *undercover* agents, their identity would be hidden. Before the crooks are punished under the law, they would have to face trial in court, and they would be *undertrial* prisoners. If they are convicted in a court of law, they would *undergo* their term in prison.

To *underline* in practical terms is to draw a line under a set of written words for emphasis; this emphasis without anything written is also *underlining* – *The principal underlined the need for all the students to take interest in sports.* An *underling* is a subordinate; the term is used in a somewhat derogatory way.

To *undertake* – *undertook* in the past tense – is to do something or to agree to do it – *He undertook to help after office hours to reduce the backlog of work*; but an *undertaker* is one who *undertakes* to handle funerals. An *undertaking*, in a formal, contractual sense, therefore, is a promise to do something – *She gave an undertaking not to pursue the matter further.* This could be a written *undertaking* or an unwritten promise. An *undertaking* may also be a governmental organization that *undertakes* to provide a service, like a *Road Transport Undertaking.*

Where *under* is not used to express an assessment, the opposite word 'over' may not apply. *Undertake* has nothing at all to do with *overtake*. There is no opposite of *underworld* as 'overworld'! But to *underestimate* is the opposite of 'overestimate'. If someone or something is *underrated*, that someone or something is not considered good enough – *He was an underrated actor, but went on to win the Oscar*; here the opposite can be correct – *He was an overrated actor*. By the way, you do not *underrate* someone, but someone may be *underrated*.

Uni- is the root word in Latin meaning *one*. And it is the basis for *unit*, *unity*, *universe* and a whole host of related, important words. A *unit* is the measure of a single quantum of any matter; it has to be a single basic amount or size or level or weight or distance. How do you measure something that is acceptable to all? That acceptable measure, which may be multiplied to get actual quantity or distance or volume or weight, is the *unit* of measurement of that measurable item. It is essential that this be acceptable to all; there would be chaos if each one of us had a different yardstick for measurement! Thus we have certain international norms – the international system of *units*, set up by the International Bureau of Weights and Measures.

Unit, of course, is related to the concept of *unity* – oneness. India speaks of its *unity* in diversity, its oneness, its togetherness despite its multitude of communities, religions, languages, traditions and cultural forms. *Unitary* pertains to a *unit*. In political systems, a *unitary*, centralized government controls the system without giving many powers to lower levels of government, as compared to a federal system. The United Kingdom is *unitary* in nature while the United States of America is a federal country, with immense autonomy for the individual States. India too is a federation, but with certain *unitary* elements. To *unite* is to bring together. The common idiom we all know is – *United we stand, divided we fall.*

Another commonly used word, *uniform*, has the same root. In schools, or in the police and the armed forces, the use of *uniforms* ensures that there is no outward differentiation among the members of that institution. The need for *uniformity* in applying rules is important for good governance. If there is no systemic *uniformity*, we might have chaos in the country. Think of how it would be if each one of us did what we wanted to do and did not bother about rules. Isn't that the state of the traffic in our cities today?

Universe, too, is one such word; it is the entire world as one – outer space, the planets, the stars, the galaxies, the Milky Way, indeed many worlds. *Universal* pertains to the *universe*, to that whole world. But *universality*? It is the presence worldwide of a certain matter or thought. One of the most well-known opening lines of an English novel is from Jane Austen's *Pride and Prejudice – It is a truth universally acknowledged, that a single man in possession of a good fortune must be in want of a wife.* Austen uses that line in an ironic way; it may be true, but many of the women in the book show that they are in want of a husband with a good fortune! A *university* comes from the Latin *universitas*, or community of scholars.

And to close this long reference to *uni*, let us mention *unique* (pronounced 'eu–neek'), *unanimity*, *unanimous* and *unilateral*. One of a kind is *unique*, when there is no other, something most unusual – *This is a unique solution*. *Unanimity* is complete agreement, harmony, where *unanimous* decisions are taken and a single view prevails. But *unilateral* is somewhat the opposite; if a decision is taken by someone without consulting others, it is a *unilateral* decision.

Up is a short word with wide-ranging use; let us discuss it in detail. It is a direction indicator. It can be an adverb, an adjective (not very common), a noun, a verb or a preposition; it is with a word like this one that the difference between an adverb and an adjective gets blurred. *Please stand up – up* is an adverb; *Your time is up* – an adjective. As a preposition – *He climbed up the ladder.* As a verb – *Let us up the ante* (put extra pressure on someone). And as a noun – *The higher-ups in his office were kind to him* (note the plural, the phrase *higher up* would refer to a position or location).

Indeed, this small word does many things. It shows the location of something above, as in the nursery rhyme *Twinkle, twinkle, little star/ How I wonder what you are/ Up above the world so high/ Like a diamond in the sky.* In indicates a position – *Please stand up* – or a direction – *We went up the hill.* It is used for doing or starting something – *You should take up a hobby*; settling something – *I will fix up a meeting*; finishing an activity completely – *He ate up all the food in the house.* It also expresses an increase – *The prices are going up every day*; a contraction of distance – *She went up to her friend*; and a stoppage – *The policeman pulled up the speeding driver*! So much in one small word. But there is more.

Up to often relates to the working of the human mind. It expresses a matter of willpower or wish – *It is up to you to decide what you want to do;* an issue of capacity – *Are you up to working an extra hour?*; a cunning device – *He was up to his scheming tricks*; a standard or norm – *His work was not up to the mark.* There are others too – *She was up to her ears in work* meaning that there was a very heavy workload.

Of course, one could literally have *up to* for a physical level – *The water came up to his chest in the pool* – or a time limit – *She would be away from home for up to four years.* In such a case, could *upto* be one word? It means *until* or *up till* (so *up until now* does not need the *up*, it is redundant). But for some reason, though the two words *up* and *to* are taken together, they are not written together. If the words are meant to be separate – *I woke up to a bright day* – there is no problem. But if they are meant to be together – *The bus does not go upto my neighbourhood* – what then? To be on the safe side, they should be treated as separate. But then, why allow *breakup* and *roundup* as single words?

Up's idiomatic use is manifold; just a few sample terms here. *The game is up* – the crook's actions have been thwarted. We have *broken up* and ended our relationship. *I am up against a wall* – unable to proceed further with what I want to do, because someone is hampering my efforts. *He was up and about* – ready to get going (in the morning). *The car was up and running* – something was working well, usually something mechanical, and possibly something that had been earlier repaired. An *up and coming* person in any profession would be one who is beginning to make a name for herself/himself. And if I was walking forward and back in a limited space such as a room or a street, I might be walking *up and down.*

There are many uses of *up* after a verb; a few which are not obvious deserve mention here. You might hear an old person saying – *My back is acting up*, that is, it is troubling him, perhaps a recurrence of an old problem. If something you hear doesn't seem logical, you might say – *It doesn't quite add up*. You might keep a *backup* of all your computer files, a duplicate copy, in case the computer crashes. The police might *beef up security* when a VIP passes their way, they would strengthen their system. To *bring up* the rear is to be at the end of a line – *The big drums brought up the rear at the march past.* To *brush up* is to recall or improve knowledge of something – *She brushed up her knowledge of ancient Greece before she went to Athens for a holiday. The bad weather might clear up*, but one may also *clear up a misunderstanding* with a friend, by explaining the matter. To fix something is to repair it, but to *fix up a meeting* is to decide on a time and inform others (you can still 'fix' a meeting, but it cannot be the other way around – you cannot repair something by fixing it *up*). *To lead someone up the garden path* is to deceive that person with a set of false statements – *He led the old lady up the garden path and got away with her money.* To *set up* is to put in place – *She set up the entire Wi-Fi system for me*; as a noun *setup* is a place that has been set *up* – *He has a very well-planned setup for his office.* Then – *What's up?* It is a slang way of greeting someone, as with *hi* or *howdy*; it is as if that person is up to something, something out of routine, some mischief perhaps! There is also *What's up with him?* – what is happening to him!

Minor differences in the use of *up* can cause major shifts in meaning. As one word, *makeup* means the cosmetics used on the face; it is also the use of cosmetics on stage or in films, with professional *makeup* artists putting on *makeup* for the actors. But to *make up* is to create a false situation – *He always makes up stories to explain why he is late to work.* To *make up to* another person is to be ingratiating; *to make up with* is to mend a relationship which is not going well. An interesting use is of *double up*. One might *double up in pain* if, say, one is hit on the groin, or *double up with laughter* seeing something very funny. But to have two persons use the same facilities meant for one is also to *double up* – *Because of the increased admissions into the hostel, even senior students had to double up*. To *live it up* is to lead a life of ease and pleasure, but to *live up to* someone's expectation may require just the opposite style of living.

As the start of a word, to create an adjective or a new verb, we add the prefix *up* to *beat, braid, end, front, grade, lift, right, roar, root, shot, stairs, start, turn, wards* and so on. The range is vast. Of this let us pick two. *Upbeat* has nothing to do with beating *up* or hitting someone; it means 'optimistic', happy in anticipation of a good result – *The cricket team's mood was upbeat after winning the first two matches*. (In music, it is a soft beat before an accented beat, but that is a matter of a musician's expertise.) *Upright* has to do with morality, an *upright person* is an honest person – it comes from the physical aspect of being erect, straight up.

The story of *up* must end here with *upon*. *Upon my word* is a phrase which indicates surprise. Many stories for young children begin with *once upon a time*. It means 'long, long ago'. It is magical in its use, it is the start of a journey through the land of stories.

Us is a pronoun, the object form of 'we'. It indicates more than one, and the speaker of the word is one of them. It is somewhat the same as 'ourselves'; the two words are generally not required together, but when used gives emphasis – *we ourselves* as with *We ourselves could not go to the concert, but we heard it was excellent*. 'Ourselves' is used if we do something for or give something to 'ourselves' – *We gave to ourselves our Constitution*, not 'gave to us'. Others give *us*, we give to ourselves.

To *utter* something, is to say something, to speak– *They noted down every word she uttered*; it is often to mutter, but not to stutter – *He uttered something so softly that we could not understand what he was saying.* In brief, *His utterances were incoherent.* It is also used for sounds which may not be actual words – *She uttered a cry of horror at the ghastly sight.* But *utter* has another meaning – 'total', 'extreme' – *He expressed his utter disgust at the proposal.* We often use it with strong emphasis – *utter nonsense*, *utter rubbish* and so on! It is thus used to describe a negative condition – *utter darkness*, but not utter light! Perhaps one can't even think of such a situation?

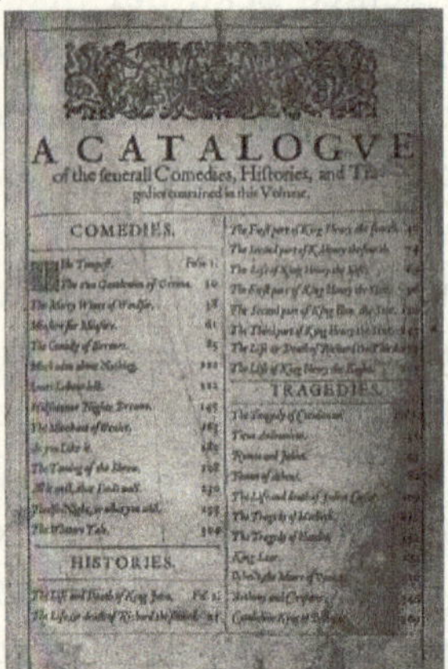
A CATALOGVE
of the seuerall Comedies, Histories, and Tragedies contained in this Volume.
COMEDIES.
HISTORIES.
TRAGEDIES.

In Shakespeare's time, the letter *U* was often written as V and vice versa. The 'catalogve' in his 1623 folio mentioned his 'seuerall' works – 14 Comedies, 10 Histories and 11 Tragedies to be precise. (You would also notice, incidentally, in the 'catalogve' alongside, the old form in print of the letter *s*.)

V

V is in the middle of the trio of letters, *u, v, w,* which are closely linked. *V* is the short form of many significant terms. A *V* sign using the index and the middle fingers is the sign of *victory*. *V* is the Roman numeral for five. This was the way to count on wood, after four single notches, the fifth number would have two lines in the form of a *V*. The letter stands for *volt* in electricity, for *volume* in geometry and for *vanadium* in chemistry. It is also the short form of *verb*, that extremely important part of grammar.

Many of us seem to have a problem in pronouncing words starting with *v*; it sounds like *w* – 'wast', 'wery', 'woice', 'wolume'. There is a trick to this. If you touch your front upper teeth lightly to the lower lip as you say the word, you will get *vast*, *very*, *voice* and *volume*.

A *verb* is the basis of all activity – all action – in English. *Go, come, eat, run, stop* – these are all verbs. A *verb* is 'controlled' by 'tense', 'aspect', 'mood' and *voice*. Having talked of 'tense' earlier, let us look at three less known terms – aspect, mood and *voice* – to get a flavour of the complexity of English grammar. *Verbs* bring with them a lot of grammar, but you need not be too bothered about that if you get the logic of it.

An 'aspect' of a *verb* presents the time of the action. Basically, aspect indicates whether an action is completed or is still continuing. This is so closely connected with 'tense', do we need 'aspect' at all? Well, it is indeed a rare aspect of grammar! Think of the word 'aspect' in some other context – *the aspect of the sun* or *a rare aspect of grammar* – and the broad concept and use, a wider view, in its comparison to 'tense', becomes a little clearer.

'Mood' explains, as expected, the mood of the action, the tenor of the description, and there are five main types. The 'indicative mood' is a simple indicator of a fact – *I go to school.* The 'imperative mode' is a command, spoken with definitiveness – *Go to school.* The 'interrogative mood' is, well, questioning – *Will/do you go to school?* Then the 'conditional mood' – *If you go to school, I will/might come with you.* And finally, the 'subjunctive' – a vague, philosophical one – where the 'if' is a speculative one – *I wonder what would have happened had I (if I had) gone to school.* This last, the 'subjunctive', is tricky; it is much like the 'conditional', and some would say that they are the same.

Voice in a *verb*? There are two, active and passive. The first is direct, the second not so – *She ate up my lunch* and *my lunch was eaten up by her.* The issue is one of emphasis – is it 'she' or 'my lunch' that is the subject? The practical difference is that the *passive voice* allows us to hide responsibility for an action – *I have lost the ball* as against *the ball is lost.* Who lost the ball may not be known in the *passive voice.* You can hide the fact that the ball was lost by me. Many people feel that the use of *passive voice* should be avoided. George Orwell (1903–1950) said, 'Never use the passive (voice) when you can use the active.' But the passive voice can be relevant. For one, it helps us to be that much more polite in our conversation. And at times, it is indeed the appropriate form. *He was elected the president* is better than *the people elected him the president*; after all, it may be obvious that it is the people who elected him, and 'the people' is such a vague, amorphous concept.

While *verb* is all about action, *verbal* is all about words. *Verbal* comes from the Latin *verbum*, meaning 'word' – the Latin phrase *verbum sapienti* means 'a word to the wise'. *Verbal* and 'oral' – what is the difference? *Verbal* pertains to 'words', 'oral' to the mouth – *verbal abuse* but *oral hygiene*. If someone has to say something, it can only be *oral* – *an oral tradition of folk songs* – but *verbal* can be used in the case of the written word, too. (Be careful, 'aural' refers to hearing). Too long-drawn a speech or an essay, with flowery language would make it *verbose*, the speaker or writer would be accused of *verbosity*, and such a speech or essay would suffer from unnecessary *verbiage*. The use of *verbal* for *verbose* is also common in colloquial or slang use – *Your essay was very verbal* – though it is best to use the correct word.

Very is a *very* common word; it indicates a high degree – *She is very rich* or *he is very proud*. That is, something much above average. But it also indicates a specific and accurate rendering – *That was the very intention of my letter* or *Those were my very words*. It also is used for emphasis – *The very idea was disgusting*. In India, the meaning of that old acronym *VIP*, *very important person*, has changed; we even have *VVIPs*!

A simple thing like a *vest*, you might feel, does not deserve mention here. It is what you wear everyday under your shirt, a singlet. But as a *verb* it becomes significant. To *vest* is to cover, or give – usually authority – *By the powers vested in him, the president commuted the prisoner's death penalty.* It is also to put on the robes of a church official. The related word 'invest' is to place power in someone – *She was invested with the position of a High Court judge.* And the ceremony to induct her to the position is the 'investiture' ceremony. To 'invest' also means to place money in a fund to receive a return on that investment.

Via is 'through' – *We went to Pune via Mumbai.* Or – *The conference was held via a satellite link.* A *viaduct* is a type of bridge, a road over waterbodies or lowland. But *viable* is very different; it means, in common use, 'that which is practical or possible' – *a viable solution.* The abstract noun is *viability* – *Have you studied the viability of this project?*

Vice and *vide*. *Vice* has two distinct meanings. At one level, it indicates a position a level below the senior-most – a *vice* chancellor of a university, where the governor of the State of even the president is the chancellor. The other is a moral wrong – *He has many vices*, suggesting that his behaviour is immoral or wicked.

Vide is a Latin word meaning to see – *vide page 54 of the reference book*. There is also *vied*, the past tense of *vie* – to compete – *The two friends vied for the post and became bitter enemies at the end.* And *void* is empty – *After he left, there was a big void in her heart*; or not valid – *The agreement was void because of some technical errors.* The phrase *null and void* is often used in a legal manner – *The court declared the election results null and void.* Think of 'avoid' and 'devoid', both related to *void* but very different in their meaning!

> Your ***vocabulary*** is the totality of all the words you know in any particular language. Obviously, the larger your *vocab* (the short form is used in slang), the better your grasp of the language. How many words do you know in English? What is the size of one's English *vocabulary*? One recent study, of two million people who did an online test[1], says that most native test takers had a vocabulary of between 20,000 and 35,000 words. Do you want to test your *vocabulary*? Try this webpage – http://testyourvocab.com/

There are only five ***vowels*** in English. Think of all the half-way sounds that could have been expressed by additional *vowels*, but their absence adds to the complexity of the language. Using a combination of *vowels* and *w* and *y* we do get a fairly wide range of sounds. But the English language is indeed very tricky, because the same set of *vowels* have different sounds in conjunction with different consonants – *put* and *cup*. Or different vowels create the same sound – *cot* and *caught*.

We do not need long words to see the power of *vowels*. They are the basis for pronunciation and stamp their authority as these five small words show – *bag, beg, big, bog* and *bug*. Each has its own *vowel*, its pronunciation and its *very* different meaning. The five words are *very* different

[1] http://www.economist.com/blogs/johnson/2013/05/vocabulary-size

from each other only because of the five *vowels* – *a, e, i, o* and *u*. Now, think of *pat, pet, pit, pot* and *put*!

But *vowels* are fun to study! Just look at French words used in English, such as *eau* (pronounced *o* and meaning 'water' as used in *eau de cologne*) or *oui* (pronounced 'we' and meaning 'yes') and *moue* (pronounced 'moo' and meaning a pout or grimace). These words have three *vowels* each together, but that is not the maximum! Here are a few other examples. *Onomatopoeia*, we have earlier seen, has four *vowels* together, and four *o*'s in the word. *Sequoia* also has four *vowels* together; it is a type of giant redwood tree, named after an American Indian leader of the Cherokee tribe. There is the repetition in *queue*, a tail of four vowels and *queueing* has five in a row. But what takes the cake is a Brazilian word, the name of a language, *Uoiauai*!

How many words have simultaneously all the *vowels* in one word? *Authorize, automobile, education, evacuation, equivocal, precaution, regulation* and *remuneration* are some common ones. And the word *simultaneous* itself! Amazingly, there are also words that have all the vowels in the order they appear in the alphabet – *abstemious* and *facetious* are two. In these words, '...ious' has, in direct order, three vowels together.

Verisimilitude, the appearance of being real, (think of 'verify', 'similar' and 'attitude'!) is the longest word in common use to have alternating consonants and *vowels*. (The longest such word, 'honorificabilitudinitatibus', that is the ability to receive honours, belongs elsewhere, in the realm of theory.)

W

This is a strange one. Why is w 'double *u*' and not 'double *v*'? The early English alphabet had no letter for *w*, the vowel-like sound softer than *v*, typically in *wide*, rather than in 'vide'. The letter used then was 'wynn', which looked somewhat like today's *p*, but the use in much of Europe was of *uu*. After the Norman Conquest of England in 1066, the 'wynn' was replaced by *uu*, and so came about the 'double *u*' of the English alphabet. It turned into double *v* along the way in print, but we still say 'double *u*'! It did not become a vowel because it is always used along with another vowel – *wait, well, wise, wore* and so on. Of course, there are exceptions; *h* can come in between, as in *what*, *when*, *while* or *whole* and there may be an *r* with *write* or *wrong* but then, there is a vowel immediately after. Incidentally, *w* is the only letter of the alphabet that has three syllables, all others have only one.

W is the abbreviation for *watt* and *west*. In cricket, it is used for *wide*, when the ball is bowled too far away from the stumps. There are a number of acronyms starting with *w*. A common one in sporting parlance, but little understood is

WAG; it stands for wives and girlfriends, of sportsmen. The *WWF* was the *World Wildlife Fund*, and retains the name in some countries, but the new version is *World Wide Fund for Nature*, to cover a wider set of objectives. The *WWF* also stands for the *World Wrestling Federation*. A number of abbreviations relate to the computer and the Internet. A *WAN* is a *wide area network*, *WAP* is a *wireless application protocol*. Then *WYSIWYG* is *what you see is what you get* and *WYSIWYP* ends with 'print' or 'pay'.

But by far the most important use of *w* in the world of computers and the Internet is in triplicate – *www*. It is the *World Wide Web*, the means of access to the totality of information that is available on the Internet through the hypertext protocol. Strangely, it takes more time to say *www* than to say *World Wide Web*!

The whole world of enquiry, of questioning, of curiosity, comes into place because of *w* – we are always asking *who*, *whose*, *whom*, *which*, *what*, *when*, *why* and *where*. These eight *w*'s also have a connection with a word that ends in *w* – *how*. This capacity to ask so many kinds of questions is *what* differentiates man from other living forms. Let us look at it as an incident being reported by a journalist. *Ramesh went home last evening and found he had lost his house keys; he realized he had left them on the bus*. *Who* is the person about *whom* the story is, to *whom* did it happen – Ramesh. *Which* is the object about which the statement is being made (if it is not only about a person) – the house keys. *What* happened – Ramesh found his keys missing. *When* did it happen – last evening. *Why* did it happen – because he had left them on the bus. *Where* did it happen – since it is about finding the keys missing – the correct answer would be that it happened at his door. The *way* it happened can answer *how* – it happened because he left them on the bus.

What, to take an example, has many roles. It is an interrogation, a question as a pronoun – *what is your name?* But it also stands as a pronoun without a question – *What he said made sense.* It is an adjective – *What book are you reading?*; an adverb – *What are you doing?*; an interjection – *What!* Can you work out a similar set of terms for the other *w* interrogators, *why*, *when* and so on?

Was, the past tense of 'is', is an interesting word. It is essential to speaking or writing, since all of our recorded fact and most fiction is of the past, and so is extensively used. The phrase *it was* starts much of what we say – *It was an easy exam*, *it was a brilliant movie*, *it was a terrible time for us*. And we have already come across Bulwer-Lytton's 'It was a dark and stormy night'!

The plural of *was* is *were*. *He was going*, but *they were going*. There are three *words* with similar sounds. – *were*, *wear* and *ware*. To *wear*, as a verb, is to put on, like your clothes, and so the noun *wear* in *outerwear* or *innerwear*. We can have, in the past tense – *She has worn the saree you gave her. Ware* was earlier used more in the plural, as items to sell – *The old woman sold her wares at the corner of the street.* But it is common now in the singular with *hardware* and *software*, words that do not need explanation here. A storage place, a godown, where things are stored for sending out to the market is a *warehouse*. Beware of two other words – *weary* and *wary*. You are *weary* when you are tired – *a weary traveller.* But to be *wary* is to be careful, cautious – *I am wary of his intentions*. You might get *weary* of being *wary*; to be always on your toes, cautious and watchful is such a strain, isn't it? *Weary* rhymes with 'teary', *wary* with 'fairy' and 'scary'.

Wear has some interesting variations; as usual an extra word changes its meaning. To *wear out* is to tire out, to cut away – *The constant drop of water wears out even rocks* or *His shoes get worn out in three months.* To *wear down* is to exhaust by putting continuous pressure – *The police wore down the terrorist who admitted to the blasts after days of interrogation.* To *wear off* is to reduce gradually – *The effects of the blast have begun to wear off after so many days.* To *wear on* one's sleeve is to display something that is actually hidden, generally used with the heart; this means the person is being open about one's feelings – *He wore his heart on his sleeve.* One's patience can *wear thin*, if one gets impatient with someone after trying to stay calm; it can also be less acceptable or believable – *His list of reasons for his poor work was wearing thin.* And then, *wearing the pants in the house* – who is the boss? The old joke goes – 'I am the boss in this house and I have my wife's permission to say so.'

Water, a molecule of which has two atoms of hydrogen and one of oxygen, covers about 70 per cent of the surface of the earth. In its natural form, *water* is the only substance that exists not just as a liquid; as ice it is solid, and as steam or vapour, it is gaseous. Most of the *water* on earth is in seas and oceans, only 2.5 per cent is freshwater and that too mostly in ice and groundwater. How precious it is!

Way is a road; it could be a tarred street in a city, a village road, a pathway through a forest, the *way* to school, the *way* to work, the *way* home. It could also be a means to finding a solution to a problem, a method, a *way*, say, to end a war. To *weigh* something is to find out its *weight*, whether it is one gram or a hundred kilograms. And then there is *wait*; to do that is to let time pass till something happens or is expected to happen. A *waiter waits* on you in a restaurant, he *waits* to take your order and then serve you; in the times of kings and queens, there were *ladies-in-waiting*, who were the queen's female assistants.

We, the plural of 'I', shows that there is more than one person, at least two, from amongst *whom* one is speaking – *We will now go to play* or *We have finished our work*. Then *we* might also say *We believe in democracy* – this *we* is a vague, general, grouping. This is the people at large. *We the people* – these are the first words of the Indian Constitution. There is a somewhat childish way of using *we* in place of 'you' – *And how are we feeling today?* Some king or queen might use *we* for 'I'; that, *the royal we* as it is called, is fortunately a fast fading style. From *we*, the subject in grammar, we have 'us', the object; 'our' is the possessive adjective and 'ours' is the possessive pronoun. *Ourselves* is the reflexive pronoun, reflecting the word we; it provides emphasis in some cases (look up 'us' in Chapter U). There is also *wee*, meaning 'small' or 'tiny', but used in only certain ways – *the wee hours of the night*, that is when the numbers are small, soon after midnight, or early morning; or a *wee bit*, a little bit of something – *He is in a wee bit of trouble* or *I am a wee bit anxious*.

A *week* is seven days – Sunday, Monday, Tuesday, Wednesday (pronounced 'Wensday'), Thursday, Friday and Saturday. Where did these days come from? The Sun and the Moon; then come four Norse gods – Tyr, Woden (Odin), Thor, Frigg and, finally, Saturn.

West is the geographical direction opposite to the earth's rotation on its axis, which causes the sun to rise in the east and set in the *west*. The east is the Orient and the *west* the Occident, from the Latin *occidens* meaning 'sunset'. The *west* has always held a strange fascination for man. The British settlers who came to the eastern coast of America, moved into the *wild west*; their adventures led to *western* novels by Zane Grey (1872–1939) and others about 'cowboy' heroes and to a whole genre of films in the early 20th century called *westerns*. Some of them were truly classics – such as, *Stagecoach* (1939), *The Magnificent Seven* (1960) and *The Good, the Bad and the Ugly* (1966).

How much the world of computing has changed our perception of common words. A *window* is that space in the wall of a house which is opened to allow in fresh air and sunshine, and closed to keep out the rain and the cold. From different *windows* one gets different views of the world outside. This simple word has been lifted into *Windows*, the computer programme which changed the way computers would be used. Different *windows* can be opened side by side in a browser, and parallel uses made of the computer and the Internet.

Will and *would* are two words we often use wrongly, especially in some parts of India. This is probably because we tend to translate from the language we speak at home as we speak in English. Many Indians say *I will go*, when they mean *I used to go* or *I would go*. The other major error is in the use of *will* with 'if' or *when* – it is wrong to say *If I will go* or *when I will go*; in both cases, the *will* must be avoided.

Will is about the future, about what has not yet happened, but there is a prediction that it *will* happen, with certainty (unless something totally unexpected happens) – *He will go to school* or *She will read a book.* None of this has happened yet. *Would* is a prediction that was made in the past, so *would* is the past version of what was then the future! *He said he would go to school*, or *she thought she would read a book*. But there are more complex differences. *Will* is simple, but *would* sometimes asks for a decision – *Will you buy this shirt* is different from *Would you buy this shirt.* In both questions the answer might be 'yes' or 'no', but in the first case, the speaker has decided on the shirt, while in the second case, the person spoken to is asked, first, whether the shirt was worth buying. In this book, *would* has been used a number of times, it indicates possibility but not certainty. The same certainty and uncertainty can be seen with 'can' and 'could'! And with 'shall' and 'should' the difference is not only between certainty and uncertainty but between a decision – *You shall go* – and a suggestion or advice – *You should go.*

Will as a noun has two meanings. The first pertains to one's strength of purpose – *I wish to do well in my studies, but do not have the will to work hard at it.* As they say, *Where there is a will, there is a way*. The other *will* is a document which is the last recorded wish of a dead person, written by him or her in his or her lifetime, indicating how s/he wished his or her earthly assets to be distributed after death. A *will* is also called a testament and the person making the *will* is the testator – the usual phrase is *last will and testament*.

There are many *words* of significance in our world that begin with *w* – *wind, water, woods*. And *word* itself. *Words* allow us to talk to each other, to communicate, to understand each other. And to *write*. We have *wandered* through this book and have *wondered* about the mysteries of the English language. The *a* in the first and *o* in the other make the two words so different. To *wander* is to move or walk slowly, without the need to go from one point to another quickly, to stroll. *Wonder* is a feeling of something unexpected or amazing, perhaps beautiful.

Words indeed are what make up a language. There would be no language if it did not have *words*. The strength of English is that it has imported *words* from a vast number of languages, from across the world. English *words* range from a single letter to many *words* with over 20 letters. The shortest *words*? *A* and *I*. The longest *word* is a matter of debate. The protein Titin has a chemical name which has 189,819 letters, surely one created for effect and not in common use! In England the opposition to the established church led to a word, *antidisestablishmentarianism*, which is possibly the longest 'standard' word in the language, with the twin negatives 'anti' and 'dis'. *We* have, in Chapter F, come across another *word*, one letter longer – *floccinaucinihilipilification*.

The *world* is the place we humans live in. It is used both for the whole universe which includes our earth, and for just the earth itself. But it is not just a geographical term. It is peopled by all of us, and the birds and the beasts, the sky, the waters, the lands, the past and present of human civilization. There are many *worlds* in the galaxies that we are now beginning to observe. And there is our own personal *world*, the totality of our own individual experiences, our own lives. So, we have the *other world*, which is our way of referring to the *world* after death – no one knows what that is. We also use the word in terms of professions or activities – the *film world*, the *fashion world*, the *world of sports* and so on. After two *World Wars*, the fear is that a third one, if it happens with the *world's* nuclear arsenal, might be the end of our *world*.

The *written word* is what you see in a book; the *writer*, that is the author, has put down his ideas in *writing*. If you did not *write*, you could not reach out to people except those immediately around you and what you wanted to say could not be recorded for the future. That is the importance of *writing*. You *write down* the list of things to buy, you *write out* a cheque, you *write off* a loan that will not be repaid, you *write up* the report that you have to present next week.

The concept of right and *wrong* is, first, a moral question – what is right and what is *wrong* is a matter of debate. Perhaps, anything we do that harms others is *wrong*, and even to think in that way is *wrong*. But that, someone might say, is too simple a way of looking at it. If someone is kept in custody illegally, it is *wrongful* confinement.

In English and its use, too, the words right and *wrong* are important, there is a right use and a *wrong* use of a word or a term. Let us look at some examples of *wrong English*.

We often translate from our mother tongue or are confused by English grammar and usage. A sample is given here of the *wrong* use of words and phrases. The correct use is given in brackets.

1. anyways [anyway];
2. are you going to come/go? [will you come/go?];
3. he is like that only [he is like that];
4. his happy birthday is today [today is his birthday, or, it's his birthday today]
5. last to last time [the time before last, or, before the last time];
6. much more quicker/easier/faster/slower [quicker/easier/faster/slower];
7. myself Mr Rao [I am Rao];
8. tell to him [say to him, tell him];

9. the teacher came in the class [the teacher came to/into the class];
10. today morning/evening [this morning/evening];
11. we enjoyed like anything [we enjoyed ourselves very much];
12. I will not leave till the game is not over [I will not leave till the game is over];
13. when I will go [If I go, or, when I go];
14. when it will be [when it is];
15. when he was alive, he will go [when he was alive, he would/used to go];
16. your good name please [your name please];
17. where you are coming from? [where are you from?]
18. you are going? [are you going?];
19. you will come, no? [will you come? or, you will come, won't you?];
20. yesterday evening/night [last evening/night (yesterday morning and yesterday afternoon is correct)].

The longest word in common use with no letter repeated is *ambidextrously*. It also has all the vowels and *y*. This word has 14 letters. The longest word not in common use, with all the vowels but no letter repeated is *uncopyrightable* with 15 letters.

The longest word with the letters in alphabetically descending order is *spoonfeed*. The longest word in alphabetical order is actually shorter and certainly uncommon – *aegilops*, which is a kind of rough grass; but this is considered by some to be a proper noun and so not eligible for this distinction.

X

The unique characteristic of *x* at the start of the word is that it is pronounced either as 'ex' and the *x* is separated from the rest of the word – as in *Xmas* – or as in z! *Xenophobia* is pronounced as 'zenophobia'. It is the only letter that does not have its own pronunciation. Letters such as *ef, em, en* and *el* can do without the *e* to start a word, but *x* turns to 'zed'.

In Roman numbers, X is 10; *XX* is 20, *XXX* is 30. Since L is 50, *XL* is 40. But *XL* in clothing size is 'extra large' and *XXL* even larger. Be careful of *XXX* other than as a number; it could imply *X-rated*, pornographic stuff. *X* or *XX* at the end of a letter or message is the sign of a kiss. But using *X* to denote a kiss in a text message is awkward if you do not intend to let it be seen as a romantic move. It is not quite a friendly gesture unless it is for someone you have known a long time, and is a good friend. *XO, XOX* or *XOXO* – the *X* and the *O* are said separately – is the Internet slang for hugs and kisses.

A corporate term that may be mentioned here is *Xerox*, with *x* at the start and end of the word. As a noun it indicates a photocopy or a photocopier manufactured by the company of that name; as a verb it is the act of photocopying. It is derived from a created word, *xerography*, meaning 'dry writing'. This is an example of a brand name taking over as a word of common use.

As an abbreviation, *Xmas* denotes Christmas, but the X is not the cross of Christ, as some people believe. It comes from the Greek letter *chi* (pronounced 'kai'), which begins 'Christ'. But the short form *Xmas* is convenient for fitting into a newspaper column, and for other such use, and so has remained popular.

X-rays were called *X-rays* because when they were discovered, the X was used to denote an unknown value. Any student of mathematics knows that the search for an unknown number or result begins with *let us call it x*. In mathematical terms again, a two-dimensional graph uses the *x* axis and the *y* axis.

Gen X, or *Generation* X, is the term used for the new breed of young men and women born after the baby boom that happened after the Second World War. Generally people born in the 1960s till mid 1980s are considered part of the *Gen X* – a new generation of youth who did not have social attitudes similar to their parents. Gen X is the generation between the 'baby boomers' and the 'millennials'.

Y

The importance of y is more at the end of words than at the start. In that position, it helps in describing something – *an airy room, a scary tale, a teary child, a wary opponent, a weary traveller* and so on. These create descriptive qualifiers. As expressions of actions, *y* is also significant, with 'ly' endings as adverbs – *The bus moved slowly; The boy ran quickly; The teacher scolded us roundly; The horse galloped wildly*. Nouns ending with *y* generally use the plural 'ies'– *lady* becomes *ladies*, *pony* is *ponies*. But, as always, there are rules and there are exceptions to rules. If the *y* is preceded by a vowel, there is a simple addition of s – *boy* becomes *boys*, *key* becomes *keys*, *way* is *ways*.

The letter *y* suffers from an identity crisis – is it a vowel or a consonant? In 'standard' English, it is a consonant, but functions, for all practical purposes, as a vowel and performs the duties of a vowel. It works as *i* in 'myth', 'ai' in 'mynah' (a combined sound called a diphthong) and so on. And it opens words with what some might call a consonant, and some a semi-vowel sound – *yen, yes, yet, you* and so on.

Let us look at these small words of common use. But before we do that, we must mention another interesting word – *yacht*. It is perhaps the only commonly used word that ends in 'cht', and the 'ch' is silent. *Yacht* rhymes with 'not', 'pot' and 'swat'. That it can be called a word in common use may be disputed, because yachts are not very common to find. They are expensive, luxury boats, or small ships, and now used mainly by very rich people for leisure. A yacht is usually longer than 10 metres and some of the longest are in the range of 140 to 160 metre.

Yen is the official currency of Japan; it is related to the Chinese word *yuan*, a round coin. But a *yen* for something is also a *yearning*, a desire for that something, a deep longing. The difference between the use of *yen* and *yearning* is perhaps seen in these two sentences – *I have a yen for chocolate* and *I yearn for the good, old days.* One could have substituted *yearning* for *yen* in the first sentence. But you cannot say *I have a yen for the good, old days*!

Yes is one of the most used words in English. It is used to agree with a statement or as a reply to a question that requires a confirmation. *Did you go to office today? Yes.* It means, *I did go to office today.* One word replaces a whole set of words, it is an efficient word. If the reply was *Yes, I did,* it actually places emphasis on the answer. Suppose the question was, *Didn't you go to office today?* If you simply said *Yes*, it would be silly, would it mean that you did go or didn't? In this case, it is better to say *Yes, I did* or *No, I didn't*. The colloquial versions of the word are many – *ya*, *yea*, *yeah*, *yo* and *yup*; other equivalent words, depending on the usage might be *sure, of course, okay, true* or even *done* in slang. *Will you please get me my book? Done!*

Yet, as you know, is a conjunction; it joins parts of a sentence. But it is much more than that, and as a conjunction itself, somewhat complex in its use. *He studied very hard, yet he did not pass the exams.* The *yet* here could be substituted with 'but'. And *yet*, there is a slight difference between the two. *Yet* has a little more emphasis in its use. It is like saying – *He studied very hard; even then he did not pass the exams.* The other aspect is the use of 'and' with *yet*, as you saw a little earlier in this paragraph. So, *yet* is not just a word that links, there is a certain emphasis that it implies. It also shows emphasis in other ways – *He is 20 years old, but he has not yet finished school.* This is to explain that he should have finished school by now and he hasn't, despite being that old. And then – *She drank yet another cup of tea, her fourth in a row.* This is also in the context of time, it implies that she might have stopped earlier!

You is the 'opposite' of 'I', the second-person personal pronoun in grammar. The speciality of the word is that it is both singular and plural – unlike *I* with 'we' and 'he/she/it' with 'they' – and uses the plural form with the verb – *you are*, never *you is*! *Your* is the possessive form, an adjective – *What is your name, please*?

An error, between *your* and *you're*, needs to be emphasized. *You're* uses the apostrophe to join *you are*. If *you* are not sure whether *you* should use *your* or *you're*, just expand the *you're* and it will be clear. There is also *yore*, the past – *Think of the good, old days of yore*. But this is not in common usage. *Yours* is the possessive pronoun – *Is this book yours*? The *s* is the difference between the pronoun and the adjective – *your* will always be before the noun, *yours* always after. And there is no word such as *your's*, never! If you tend to use that, think of 'your is' and you will know you are making a mistake.

Youth is an abstract noun, it cannot be counted. It is the state of being *young*, not a child but certainly not old. *He wasted his youth in bad company.* It is now correct, however, to say *Two youths were caught stealing* and this has come into common use, though it is better to say *two young men/persons/people*. Strangely, for two *young* women, we do not say two *youths*!

Z

This last chapter, on *zed*, must begin with a mention of the American way of saying it, which is *zee*, not *zed*.

Zap, *zip* and *zoom* are onomatopoeic words, related to speed, and at times used together. *Zap* is to strike with rapid force. In common parlance it is to surprise – *I was totally zapped by the question and could not think of an answer. Zapping* is also channel surfing on the television.

Zip is a quick movement – *He zipped past me into the dining room to devour the food*. But the word has other uses. A *zip*, as you know, is also a *zipper* or *zip fastener*; one has to *zip* or pull together (*zip* as a verb here) to join two parts of a piece of clothing – such as the *zipper* on a pair of trousers. The opposite would be to *unzip*. The concept has been borrowed in computer jargon; to *zip* a file or a set of files is to compress using a *zip* utility programme and so use less space for storage; here, too, we can *unzip* the contents using an *unzip* programme. *Zip* is also a synonym for vigour, for pep – his speech had no *zip* in it. Speed, verve, enthusiasm is the common context in all these uses. But *zip* is also slang for 'nothing' – *His efforts brought him zip in return*; the word *zilch* has the same meaning. The postal system in the USA uses a *zip code* to identify a postal address; it is an acronym of *zone improvement plan*.

Zoom has both audible and visual meanings, at times together. When a jet plane *zooms* into the sky, it does so with great speed and creates a terrible amount of noise in the process. *Zoom* is also to focus on a subject as through a camera's *zoom* lens; one might also search through a pile of material and *zoom in* to focus on something relevant, specific or important – *He read my long dissertation and zoomed in on the weakest part of my analysis*. One might *zero in*, also!

Zeal (to rhyme with 'feel' and 'meal') is the enthusiasm with which something is done, a cause espoused. You might *zealously*, (now the *zeal* is pronounced 'zel' to rhyme with 'fell'), passionately or enthusiastically, guard a secret or pursue a career in music. But a *zealot* is a negative person, one who is *overzealous* in one's views about an issue. The term comes from a sect, the *Zealots*, founded by Judas, their philosophy was *zealotry*; the term now stands for the strong views of a *zealot*. Strangely, a herd of *zebras* is also called a *zeal* of *zebras*! Or a dazzle of *zebras*.

The *zero*, perhaps the most important of numbers, signifies the absence of any entity. It is spoken of as 'nil', 'nought' or even *o*. In cricket it could be a duck; in tennis it would be love. In mathematics, it is both a number in itself, as well as a place holder. In simple addition or subtraction, it has no impact on the result; in multiplication the result is *zero* and in division, the *zero* as the denominator results in infinity, or the undefined. The placing of *zeros* is critical, and its placement calls for precision! That the *zero* can be both nothing and infinity is a philosophical concept. The *zero* is round, like the universe, there is no extremity, no end, nothing at all and everything.

> A strange word is *zeugma*; it is a little known, uncommon, figure of speech. It is used to put together two or more different matters, concepts or conditions. *Eggs and oaths are soon broken* is an English proverb, an example of a *zeugma*.

A *zone* is an area, often an administrative segment of a geographically contiguous area. *Zoning* is a method of planning for and permitting different activities in different parts of an area, such as a city – an industrial *zone*, a commercial or a residential *zone;* these are governed by municipal *zoning laws*.

In geography, *zones* may be both latitudinal and longitudinal. One would come across the torrid, temperate and frigid *zones*, moving from the Equator to the Poles, with their approximate temperature-based regions. On the other hand, *time zones* cover areas that 'use' the same time, with the 24 hours of a day being broken up as *time zones* to cover areas within a 15° longitude, starting with 0° at Greenwich in England. At 0° we have the Greenwich Mean Time (GMT) and *time zones* shift forward or back from there. But the actual time 'used' may depend on the convenience of a people, of the country's requirements. India uses one *time zone* for convenience, even though the eastern end of Arunachal Pradesh and the western tip of Gujarat are nearly 30° apart. *Zoned out*, as a slang term, means to fall asleep or lose concentration or consciousness – *I zoned out listening to the professor's long lecture.*

The last word in the English language, according to some dictionaries, is *zyzzyva*. It is remarkable because it has three *z*'s, and two *y*'s and a *v* to boot. Interestingly, like *zebra*, it begins with the last letter of the alphabet and ends with the first letter! It is an insect found in South America.

> The last word, we believe, is not *zyzzyva*, but a word with no vowel at all! To denote deep sleep, and the sound of a soft snore, one repeats *z*, with *zzzzz*.... That surely, is the last word!

Dedication and Acknowledgements

This book is for someone who fills my life. Poile Sengupta, my wife, my best friend. Novelist, playwright, children's writer, actor, teacher. This book could not have been written without her gentle advice and quiet support.

It is also for Amaya Sengupta, our five-year-old granddaughter. I hope, one day soon, she will read this book and discuss the nuances of English with me.

Then Anasuya, Ashwin, Aditya and Anindita, each one of them knows English better than I do. Their love I cherish.

And many, many thanks to Vatsala Kaul Banerjee of Hachette India, who amazed me with her faith in me.

Notes

'The English language is nobody's special property. It is the property of the imagination: it is the property of the language itself.' – Derek Walcott

Notes

'Speaking English is like a tongue-twister for me. I can speak each word perfectly, but then you have to string them together, like "Blah, blah, blah." That's when I get crazy.' – Jackie Chan

Notes

'If you talk to a man in a language he understands, that goes to his head. If you talk to him in his own language, that goes to his heart.' – Nelson Mandela